John William Edward Conybeare

A History of Cambridgeshire

John William Edward Conybeare

A History of Cambridgeshire

ISBN/EAN: 9783337338374

Printed in Europe, USA, Canada, Australia, Japan

Cover: Foto ©ninafisch / pixelio.de

More available books at **www.hansebooks.com**

POPULAR COUNTY HISTORIES.

A

HISTORY OF CAMBRIDGESHIRE.

BY

REV. EDWARD CONYBEARE,
Vicar of Barrington, Cambs.

LONDON:
ELLIOT STOCK, 62, PATERNOSTER ROW, E.C.
1897.

PREFACE.

§ 1. MORE and more, with the wonderful development in scientific accuracy which is the most marked intellectual characteristic of our age, does the popular treatment of any subject appear weak and superficial. And especially has this come to be the case with regard to history. The application to that study of increasingly scientific methods has brought with it a somewhat undue depreciation of the old picturesque style of representing the past. Minute research, elaborate verification, scrupulous balancing of evidence, critical acquaintance with every rival theory; these are the notes looked for in " up-to-date " historical treatises.

§ 2. Too much of this, however, obviously tends to make a history less " popular "—less of a pleasant book to while away the time withal. And the first object of a popular history is, I take it, to be readable. My aim, in the following pages, has therefore been more especially to make them so; to associate local details with the general outline of English history, and to refer such of my readers as wish to go more deeply into the subject to the various exhaustive works on its various sections, which the industry of other authors has so abundantly provided. At the same time, as will be seen, constant use has been made of the original authorities for each period, and every statement verified by reference to them.

§ 3. Nowhere, however, will be found in this work the cheap suggestion of familiarity with these original authorities which is implied by that affected spelling of well-known names in antiquated form, so fashionable of late amongst historical writers. Such words as Ælfred, Eadward, Æthelthryth, Knut, and the like, are given in the old-fashioned shapes which the general consent of English writers has assigned to them, departure from which is a totally needless and wholly objectionable break in the continuity of English literature. "Britons," "Saxons," "Danes," and "Normans" are also, in this work, spoken of in the time-honoured manner, rather than with the new-fangled precision in nomenclature by which various authors are prone to show their acquaintance with the latest theories of our complex nationality.

§ 4. No historian of Cambridgeshire can avoid devoting a considerable portion of his space to the development and vicissitudes of that great institution which has made the County name so famous—the University of Cambridge. At the same time a County history is not a history of the University, of whose development my object has been rather to introduce a series of sketches than to tell the complete tale, already so well told by others. Only where these sketches have involved the use of hitherto unpublished material have I endeavoured to make them anything more than an outline.

§ 5. Cambridgeshire is commonly held to be a district singularly devoid of interest, both physically and historically. This estimate is unjust. The County does not, indeed, present the marked natural features of Devonshire or Yorkshire, nor has it had any special share in the great military and political cataclysms of English history. But—to say nothing of the glories of Ely, and of Cambridge itself—there are few parts of England where can be found fairer pictures of English rural life. Ancient churches of rare architectural beauty, thatched cottages gleaming around village greens, breezy meadows beside bright streams, golden harvest-fields, whence the gleaners may yet be seen, as of old, returning at eventide with their sheaves, combine to make up a landscape delightsome and restful to eye and soul. And the following pages will, I trust, show that the tale of "the slow-ground ages," whose "grist" such scenes are, is likewise, in no small degree, full of pleasant and unflagging, if quiet, interest.

CHRONOLOGICAL TABLE.

B.C.		PAGE
?	Palæolithic period	7
	River-bed men, along with elephants, etc.	7
	Cut bones. Flint implements	7
2000 (?).	Neolithic period	8
	Polished flint weapons	8
	Ugrians	9
	Jadite axe-heads	10
500 (?).	Britons reach district	11
359	Philip of Macedon	13
250 (?).	Rise of Iceni	12
	Icknield Way	12
	The Five Dykes	14
55.	Invasion of Julius Cæsar	16
	Rise of Trinobantes	16
A. D.	Cunobelin ("Cymbeline")	16
46.	Roman Conquest begun	18
50.	First Icenian revolt crushed by Ostorius	18
51.	Roman Conquest completed by overthrow of Caractacus	18
61.	Boadicea's rebellion	21
	Cambridgeshire wasted by Romans	22
	Pax Romana, Cambridgeshire flourishing and populous	22, 26
	Cambridge (? Camboritum) a Roman town	25
138.	Antoninus Emperor. Itinerary	24
277.	Probus deports Vandals to Britain. Vandlebury (?)	29
284.	Diocletian Emperor	29

b

A.D.		PAGE
286.	Carausius assumes diadem in Britain	29
293.	Allectus murders and succeeds him	29
	First importance of British fleet	29
296.	Allectus overthrown by Constantius Chlorus, Cæsar of the West	29
312.	Battle of Milvian Bridge won by Constantine	30
	Christianity established in Britain	30
353.	Magnentian rebellion. Battle of Mursa	31
383.	Maximus leads British army against Gratian	31
395.	Honorius Emperor	32
402.	Legion withdrawn from Britain	31
403.	Notitia compiled	23
406.	Stilicho withdraws Roman troops from Rhine. Gaul overrun by barbarians	31
407.	British army tries to save the West, and, under another Constantine, conquers Gaul and Spain	32
411.	Constantine slain. Britain left defenceless to raids of Saxons, Picts, and Scots	32
425.	Valentinian III.	27
446.	Last vain appeal of Britons for Roman aid	32
449.	They invite Saxons to settle in island	33
450.	Saxons defeat Picts at Stamford	35
	Saxons exterminate Cambridgeshire Britons, who are driven into Fens and set up Girvian kingdom	41
	Rest of County chiefly East Anglian	43
575.	Uffa, first King of East Anglia	44
597.	Roman Mission, under Augustine, begins conversion of England	44
599.	Redwald, King of East Anglia, a semi-Christian	45
617.	Earpwald succeeds, as heathen	45
626.	Penda, King of Mercia, champion of heathenism	46
627.	Edwin, King of Northumbria, baptized by Paulinus	46
628.	Earpwald converted, and slain. Heathen reaction	45
631.	Sigbert succeeds; a zealous Christian	45
	St. Felix, the Apostle of East Anglia, founds monastery at Soham	46
633.	Penda conquers Northumbria, and stamps out Roman Mission	46
634.	Sigbert retires to monastery. Egric succeeds	46

A.D.		PAGE
636.	Celtic Mission, under Aidan, restores Northumbria to Christianity	45
637.	Mercian attack on East Anglia. Sigbert and Egric slain	47
	Anna, of Exning, succeeds to East Anglian throne	47
642.	Penda again overthrows Christianity in Northumbria	46
645.	Kenwalk, King of Wessex, expelled by Penda	46
647.	St. Felix dies, and is buried at Soham	46
652.	Etheldred, daughter of Anna, weds Tonbert, King of the Girvii	47
654.	Anna destroyed by Penda, who makes Ethelhere, a heathen, King of East Anglia	47
655.	Battle of Winfield. Penda and Ethelhere slain by Oswy of Northumbria	47
	Ethelwald restores Christianity in East Anglia	47
	Tonbert dies. Etheldred sole ruler of Girvians. Ovinus her Prime Minister	53
656.	Wulfhere, son of Penda, first Christian King of Mercia, weds Ermenilda, niece of Etheldred	48
657.	Abbeys of Peterborough and Thorney founded	49
660(?).	Etheldred weds Egfrid, son of Oswy, and aids Hilda to restore Northumbrian Christianity	51
664.	Adwulf, son of Anna, succeeds to East Anglian throne	51
	Birth of Venerable Bede	54
668.	Theodore of Tarsus made Archbishop of Canterbury	53
669.	St. Chad, the Apostle of Mercia, dies at Lichfield	54
670.	Egfrid, King of Northumbria. Etheldred leaves him, and takes veil under St. Wilfrid of York	51
673.	Etheldred returns with Wilfrid to her own kingdom, and founds monastery at Ely	51
679.	Etheldred dies. Her sister, Sexburga, Queen of Kent, succeeds as Abbess	51
685.	Egfrid of Northumbria dies	48
690.	Archbishop Theodore dies	53
695.	A coffin for St. Etheldred found amid ruins of Cambridge	52
699.	Ermenilda, Queen of Mercia, Abbess of Ely	280
731.	Venerable Bede concludes his History	54

	All England south of Humber under Mercian supremacy	54
755.	Offa, King of Mercia	63
784.	Cynewulf, King of Wessex, slain	66
787.	First Norse pirates land in England	56

Chronological Table.

A.D.		PAGE
808.	Northumbria and Kent under Charlemagne	63
823.	Egbert frees Wessex and East Anglia from Mercians	56
827.	Mercia and Northumbria conquered by Egbert, thus uniting England under his sceptre	57
	Cambridge rebuilt	57
832.	Danish invasions begin	57
866.	Danes "horsed" in East Anglia	58
867.	Northumbria ravaged by Danes	58
870.	On their return they destroy Ely and Soham, and conquer East Anglia. Murder of St. Edmund	58
	Burgraed, King of Mercia, seizes Isle of Ely	73
871.	Alfred the Great	58
875.	Cambridge Viking stronghold	58
878.	Peace of Wedmore. Cambridgeshire ceded to Danes	59
?	College of Ely set up by Alfred	72
894.	East Anglians, with Danes, ravage England	58
901.	Edward the Elder	59
905.	Last Cambridgeshire battle at Dykes	60
912.	Edward and Ethelfled begin reconquest at Danelagh	60
921.	Cambridge submits to Edward. Cambridgeshire created	61

Peace and prosperity under great Dynasty of Alfred - 61

958.	Edgar the Peaceful, King of English	64
970.	Abbeys refounded at Ely, Thorney, and Peterborough	73
973.	Edgar Basileus of Britain	64
979.	Coronation of Ethelred the Unready	65
980.	Danish invasions begin again	65
991.	Danish attack on East Anglia foiled, at Battle of Maldon, by Brithnoth	66
1002.	Massacre of St. Bryce	75
1004.	Second Danish attack repulsed by Ulfcytel	76
1010.	Battle of Ringmere. Cambridge destroyed, and Cambridgeshire ravaged by Danes	77
1016.	Edmund Ironside	78
	Battle of Assandun won by Canute	81
1017.	Canute, first "King of England," specially favours Ely	83
?	St. Benet's, Cambridge, built	87
1035.	Death of Canute. England divided	86
1036.	Alfred the Etheling murdered at Ely	86
1042.	Edward the Confessor	85
1066.	Battle of Hastings	93

Chronological Table.

A.D.		PAGE
1068.	William the Conqueror builds Cambridge Castle	98
1070.	English revolt in Fenland. Ely "Camp of Refuge."	
	Hereward	95
	Lanfranc, Archbishop of Canterbury	120
1071.	Capture of Ely by William	99
1078.	Tabula Eliensis	101
1081.	Abbot Simeon begins existing church at Ely	110
1086.	Assize of Salisbury	112
	Doomsday Survey	90
1087.	William Rufus	112
1090 (?).	Royston Cross set up	113
1092.	Canonry of St. Giles, Cambridge, founded	110
1093.	Anselm, Archbishop of Canterbury	120
1095.	First Crusade	116
1099.	Knights of St. John (Hospitallers) established	128
1100.	Henry I.	105
1106.	Norman church of Ely completed	112
1107.	Bishopric of Ely founded	111
1112.	Barnwell Abbey founded	110
1116.	University of Bologna begun	121
1118.	Templars established	116
1120.	Church of Holy Sepulchre, Cambridge, built in the Jewry	110
1133.	Priory of St. Rhadegunde founded	119
1135.	Stephen	113
	St. John's Hospital, Cambridge, founded	116
1140.	University of Paris begun (?)	121
1143.	Geoffrey de Mandeville seizes Ely and sacks Cambridge	114
1149.	University of Oxford begun (?)	121
1154.	Henry II.	113
1170.	Murder of Thomas à Becket	113
	Royston Priory founded, and hermitage in cave	113
1187.	Jerusalem taken by Saladin	130
1189.	Richard I.	127
1190.	Oxford already a University	122
1192.	Cambridgeshire under Episcopal Interdict	127
1199.	John	137
1207.	Cambridge incorporated	137
1208.	Papal Interdict on England	128
1209.	Cambridge University begun by students from Oxford	122
1215.	Galilee of Ely completed	130
	Barons' War. Magna Charta	130
	Ely ravaged by royal mercenaries	130

A.D.		PAGE
1216.	Cambridge taken by Barons	131
1216.	John's army overwhelmed by tide at Wisbeach	131
1224.	Franciscan Church built at Cambridge	120
1229.	University increased by immigration of students from Paris	123
1231.	Royal charter for University privileges	125
1232.	Guarinus, Grand Master of Hospitallers	130
1234.	Cyclone at Eltisley	133
1240.	Second immigration of Oxford students	123
1260.	Attempt to found University at Northampton	123
1261.	Town and Gown riot	122
1265.	Battle of Evesham. Ely seized by patriots	131
	Henry III. fortifies Cambridge with King's Ditch	137
	Mayoralty of Cambridge inaugurated	127
	Merton College founded at Oxford	127
1268.	Ely patriots crushed by Edward	133
1272.	Edward I.	133
1284.	Peterhouse founded	127
1299.	Cambridge dowry of Queen Margaret	138
1307.	Edward II.	163
1312.	Templars suppressed	143
1321.	Ely Lady Chapel begun	158
1322.	Fall of central tower at Ely. Alan de Walsingham begins Lantern	157
1324.	Michaelhouse founded	162
1326.	University Hall founded	162
1327.	Edward III.	163
1330.	Attempt to found University at Stamford	123
1337.	King's Hall founded	163
1338.	Report of Shingay Bailiwick	128
1347.	Pembroke Hall founded	162
1348.	Gonville Hall ("College of the Assumption") founded. Lantern completed at Ely	158
1349.	Ely Lady Chapel completed	158
1350.	Trinity Hall founded	162
	The Black Death. Ashwell inscription	157
1352.	Corpus Christi College founded	162
1359.	Clare College founded	162
1370.	Gregory XI., Pope	145
1377.	Richard II.	154
	The Poll Tax	152
1379.	Archbishop Sudbury regulates clerical fees	288

Chronological Table.

A.D.		PAGE
1380.	Grantchester Vicarage	151
1381.	Wat Tyler's rising	154
1414.	Council of Constance	167
1417.	Martin V., Pope	145
1429.	Joan of Arc	161
1430.	Assize of Barnwell	167
1431.	Eugenius IV., Pope	167
1438.	Council of Florence	167
1440.	Eton College founded	169
1441.	King's College founded	169
1448.	Queen's College founded by Margaret of Anjou	173
1450.	Cade's rebellion	173
1453.	Fall of Constantinople	184
1455.	Wars of Roses begun	173
1457.	Bishop Pecocke imprisoned at Thorney	176
1471.	Death of Henry VI.	174
1473.	St. Catharine's College founded	176
1475.	Queens' College completed by Elizabeth Woodville	174
1478.	Morton, Bishop of Ely, attempts drainage of Fens	248
1483.	Richard III.	166
1485.	Henry VII.	174
1486.	Alcock, Bishop of Ely	176
1496.	Jesus College founded	176
1497.	Fisher, Master of Michaelhouse	186
1498.	Bassingbourn Parish Accounts (to 1534)	178
1503.	Lady Margaret Professorship founded	186
1505.	Fisher, President of Queens' College	186
	Christ's College founded	186
1508.	Fisher, Chancellor of University	186
1509.	Henry VIII.	184
1511.	Erasmus at Cambridge. Study of Greek introduced	186
	St. John's College founded	186
1514.	Erasmus leaves Cambridge	187
1515.	West, Bishop of Ely	185
1530.	Sanction of "Divorce" by University	193
1533.	Cranmer, Archbishop of Canterbury	193
1534.	Papal supremacy cast off	63
	Goodrich, Bishop of Ely	188
1535.	Fisher executed. Thomas Cromwell, Chancellor	188
1536.	King's College Chapel completed	174
1539.	Abbeys suppressed	189
1540.	Regius Professorships founded	195

Chronological Table.

A.D.		PAGE
1541.	Destruction of shrines	191
	Parish of Royston founded	189
1542.	March Parish Accounts (to 1566)	207
	Magdalene College founded	194
	Parker, Master of Corpus	196
1546.	Trinity College founded	194
1547.	Edward VI.	195
1548.	Chantries suppressed	199
	Parish Guilds suppressed	196
1549.	Altars broken down	200
1550.	Peasant revolts in many counties	202
1551.	University and College libraries destroyed	195
1552.	Parish churches despoiled	197
1553.	Escape of Mary Tudor at Sawston	203
	Proclaimed Queen at Cambridge. Catholic reaction	204
	Altars set up again	208
1555.	Martyrdom of Ridley and Latimer	205
1558.	Caius College founded	209
	Elizabeth succeeds. Protestantism again dominant	206
	Altars finally overthrown	208
1559.	Parker, Archbishop of Canterbury	196
	Thirlby, last Roman Catholic Bishop of Ely, deposed	212
1560.	Episcopal Manors confiscated by Elizabeth	167
1564.	Elizabeth visits Cambridge	213
1570.	Elizabethan Statutes	245
1573.	Dr. Caius driven from Cambridge	210
1574.	First plan of Cambridge	194
1580.	Survivors of Roman Catholic Hierarchy imprisoned at Wisbeach	212
1584.	Emmanuel College founded	210
1585.	Feckenham, last Abbot of Westminster, dies at Wisbeach	213
1589.	Lancelot Andrewes, Master of Pembroke College	213
1595.	Sidney Sussex College founded	210
1603.	James I. succeeds	214
1605.	Gunpowder Plot	184
1609.	Lancelot Andrewes, Bishop of Ely	218
1610.	Hobson's Conduit	268
1615.	James I. resides at Royston	218
1623.	Charles starts thence on Spanish wooing	214
1625.	Charles I. succeeds. Wren, Master of Peterhouse	217
1630.	Draining of Fens begun	251

Chronological Table. xix

A.D.		PAGE
1633.	Laud, Archbishop of Canterbury	213
1635.	Peterhouse Chapel built	217
1638.	Wren, Bishop of Ely	217
1640.	Ship-money riot at Melbourn	222
1642.	Civil War begun. Associated Counties	214
	Wren imprisoned by Parliament	218
1643.	Churches desecrated by Dowsing	215
	Prayer-Book proscribed	226
	Covenant enforced	289
	Parsons ejected	218
	Cambridge fortified by Roundheads	223
1645.	Battle of Naseby. Cavalier march through Cambridgeshire	215
1646.	Fall of Oxford. Charles escapes through Cambridgeshire in disguise	291
1647.	Roundhead army on Triplow Heath	224
	King captured and confined at Newmarket	224
	King detained at Royston	226
1653.	Cromwell, Protector	226
1657.	Fuller, Prevaricator	229
1660.	Restoration	232
1661.	Prayer-Book brought back	233
1662.	Monmouth visits Cambridge	230
	Fire in Trinity Chapel	231
1664.	Conservators of Fens incorporated	252
1685.	Revocation of Edict of Nantes	263
	Archidiaconal Visitation. State of churches	260
1687.	James II. attempts toleration	262
1688.	Revolution	262
1704.	The great storm	264
1715.	Cambridge Hanoverian. Library enlarged by George I.	247
1730.	Senate House built	247
1740.	"Mr. Tripos" abolished	245
1753.	Carter's "History of Cambridgeshire"	236
1769.	Square caps introduced	247
1800.	Downing College built	265
	Enclosures beginning	256
1802.	"Sunday" School Union formed	266
1804.	French invasion threatened	72
1805.	Trafalgar	72
1811.	National Schools established	267
1816.	Littleport Riots	256

Chronological Table.

A.D.		PAGE
1824.	Classical Tripos begun	264
1827.	Oxford and Cambridge cricket match begun	266
1829.	Oxford and Cambridge boat race begun	266
1830.	Rick-burning	259
1837.	Accession of Queen Victoria	259
1839.	State aid to Elementary Schools begun	267
1840.	Penny Postage	236
1845.	First Cambridgeshire railway (G.E.R. main line) opened	279
1850.	Coprolite-digging begun	259
1851.	Natural and Moral Science Triposes begun	264
1856.	Law Tripos begun	264
1858.	New Statutes. Religious restrictions abolished	265
1870.	Elementary Education Act	267
1873.	Girton College founded	265
1874.	Theological Tripos begun	264
1875.	Newnham College founded	265
	History Tripos begun	264
1879.	Agricultural disasters. Depression sets in	268
	Ridley Hall founded	265
1881.	Selwyn College founded	265
1885.	Cement manufacture introduced	269
1894.	Local Government Act	268
1897.	Roman Catholic and Presbyterian Colleges founded	265
	Newmarket and Royston secede from Cambridgeshire	269

TABLE OF CONTENTS.

CHAPTER I.
INTRODUCTORY.

                                                  PAGE

Creation and dimensions of Cambridgeshire—Natural divisions—The Fenland—Southern region—River system—Geological formations—Flora—Coprolites . . . 1—6
Primæval Cambridgeshire—Evidence from fossils—The Fenland forest—Extinct fauna—"River-bed men"—Sawn deer-horns—Palæolithic weapons - - - - - 6—8
Great stride to the Neolithic period—No further break in the history of mankind—The Ugrian race—Brownies and pixies—Jadite axe-heads—Flint gradually superseded by metal—Brandon flint workings—Royston Cave . . 8—11
Incoming of the Britons—First record of Britain—The Iceni—British coinage—Cunobelin—British earthworks—British villages - . . . . . . 11—15

CHAPTER II.
ROMANO-BRITISH PERIOD.

Beginning of authentic history—Invasion of Julius Cæsar—Roman conquest of Britain—Cambridgeshire friendly—Rebellion against disarmament—Battle of the Dykes . 16—19
Roman oppression—Rebellion of Boadicea—Devastation of Cambridgeshire . . . . . . 19—22
The Pax Romana—Roman roads in Cambridgeshire—Identification of sites—The Notitia—Itineraries of Antoninus . 22—24

Camboritum — Romano-British remains — Ash-pits — Pottery —
Thimbles — Coins - - - - - - 25—27
The Diocletian system — Position of Cambridgeshire — Romano-
British army — Vandlebury — Allectus — British fleet — Constantine the Great — Magnentius — Maximus — The last Constantine — Geraint — Britain denuded of soldiers — Barbarian
inroads - - - - - - - 27—33

CHAPTER III.

ANGLO-SAXON PERIOD—I.

Origin of Saxon name — English march through Cambridgeshire
— Picts defeated at Stamford — Romano-British civilization
stamped out - - - - - - 34—36
Existing villages founded — Common fields — Eorl and churl —
Marks — Anglo-Saxon cemeteries — Ornaments — Weapons —
Currency — Spindle-whorls - - - - 37—39
Fate of Britons — The Fens still British — Girvii — British names
surviving — Basket-work - - - - - 41—42
Southern Cambridgeshire — Mercia and East Anglia — Local
dialect — Bretwaldas — Conversion of East Anglia — Bishop
Felix - - - - - - - 42—46
Last struggle of heathenism — Penda — King Anna and his
family — St. Etheldred — Foundation of Ely and Thorney —
St. Wilfrid — Burial of St. Etheldred — Her rule of the Isle
— "Families" and "hides" — Theodore of Tarsus — Parishes
formed — The cross of Ovinus — The Heptarchy - - 46—54

CHAPTER IV.

ANGLO-SAXON PERIOD—II.

Bede's forecast — England under Egbert — Mint at Cambridge —
Danish invasion — East Anglia their fastness — Great raid
of 870 — Ely destroyed — Death of St. Edmund — Vikings at
Cambridge - - - - - - 54—58
Peace of Wedmore — Last Cambridgeshire battle — Cambridgeshire in the Danelagh — Reconquest by Edward — Creation
of the county — Hundreds and tithings — Fight at Chesterford (?) - - - - - - - 59—62
Edgar the Peaceful — Ethelred the Unready — Danish inroads
recommence — Battle of Maldon — Brithnoth at Ely — Refounding of the abbey — Shrines - - - - 64—74

Sweyn's invasion—Ulfcytel the Ready—Battle of Ringmere
—Cambridgeshire separate from East Anglia—Ravaged by
Danes—Sack of Cambridge—Massacre of Balsham—Bar-
rington Ford—Bracteates   -   -   -   - 75—78
Edmund Ironside—Battle of Assandun (Ashdon)—Arguments
for its locality—Order of battle—English colours—
Edmund's charge—Treason of Edric—Canute's minster   78—82
Canute first King of England—Earlier royal titles—His favour
for Ely—Prosperity of the abbey—Officers—Schools—
Royal pupils   -   -   -   -   -   - 82—85
Alfred the Etheling—Rebuilding and expansion of Cambridge
—St. Benet's   -   -   -   -   -   - 86—87

CHAPTER V.

NORMAN PERIOD.

Cambridgeshire specially ruined by Conquest—Doomsday—No
Thanes in county—No English landholders—Destruction
and oppression of Cambridge   -   -   -   - 88—92
Reasons for this—William's theoretical position—Wholesale
confiscation of land   -   -   -   -   - 92—94
Revolt of Fenland—Danes at Ely—Camp of Refuge—Here-
ward—Capture of Ely—Tabula Eliensis—Nomenclature—
English stamped out   -   -   -   - 95—104
Good results of Conquest—Extinction of slavery—Revival of
religion—William of Malmesbury   -   -   105—106
Norman churches—Ely a bishopric—New cathedral—Royston
—Thomas à Becket   -   -   -   -   109—113
Anarchy under Stephen—Galfrid de Maundeville—Bishop
Nigel—Rise of existing Cambridge   -   -   113—116

CHAPTER VI.

EARLY ENGLISH PERIOD.

Burst of progress in the thirteenth century—Church-building
—Friars in Cambridge—Educational movement—Literary
development of the thirteenth century—English historians—
Foreign dialecticians   -   -   -   -   118—121
First universities—Bologna, Paris, Oxford, Cambridge—Earliest
University organization—Course of study—Trivium and
Quadrivium—Proctors—Collegiate system begun—Its ad-
vantages—Merton, Peterhouse   -   -   -   121—127

xxiv   *Contents.*

Bishop Longchamps—Interdicts—Queen Eleanor—Papal ban
—Exemption of preceptories—Shingay—"Fairy-cart"—
Report of bailiwick . . . . 127—128
Barons' War—Cambridgeshire a national stronghold—Ravaged
by Royalists—Recovered by Barons—John's march from
Wisbeach—Patriot defence of Ely . . 130—133
Historians of the period—Local anecdotes—Eltisley cyclone—
Matthew Paris—His notes on the weather and the
crops . . . . . . 133—135
Growth of Cambridge—The King's Ditch—Monastic buildings
—Religious Houses throughout the county—Hospitals—
Hermitages—Our Lady of Whitehill—Papal Bulla 140—145
Episcopal registers—Vicarage of Grantchester—The poll-tax—
Wat Tyler—The Black Death—Ashwell inscription—Ely
lantern—Lady Chapel . . . . 146—158

CHAPTER VII.

"PERPENDICULAR" PERIOD.

Results of the Black Death—Free labour—Perpendicular
architecture—Insularity—John Bull . . 160—161
The first colleges—Peterhouse—Michaelhouse—King's Hall—
Early collegiate life—Special studies—Pembroke—Clare
—Assize of Barnwell—Ely manors—Stock—"Smoke
farthings"—Spoliation of the see - . . 162—168
Foundation of King's College—Henry VI.—Eton—Will of King
Henry VI.—Queens' College—Wars of the Roses—Completion of King's College Chapel—Milton's and Wordsworth's descriptions of it - . . . 168—175
Heralds of the Reformation—Reginald Pecocke—Jesus College
founded - . . . . . 175—176
Bassingbourn accounts—Inventory—The Use of Sarum 178—182

CHAPTER VIII.

REFORMATION PERIOD—I.

Length of Reformation drama—Causes of Reformation—Fall
of Constantinople—Renaissance—Bishop West—Fisher—
Christ's and St. John's founded—First pensioners—Erasmus
—Sir Thomas More—Greek pronunciation - 183—187

Cromwell Chancellor—Change of curriculum—Despoiling of University—Bishop Goodrych—Suppression of Abbeys—Grievances following—Royston Priory—Latimer's protest—Destruction of shrines—Popular revolts—Cambridgeshire Protestants . . . . . 188—192
'Germans' at Cambridge—Magdalene—Trinity—Regius professorships—Bishop Cox—Libraries destroyed - 193—196
Parish guilds suppressed—Church goods confiscated—Barrington Inventory—Overthrow of morality—Peasant risings 196—202
Mary at Sawston—Proclaimed at Cambridge—Catholic reaction—Dr. Perne—Marian persecutions—Ridley's farewell to Cambridge - - - - - 203—205
Elizabethan counter-change—Disastrous effect of unsettlement—March parish accounts—Caius—Emmanuel—Sidney 206—210

CHAPTER IX.

REFORMATION PERIOD—II.

Oliver Cromwell at Sidney—The prisoners of Wisbeach—Protestantism loses favour—Elizabeth at Cambridge—Lancelot Andrewes—Reactionary movement—James I. and Charles I. at Royston - - - - 211—213
Civil War—Associated counties—Royalist march on Cambridge—Ecclesiastical disturbances—Dowsing—Profanation of churches—Ejection of incumbents—Ship-money—Cromwell at Cambridge - - - - - 214—223
Lack of funds—Discontent of the army—Triplow Heath—Cornet Joyce—Charles at Newmarket—March on London—King detained at Royston - - - 223—226
Changes at Cambridge—Prayer-Book torn up—"Oliva Pacis"—Puritan license—Mr. Tripos—University humour—Thomas Fuller—Ode to Monmouth - - - 226—230

CHAPTER X.

MODERN PERIOD.

Modern England begun at Restoration—Political conditions—Ecclesiastical—Social—Coinage—First coppers—Earlier tokens - - - - - - 232—235
First public vehicles—First postal deliveries—First newspapers - - - - - - 235—236

xxvi   *Contents.*

                                                                PAGE
Newmarket Races—Stourbridge Fair-   -   -   237—240
University progress in eighteenth century—The Tripos—
   George I. enlarges the Library—Epigrams   -   245—247
Draining of Fens—Early objections—Attempt by Charles I.—
   Bedford Level—Cromwell—Conservators—Wicken Fen—
   Decoys   -   -   -   -   -   -   247—253
Enclosure of wastes—Effect on peasantry—Agrarian discontent
   —Rising at Ely—Rick-burning—Victorian prosperity   256—259
Church restoration—Earlier decay—Visitation of 1685—State
   of fabrics—Services—Education—Nonconformity—Briefs—
   The great storm   -   -   -   -   -   259—264
University changes in nineteenth century   -   -   264—266
Elementary education—First (Sunday) schools—Local Government—Water-supply—Hobson's conduit—Present agricultural depression   -   -   -   -   266—269
APPENDICES   -   -   -   -   -   -   270—291
INDEX   -   -   -   -   -   -   -   292—306

PRINCIPAL WORKS ON CAMBRIDGESHIRE.

Babington : " Ancient Cambridgeshire "	1883
„ " Flora of Cambridgeshire "	1860
Blomefield : " Collectanea Cantabrigiensis "	1750
Bonney : " Cambridge Geology "	1875
Carter : " History of Cambridgeshire "	1753
Clark, J. W. : " The Observances in Use at the Augustinian Priory of St. Giles and St. Andrew at Barnwell "	1897
Cooke : " Tourists' Pocket Directory "	1807
Kingston : " East Anglia and the Great Civil War "	1897
Lysons : " Magna Britannia," vol. ii., part i.	1808
Nichols, J. : " History of Barnwell Abbey "	1786
Powell : " The East Anglian Rising, 1381 "	1896

ON CAMBRIDGE ITSELF AND THE UNIVERSITY:

Caius : " Historiæ Cantabrigiensis Academiæ "	1574
Clark, J. W. : " Architectural History of the University of Cambridge "	1885
Clark, J. W. : " Historical and Picturesque Notes "	1890
Cooper, C. H. : " Annals of Cambridge "	1842
Dyer, G. : " History of Cambridge "	1814
Fuller, T. : " History of the University to 1634 "	
Logan : " Cantabrigia Illustrata "	1688
Mullinger, J. : " History of the University "	1888

On Ely and the Isle:

Bentham, J.: "History of Ely"	1771
Clements, J. H.: "Brief History of Ely and its Villages"	1868
Elstobb, W.: "Historical Account of the Great Level"	1793
Miller and Sketchley: "Fenland, Past and Present"	1878
Stubbs: "Historical Memorials of Ely Cathedral"	1897
Warner, H.: "History of Thorney"	1878
Wells, S.: "History of the Draining of the Bedford Level"	1830

See also The Proceedings of the Camden Society and of the Cambridge Archæological Society *passim*.

HISTORY OF CAMBRIDGESHIRE.

CHAPTER I.

INTRODUCTORY.

§ 1—8. Creation and dimensions of Cambridgeshire—Natural divisions—The Fenland—Southern region—River system—Geological formations—Flora—Coprolites.

§ 9—11. Primæval Cambridgeshire—Evidence from fossils—The Fenland forest—Extinct fauna—" River-bed men "—Sawn deer-horns—Palæolithic weapons.

§ 12—19. Great stride to the Neolithic period—No further break in the history of mankind—The Ugrian race—Brownies and pixies—Jadite axe-heads—Flint gradually superseded by metal—Brandon flint workings—Royston Cave.

§ 20—25. Incoming of the Britons—First record of Britain—The Iceni—British coinage—Cunobelin—British earthworks—British villages.

§ 1. THE county of Cambridge is one of those purely artificial divisions which render the boundaries of our Midland shires so much less interesting than those of Northern, Eastern and Southern England. In these last the limits of the modern county mostly correspond, roughly at least, and sometimes very closely indeed, with those of some ancient British or Anglian or Saxon principality. Northumberland and Cumberland,

Norfolk and Suffolk, Essex, Middlesex and Sussex, Kent, Dorset and Devon, all these were formed, not by arbitrary mapping out, like the present departments of France, but by historical development, like her old provinces. Their very names tell the tale of their origin and of their growth. They are the original entities, the gradual accretion of which has issued in the formation of England. Such counties never bear the name of their chief town; for town and county arose independently, and when their names resemble each other (*e.g.*, Dorset and Dorchester), it is the town that is called after the shire rather than the shire after the town. A few exceptions are, indeed, to be found. Lancashire, Yorkshire, and, most remarkably of all, Hampshire—the county of Southampton—are evidently mere administrative divisions, created by the government of an already existing England, not factors in the evolution of England. The original divisions have here been erased, only a few distinct names, such as Furness, Holderness and Craven, lingering on in tradition to tell us what they were. And this is the arrangement which in the Midlands we find general. Save one county only, and that the latest formed of all, Rutland, all are artificial administrative divisions named after a chief town, with here and there a faint traditional remembrance (as in Lindesay, Kesteven, and Elmet in Lincolnshire) of the older state of things still surviving in East Anglia and Wessex. Not that the Midland counties are creations of yesterday—far from it. Rutland itself dates from the Norman Conquest; and the very difference between the nomenclature of the Midland shires and the older districts around them tells us the tale of those fearful Danish invasions which swept away all previous government throughout Central England, and of the glorious energy and statecraft wherewith Central England was reconquered and welded together with the surrounding lands into an integral and indivisible whole by the children of the Great Alfred, Edward the Elder and his sister, the Lady of the Mercians.

§ 2. These illustrious princes have received scant justice from history; but of the brother in particular it is not too much to say that, with the single exception of his heroic and saintly father, no English king has ever deserved so nobly of his country. If the father, by his unconquerable devotion and patriotism, saved the very existence of the realm, it was the son who brought to harvest the good seed sown by the father's efforts; and without such a son and successor those efforts would have been in vain. Edward succeeded to the desolated and half-ruined heritage of Wessex; at his accession half the English people were groaning beneath an alien and heathen yoke. He left to his heir the throne of a united and Christian England, and the overlordship of the whole Island of Britain. Rightly does Florence of Worcester, the leader of that wonderful choir of national historians which adorned our country in the twelfth century, speak of him as "dignitate potentia pariter et gloria superior" even to Alfred himself, and inferior to him in nothing except those literary labours which were so peculiarly Alfred's own.[1]

§ 3. It is to this monarch, then, and to his sister, that we owe the creation of Cambridgeshire: a long strip of territory, bounded on the east by the ancient East Anglian counties, and elsewhere by arbitrary lines, the exact delimitation of which was due, doubtless, to long-forgotten local reasons of the tenth century. Its greatest length from north to south is about fifty miles, its greatest breadth about twenty-five, either line of greatest dimension passing through the town of Cambridge.

§ 4. The county is divided by Nature into two regions of about equal size, but very different in character, the Fenlands in the north, and the low chalk uplands in the south. The latter, strictly speaking, form the actual shire

[1] See Freeman's "Norman Conquest," vol. i., p. 56.

of Cambridge, the former having to a great extent a legally independent recognition, under the name of the Isle of Ely.[1] This recognition is the last relic of the quasi-palatinate jurisdiction formerly exercised by the Bishops of Ely, against whose " peace " (and not that of the King, as elsewhere in England) evildoers in that district were held to offend, and before whose tribunal they were summoned. The region thus privileged is now a vast alluvial plain, almost treeless, intersected in every direction by a network of ditches, locally called "lodes," from which the water is pumped by steam-power into the sluggish channels along which it makes its way into the sea. The whole district is only kept dry by artificial means, for it is well below sea-level, and even within living memory was one vast morass, tenanted by innumerable wild-fowl. To this day it remains sparsely inhabited, the few towns and villages located on the almost imperceptible rises marking what were once islets amid the marsh. The elevated ground on which Ely itself stands formed an island of greater height and of respectable size, giving space for a whole group of villages. It is still surrounded by water, various branches of the Ouse stagnating round it.

§ 5. The Southern Region consists of low chalky uplands, through which the Cam, and its sister stream the Granta, with their various tributaries, have eroded marvellously broad valleys for such petty rivers. The former, also called the Rhee, has its source in a lovely group of springs at Ashwell, in Hertfordshire, just across the county boundary; while the latter, in like manner, rises just outside the county, near Saffron Walden, in Essex. The southern boundary of their basin is formed by the escarpment of the great chalk plateau, which sweeps through England from the Yorkshire Wolds to the coast of Devon, and is so conspicuous a feature in the geological map of our island; and which at this part of its

[1] See Chapter IV., § 24.

course forms the watershed between the valleys of the Thames and the Ouse. The river gravel deposited by these streams rests usually upon the Gault, a bluish clay very finely comminuted and tenacious, and specially impervious to water. This bed is usually of considerable thickness, averaging 200 feet, and rests in turn on the Lower Greensand, which crops out at the western side of the county, and furnishes an abundant supply of excellent water, frequently rising in a fountain when artesian wells are pierced through the Gault. The chalk outliers are often capped by boulder clay, containing many travelled fragments of rock, usually ice-marked. The chalk itself is locally called "clunch," and is much used for building, some of the churches (*e.g.*, Barrington) being entirely constructed of this material.

§ 6. The flora of Cambridgeshire is now poor in the extreme. Not a single fern, and very few wild-flowers, are to be found; while the interesting plants which once existed in the fens and on the chalk downs have vanished before the spread of cultivation, like the wild-fowl of the former and the bustard of the latter regions. The Great Copper butterfly, too, no longer brightens the reed-beds, and its companion, the Swallow-tail, is only found in remote nooks here and there.

§ 7. The whole county is rich in fossils; the river gravel furnishing remains of elephant, rhinoceros, hippopotamus, lion, hyæna, cave-bear, etc., and the secondary strata many species of birds, saurians, crustacea, and mollusca, with, in comparison, but few fishes, though sharks' teeth are found in extraordinary abundance, beautifully polished and as sharp as ever. These relics are chiefly contained in the Upper Greensand—a very thin stratum, full of green grains of glauconite and innumerable formless phosphatic nodules, locally, though mistakenly, called coprolites. They are probably concretions from the softer tissues of various animals and plants flourishing in a shallow sea, and are so numerous and so rich in phosphate of lime that it has been found worth while to unearth and grind them for manure wherever they occur within twenty-five feet of the surface. A very large area of the Cam Valley has thus been turned over within the last half-century, to the great profit of the land-owners, these coprolites being usually worth some £150 per acre.

§ 8. To the coprolite industry we owe most of the materials for our sketch of the county in prehistoric periods. The systematic upturning of very large areas to the depth of from five to twenty-five feet has brought to light all relics of the past contained in the overlying soil; and though many objects of rare interest were lost or destroyed, especially in the earlier years of the excavation, by the ignorance and cupidity of the workmen, yet enough have been preserved in the University museums and in the custody of intelligent collectors to throw an unusual amount of light on the by-gone condition of the district.

§ 9. By the light thus afforded we get our earliest view of Cambridgeshire as a region of forest, sparsely wooded in the southern uplands, densely over the northern levels of the Fenland. It is strange to contrast the utterly treeless state of these reclaimed fens with what they were before they became fen. Below the peat of the marshes a forest bed covers the whole country, the stems and roots of oak, beech, hazel, and alder being found in abundance. The plain must therefore have been at that time not below the sea-level, as now, but sufficiently above it at least for the growth of all this timber. It is, indeed, fairly certain, on geological grounds, that the entire bed of the North Sea was then dry land—a vast plain through which our Eastern rivers meandered till they joined the great estuary of the Rhine near the present coast of Norway. Over this plain and through these forests wandered the rich fauna of the Pleistocene period: elephant, rhinoceros, and hippopotamus wallowing in the swamps and browsing along the rivers; the red deer and the Irish elk, with his mighty horns, haunting the glades, along with the bison, the gigantic wild-ox (*Bos primigenius*), and their diminutive ally (*Bos longifrons*); while these and other ruminants furnished abundant prey to the great carnivora—lion, bear, and hyæna—whose remains are found intermingled with theirs in the débris of their native streams all over the county.

§ 10. Nor are traces wanting to show the presence, even in those remote times, of human intelligence. The roughly-shaped unpolished flint axe-heads and arrow-heads, ascribed by archæologists to the "river-bed men," are found in the same strata as the bones of these extinct monsters. The bases of stag's horns—sometimes shed in the course of nature, sometimes broken from the skull—are also found in these strata, with the antler laboriously sawn off by the repeated cuts of some soon-blunted implement (such as a fragment of oyster-shell might be). Some specimens of these, dredged up off the coast of Essex, are in the British Museum. In the gravels of the Cam they are numerous, and, from the uniformity with which they have been treated, were evidently in common use amongst the savages of that period, though what purpose they can have served is still an undiscovered problem in archæology. But it is interesting to note that reindeer horns are to this day habitually so treated by the Esquimaux, with a view to utilizing the upper part of the antler. A pair of these sawn-off deer's horns form an essential part of the equipment of every dog-sledge. When the hunter has occasion to leave his team for a while, he drives these antlers deep into the snow, and thus anchors the sledge, which the dogs would otherwise be very likely to run away with.

§ 11. As the ages passed on, land and sea assumed their present boundaries. Britain became an island, with the hills and dales, the shores and the rivers, which still endure. The larger animals earliest became extinct; but the bear, the elk, and the wild-bull survived almost to historic times in the district. The skull of one of the last-named, wounded by a flint implement, a portion of which still remains embedded in the bone, was found in Burwell Fen in 1863, and is now in the Woodwardian Museum at Cambridge.

§ 12. The fashion of this implement shows a marked change from those met with in the earlier periods. It is no longer a mere flake, roughly chipped into the desired shape, as of old, but a smoothly-polished weapon ground to a fine edge and bespeaking in its manufacture a great advance in art and intellect. This passage from the Palæolithic age of rough flakes to the Neolithic, with its well-wrought implements, marks, in fact, a greater step in human progress than any other change within our ken. From the "river-bed" savages we are separated by an absolute gulf; we know neither whence they came nor whither they disappeared, nor whether they were the progenitors or the victims of the later race whom we find occupying their ground. Some writers, indeed, have identified them with the Lapps and Esquimaux of our Arctic regions, but on such slender grounds as to be little better than pure conjecture. But from the Neolithic period onwards the advance of the human race can be traced; we meet with no further break in its history. Stone was succeeded by bronze, and bronze by iron, in the armoury of mankind, but each age passed gradually into the next, with no such gulf between as severs the two Stone Ages.

§ 13. The Neolithic weapons found in Cambridgeshire are sometimes discovered by the plough in the open fields, sometimes unearthed from the tombs of those who wielded them. These tombs are oblong barrows distinguishable by their shape from the round tumuli of the subsequent Celtic interments, and the skulls of their occupants show the same diversity. It is, indeed, a rule in archæology: "Long barrows, long skulls; round barrows, round skulls." This long-skulled race of flint-users is commonly known by the name of Ugrian, and tradition has preserved, in the fairy-tales of our childhood, many of its characteristics. The savage Ogre, the spiteful woodland Brownie, the crafty subterraneous Pixie, are reminiscences, filtered through many a tale round the winter fire, of the cannibalism, the complexion, the character, the habitations, and the stature, of this early race.

§ 14. We can picture them to ourselves, by the flickering light of these old traditions: brown-skinned beings, sometimes of huge stature (as the owner of the famous Neanderthal skull must have been), but mostly diminutive, dwelling in the recesses of the forests, like the brown dwarfs (not improbably of the very same race), in Central Africa at this day, and like them savage, spiteful, crafty, skilful in the manufacture of murderous weapons, and thus dreaded by the superior races forming settlements amongst them.

§ 15. The legends which tell how Brownie and Pixie would flee from the very sight of iron teach us by what means the prehistoric flint-wielders were exterminated, driven to seek refuge in the chalk-pits whence their flints were procured, forced to remain unseen during the day, and only venturing above ground at nightfall, till finally the race became utterly extinct. The iron weapons of the incoming Aryan tribes, and their vast superiority both in physical force and in civilization, proved atogether too much for the earlier savages. Yet their extinction was probably a matter of centuries; and, indeed, there are not wanting authorities who contend that to this day there remain, notably in Ireland, many non-Aryan characteristics amongst the population of our islands, derived from this forgotten source.

§ 16. In Cambridgeshire, however, the only traces of their existence remaining are their sepulchral barrows and their weapons, sometimes formed of local flint, sometimes of such as is more usually found in the North of England (which may, however, have been obtained from the boulder clay of the neighbourhood); while specimens are not unknown of the beautiful jadite axe-heads, whose existence tells us so much concerning prehistoric civilization.

§ 17. In these we have the very earliest evidence of trade; and that not mere local barter, but an interchange of commodities between regions very widely separated. The only known locality where the material of which these axe-heads are composed is to be found is in the Chinese Empire; but the axe-heads themselves are met with all over Europe, and also in North America, proving that trade routes existed throughout the greater part of the Northern Hemisphere; while the wonderful finish of the articles, and their manufacture from so intractable a material, speaks much for the degree of skill to which their makers had attained.

§ 18. With the coming in of the Celtic races flint was everywhere superseded by metal, first bronze, and then iron, but so gradually and with so little breach of continuity that we find flint weapons still in use as late as the Battle of Hastings (where William of Poitiers mentions "lignis imposita saxa" as amongst the arms of the English militia); while the chalk-pits at Brandon in Norfolk bear evidence of having been continually worked for flints from prehistoric times to the present day. Now these pits only supply the guns of negro slave-hunters; but the piles of chippings and flakes around tell of the days when Europeans fought with flintlocks and struck their light by means of tinder-boxes, no less than of the more distant Ugrian period. Nay, the very implements still used in the pits, with their peculiar shape, are but copies in wood and iron of the stone heads fixed into deer-horn hafts which are now and then found in some fallen-in adit, along with the bones of their prehistoric owner.

§ 19. Like workings, though now quite disused, are also found in the South Downs, and Cambridgeshire has one very remarkable example in the Royston Cave. Though modified by subsequent use for the purposes of Christian worship, there can be little doubt that this interesting excavation was originally made by flint-seekers. It presents the usual features of their pits: a perpendicular shaft some twenty feet deep, narrow enough to be climbed by means of footholds cut in the sides, and gradually opening out into a circular chamber, widened as the flints and the surrounding chalk were dug away, the whole cave thus being shaped like a bottle.

§ 20. The first Aryans who reached our island belonged to the Celtic races, the earliest swarm, in all probability, cast off by the parent stock from its home in Central Asia. Pushing across the Russian steppes, exterminating and driving before them whatever previous inhabitants they met with in their course, these races in wave upon wave poured in upon our shores. The first inrush was probably that of the pure Celts, or Goidels, the latest that of the Britons, or Cymry (an appellation signifying simply 'confederates,' and probably the 'Gomer' of Genesis x. 2), who on their march had left their name abidingly attached both to the Crimea and to the Cimbric peninsula of Denmark; and, each tribe being quite as ready to make room for itself at the expense of its Aryan kindred as at that of the aboriginal savages, it was by the Britons that the region now called England was finally occupied.

§ 21. Nor does this final occupation appear to have been of more than a few centuries' standing, when the conquests of Julius Cæsar first bring the country into connection with classical history. We there find that it was at that time divided amongst some score of Cymric clans, small and great, of the same blood, speech, and religion as those of Gaul;[1] sometimes, indeed, even of the same name, for there were Parisians settled on the Humber. Cambridge formed the western march of the dominions of the Iceni (as the name is usually written, though their own spelling of it, as their coins testify, was Ecen, while its many survivals in local topography show it to have been unquestionably pronounced *Ickn*), the most powerful, perhaps, of all the clans, themselves occupying the whole of Norfolk and Suffolk, and exercising over neighbouring tribes an influence so widely felt that Cæsar knew them as the Cenimagni—'the great Iceni'—while their military frontier road, the Icknield Way, extended right down to the Thames near Reading. This road followed the line of what are usually called the East Anglian Heights, its course testified to by such names as Ickborough in Norfolk, Icklingham in Suffolk, Ickleton in Cambridgeshire, and Ickleford in Herts, found along it.

§ 22. The existence of engineering works on so large a scale would alone be sufficient to prove that the Britons were not the mere savages which, until quite recently, historians have depicted them. Cicero, indeed, declares, in belittling Cæsar's doings, that Britain could produce no plunder worth lifting except slaves, "and quite uncultured slaves too"; but Cæsar himself and other writers, as well as the few undisputed relics of the pre-Roman British period, tell a different tale. The Britons had for many years been sufficiently civilized to have a coinage of their own,[2] of native Welsh and Cornish gold, rudely

---

[1] Cæsar, "Bell. Gall.," v. 12.

[2] Cæsar speaks of this coinage as follows: "Utuntur aut ære aut nummo aureo, aut annulis ferreis ad certum pondus examinatis pro nummo." This passage was deliberately corrupted by Scaliger in the seventeenth century to deny the use of money amongst the Britons, and he was followed by editors for 200 years.

imitated from the staters of Philip of Macedon. To his equestrian device the Iceni added their own tribal badge, a crescent and a star, their coins, which are not uncommon, being mostly small thick saucers of gold, weighing about as much as a sovereign, with more rare examples of thinner and smaller specimens only one-fourth of that weight. These coins were probably introduced in the first instance through the Greek traders of Marseilles, to whom the British Druids were also most likely indebted for the Greek alphabet,[1] and possibly for the Greek language, at that time the *lingua franca* of commerce and civilization throughout the world. The Britons were even sufficiently advanced to have fraudulent coiners amongst them, spurious imitations, composed of base metal gilded over, being sometimes found amongst their hoards. At the same time, the increasing rudeness of their devices, which begin with a perfectly recognisable copy of their Greek original, and degenerate into a series of unintelligible scratches, testify to their lack of artistic ability, till Roman influence began to make itself felt in the first century before Christ. Under that influence we see a fresh development take place; the unintelligible scratches are superseded by devices of no small merit—a vine-leaf, or an ear of corn, or a wild-boar, or a bull, or an armed warrior; while Cunobelin, who reigned in Britain about the time of the Christian era, with such sway that his name alone of independent British monarchs has been echoed down by tradition (in the form of Cymbeline), added a Latin superscription above the figure presumably meant for his image, and used silver and bronze as well as gold in his mint.

§ 23. Cambridgeshire has supplied various examples of his coinage, as well as of the earlier Icenic gold; and has likewise preserved indications of its British period, not only in the Icknield Street (which runs across the

[1] Cæsar, "Bell. Gall.," vi. 13.

south-eastern corner of the county, and in the town of Royston is still called by its ancient name), but in the earthworks of Castle Hill at Cambridge, of Vandlebury on the Gog Magog Hills, of the Round Moats at Fowlmere, and, probably, in those at Shuckburgh Castle and at Grantchester. The four (or five) great dykes which cross the Icknield Way at right angles may also be assigned almost with certainty to this period. Excavations show them to be of later age than the street itself, and to be intended for its defence against invaders from the westward. All begin from the low marshes fringing the course of the Cam, and run south-eastwards for a few miles, thus completely crossing the narrow strip of open chalk slopes which must always have existed between those marshes and the primæval forest on the East Anglian Heights. That narrow strip would form the natural path into the land of the Iceni, and was thus at once the line of their military road and a jealously-guarded military frontier. An invader endeavouring to advance along the road would first have had to force the passage of the Brand Ditch, running from the boggy region between Melbourne and Fowlmere (still full of springs) to Heydon on the summit of the Thames watershed; then that of the Brent Ditch near Abington; then (according to the very probable view of Professor Hughes) that of the so-called Worsted Street, with its north-western flank protected by the great fort of Vandlebury; then that of the Fleam Dyke, running from Fen Ditton (a name probably derived from Ditch End) to Balsham; and finally the yet more formidable line of the famous Devil's Dyke across Newmarket Heath. This stupendous fortification extends for nearly ten miles, from the fen at Reach to the forest at Wood Ditton. The rampart (here, as in all the other defences, on the eastern side), is thirty feet above the bottom of the ditch, and was doubtless surmounted by a palisade of heavy timbers, forming an obstacle which would to this day prove formidable to troops, especially if unprovided with artillery. The names of most of these dykes, Brand, Brent (*i.e.* burnt), Fleam (? flame), and Worsted (the place of war), bear testimony to the traces of battle and conflagration still visible along their course when our English ancestors entered the land and bestowed upon them these abiding designations.

§ 24. Besides these relics of warlike handiwork, there have here and there been found in the county traces of the ordinary village life of the Britons. These have been chiefly unearthed for a moment during the process of coprolite digging, and have unhappily been almost always destroyed in that process without being seen by any but the diggers. One such, however, at the village of Barrington, was carefully watched during the work, and was found to consist of a collection of circular pits, from twelve to twenty feet in diameter, and from two to four feet in depth, cut out in the chalky clay, and usually with a small drain running from each for a few feet down the gentle slope on which the whole were built. The entire settlement was surrounded by a four-foot ditch and rampart. These pits were doubtless the dwelling-places of the ancient British villagers, a superstructure of wood and thatch completing them into very passable wigwams for the scanty population, who supported themselves partly by hunting, but more particularly by the pasturage which the open chalk lands afforded for their sheep and their scarcely larger oxen, and by the rude tilth immediately around each little community.

§ 25. From these and such-like relics we can in some degree reconstruct the physical and ethnological development of our county in the remote and unrecorded past. But not till we find ourselves brought into contact with the great name of Rome do we enter the regions of its actual history.

CHAPTER II.

ROMANO-BRITISH PERIOD.

§ 1—4. Beginning of authentic history—Invasion of Julius Cæsar—Roman conquest of Britain—Cambridgeshire friendly—Rebellion against disarmament—Battle of the Dykes.

§ 5—7. Roman oppression—Rebellion of Boadicea—Devastation of Cambridgeshire.

§ 8—11. The Pax Romana—Roman roads in Cambridgeshire—Identification of sites—The Notitia—Itineraries of Antoninus.

§ 12—16. Camboritum—Romano-British remains—Ash-pits—Pottery—Thimbles—Coins.

§ 17—24. The Diocletian system—Position of Cambridgeshire—Romano-British army—Vandlebury—Allectus—British fleet—Constantine the Great—Magnentius—Maximus—The last Constantine—Geraint—Britain denuded of soldiers—Barbarian inroads.

§ 1. AUTHENTIC history begins for our island with the enterprise of Julius Cæsar, undertaken, as it would seem, rather with a view to making a sensation at Rome by carrying the eagles to so distant a region, than with any idea of permanently occupying the country. But the first wave of Roman invasion, which thus, in 55 B.C., broke upon the shores of Britain, spent its force just before it reached the borders of Cambridgeshire. The stronghold of the chieftain who then stood forward as the British champion—Cassivellaunus (as Cæsar Latinizes his native name Caswallon)—is commonly supposed by antiquaries to have been somewhere in the neighbourhood of St. Albans. At all events, he was not an Icenian; and when, a century later, the Romans again entered the land, this time as permanent conquerors, the Iceni not only submitted, but co-operated as "friendlies" in the earlier campaigns of the invaders. Thus, while other clans were subdued and disarmed as a result of the operations of 46 and 47 A.D. (in which Vespasian, the future Emperor, was singled out, in the words of Tacitus, by his courage and resource, for the high destiny awaiting him), the inhabitants of Cambridgeshire retained their military strength unbroken. Indeed, they were, in all probability, positively the freer for the advent of the Romans, having been previously to some extent kept down by the widespread power of Cunobelin,[1] Prince of the rival sept of the Trinobantes, whose home territory comprised Essex and Middlesex, while his suzerainty seems to have been acknowledged by at least the whole of Southern and Eastern Britain. Already, in the days of Julius Cæsar, had the Trinobantes become "prope firmissima omnium ejus regionis civitatum,"[2] and since his date their power had enormously developed, probably by that adoption of Roman culture to which their coins bear witness. The capital fastness of Cunobelin was no further off than Camelodunum (Colchester), and the deep impression made by the sway which he thence exercised is shown in its lasting effect upon local and national tradition. Not only was Camelodunum the only site in Britain deemed worthy to be advanced to the dignity of a Roman colony (whence its present name of Colchester = Colonia-ceastre), but the remembrance that it had once been the seat of British royalty was handed down from bard to bard, till "Camelot" became the capital city of their ideal British monarch, King Arthur, and was finally iden-

[1] See Chapter I., § 22.
[2] Cæsar, "Bell. Gall.," v. 20.

tified by the mediæval romancers with the most ancient historic capital known to them, the West Saxon royal city of Winchester. The Iceni had, doubtless, submitted with little pleasure to the eclipse of their ancient greatness by this rise of a rival clan, and rejoiced to see the power of the Trinobantes fall before the invading Romans. If they were to be subject-allies, it was better to stand in that relation to these world-wide conquerors than to upstart neighbours of their own.

§ 2. But when Ostorius, in A.D. 50, succeeded Aulus Plautius in the proprætorship of Britain, the Iceni began to feel the pressure of the foreign yoke. On the excuse that the unsubdued clans were raiding the districts well affected to Rome, he not only, by swift and unexpected manœuvres, cut to pieces the raiders, but determined upon a general disarmament of all Britons alike — "friendlies" as well as "hostiles." On this point the Iceni doubtless felt as the kindred Highlanders felt towards similar measures adopted by the government of George II. To such freeborn warriors the surrender of their arms was a degradation intolerable. Not only did they themselves refuse the demand of Ostorius, but they hastily organized a confederacy of the clans around and bade him defiance.

§ 3. The spot on which they drew together to await his onset was well chosen. Tacitus ("Ann.," xii. 31) describes in forcible words the earthen rampart and the narrow strait through which the Romans had to force their way; and though his brief narrative makes it impossible with certainty to identify the ground, yet it is more than probable that those four great dykes mentioned in our last chapter played a decisive part in the struggle.[1] We have no reason to suppose that they were made for the occasion, for the strait between fen and woodland which they defended was the old and only entrance to the Icenian

[1] See Chapter I., § 23.

realm, and had doubtless witnessed many a stout prehistoric struggle. But they would now be repaired and garrisoned, and would present a formidable obstacle to the advance of the Roman forces, which Ostorius, without delay, led to crush the movement. His natural line of march would be along the Icknield Way; and by it, at the head of his auxiliary forces (for he had no legionaries with him), he flung himself upon the British army. The first dyke which barred his way was impetuously assailed along its whole length at once, and the Britons behind it put to headlong flight. They had intended, presumably, to retreat from rampart to rampart, defending each in turn, but the impetuosity of the Roman charge carried all before it. Once the first dyke was stormed, those behind proved only obstacles to embarrass the rout of the defenders, and the space between no better than a death-trap. Shut in between the forest to the east and the fen to the west, those fugitives only escaped who had the good fortune to force their way through the mad crush at the narrow entrances of Balsham Dyke and the Devil's Ditch. The rest were caught by the pursuing enemy and slaughtered wholesale, by way of express warning to such Britons as were still hesitating whether or no to join the anti-Roman league thus lucklessly inaugurated by the unhappy Iceni.

§ 4. The lesson was evidently not taught in vain. During the great campaign of the following year, which, by crushing Caractacus (or Caradoc, as his countrymen called him), completed the conquest of Britain, we hear of no movement in the eastern districts of the island, such as that which broke out with such fury in the rear of the invaders twelve years later. The Iceni and their neighbours had had enough of fighting for a point of honour, and had not yet been driven to fight by despair. Tacitus speaks of them at this date as "domiti ut pareant, nondum ut serviant."

§ 5. But to this point they were year by year brought nearer, as year by year the arrogance, the brutality, and above all the insatiate greed, of the Roman officials and adventurers, who swooped down to exploit the newly-won province, kindled in the hearts of the Britons such feelings of exasperation as are declared by Lord Macaulay, in his essay on Warren Hastings, to have followed upon like misdoings under like circumstances when India first fell a prey to England. "On the one side was a band of English functionaries, daring, intelligent, eager to be rich. On the other side was a great native population. . . . And then was seen what we believe to be the most frightful of all spectacles—the strength of civilization without its mercy. To all other despotism there is a check—imperfect indeed and liable to gross abuse, but still sufficient to preserve Society from the last extremity of misery. A time comes when the evils of submission are obviously greater than those of resistance, when fear itself begets a sort of courage, when a convulsive burst of popular rage and despair warns tyrants not to presume too far on the patience of mankind. But against misgovernment such as then afflicted Bengal it was impossible to struggle. The superior intelligence and energy of the dominant class made their power irresistible. The only protection which the conquered could find was in the moderation, the clemency, the enlarged policy, of the conquerors. That protection at a later period they found. But at first English power came among them unaccompanied by English morality. There was an interval between the time at which they became our subjects and the time at which we began to reflect that we were bound to discharge towards them the duties of rulers. During that interval the business of a servant of the Company was simply to wring out of the natives a hundred or two hundred thousand pounds as quickly as possible. . . . Imagine what the state of our country would be if it were enacted that any man, by merely swearing that a debt was due to him, should acquire a right to insult the persons of men of the most honourable and sacred callings and of women of the most shrinking delicacy, to horsewhip a general officer, to put a bishop in the stocks, to treat ladies in the way which called forth the blow of Wat Tyler."

§ 6. So far as we can judge from contemporary evidence, this eloquent passage describes almost exactly the state of things introduced into Britain during the first years of the Roman occupation. There, too, we meet with like outrages on high rank and female honour, with like abuse of the forms of law for the plunder of the provincials. Money-lenders at Rome (amongst whom it is sad to find mentioned the enlightened Seneca) by extortion and chicanery ground down the humbler British landowners, whom the oppressive taxes left no choice but to apply to them. The Icenian chieftain, Prasutagus, a man of great wealth, could see no other chance of leaving any of it to his family than by declaring the Emperor his heir along with his widow and orphans. But this compliment, though sometimes effectual when paid by a Roman, only hastened the ruin of the hapless tributaries. The district was declared a Roman fief, the property of Prasutagus confiscated, his palace plundered, his daughters outraged, and his widowed Queen, Boadicea, subjected to the ignominious cruelties of a Roman scourging.[1]

§ 7. Then followed the "convulsive outburst of popular rage and despair." The wrongs of Boadicea kindled the smouldering fury of the Britons into madness, and almost immediately she found herself at the head not only of her own Icenian tribesmen, but of tumultuous levies from all the clans of the Eastern coast and of the Midlands. Men from Cambridgeshire undoubtedly took part in the stirring scenes which followed — the destruction of the Ninth Legion, the great battle still commemorated by Battle

[1] Tacitus "Ann.," xiv. 29 *et seq.*

Bridge Road in Islington (near King's Cross railway-station), the successive and awful sacking of Camelodune, London, and Verulam. And when the rebellion was finally crushed by Suetonius in that crowning battle where 80,000 half-armed Britons fell, and the very baggage animals were slaughtered by the ruthless conquerors to swell the heaps of slain, the British villages of Cambridgeshire felt the whole sweep of Roman vengeance, and the district was so dealt with that never again could despair itself dare to rise against the mighty conquerors. We may with great probability ascribe to this campaign the utter destruction of the British hamlet at Barrington (mentioned in our preceding chapter), which was so wholly blotted out that its very existence had been forgotten a few centuries later, when we find an Anglo-Saxon cemetery on its site.

§ 8. After the Roman war came the Roman peace. From whatever cause, it is certain that the provincials throughout the Empire were, as time went on, treated with less and less of the intolerable tyranny which marked the first setting up of the Roman power in each region, and became less and less discontented with their subjection to Rome; a state of things which reminds us again of our English dominion in India. And in Britain, as in India, the strong hand of the conquerors showed itself in the material prosperity of the conquered. With the prohibition of intertribal war, and the security of the island from invasion, the country became constantly more and more advanced in civilization. Fens were drained, rivers were embanked, land was brought into cultivation, till Britain became one of the great wheat-growing provinces of the Empire. Villas and towns sprang up everywhere, and, above all, those great roads were pierced through wood and waste which remain to this day the standing monuments of the mighty hand of Rome. Our familiar phrase, "the King's Highway," still echoes the official designation (*Via Regalis*)[1] of these roads, offences committed on which continued for many centuries to be specially punishable, as committed specially against the majesty of the Crown.

§ 9. Of these roads, two of the chiefest passed through Cambridgeshire. Ermine Street (now the Old North Road), always the main route between York and London, entered the county between Godmanchester and Caxton, to leave it at Royston on crossing the Icknield Street; and the Via Devana, from Colchester (Camelodunum) to Chester (Deva), passed through Cambridge itself, and crossed the Ermine Street at Godmanchester (Durolipons). At Cambridge (Camboritum) this so-called Via Devana—a name for which there is no ancient authority, and which seems to have been invented by some unknown antiquary—was crossed at right angles by the Akeman Street, which ran from the north coast of Norfolk to Cirencester (Corinium), where it joined the great Foss Road from Lincoln (Lindum) to Seaton (Moridunum), on the coast of Devon.

§ 10. This "Akeman Street" also passed through Ely, which, however, cannot be identified with any known Roman station. The claims, indeed, of Cambridge itself to be the Roman Camboricum or Camboritum, in spite of the similarity of the names, are not unchallenged. The difficulty of identifying all but the chiefest Roman sites in Britain is well known. Our only remaining authorities are (1) the Notitia, a civil and military survey of the Empire compiled at the beginning of the fifth century A.D., giving the names of the forces at each station; and (2) the Itineraries, telling the distances between certain stations on certain often very roundabout routes. Of these the former is by far the surest guide. When, for example, we read there that a Spanish cohort was quartered at Axelodunum on the Wall of Severus, and a Dacian cohort at

[1] See Ramsay, "The Church in the Roman Empire," p. 31.

Amboglanna, we know that the spots beside the wall where inscriptions relating to these troops are found must represent Axelodunum and Amboglanna respectively.

§ 11. But in Cambridgeshire the Notitia gives µs no help, and we are driven back on the Itineraries. Here one of the routes given unquestionably passes through the county, and one of the stages mentioned is Camboritum. The route in question is Iter V. of Antoninus, who gives it thus:

ITER A LONDINIO LVGVVALLIO AD VALLVM (Carlisle) M.P. CCCCXLVIII.

I. A LONDINIO CÆSAROMAGO (Chelmsford) - M.P. XXVIII.
II. CÆSAROMAGO COLONIÆ (Colchester) - - M P. XXIII.
III. COLONIA VILLÆ FAVSTINI (Dunmow?) - M.P. XXXV.
IV. VILLA FAVSTINI ICIANOS (Chesterford?) - M.P. XVIII.
V. ICIANIS CAMBORICO (Cambridge?) - - M.P. XXXV.
VI. CAMBORICO DVROLIPONTI (Godmanchester?) M.P. XXV.
VII. DVROLIPONTE DVROBRIVAS (Caistor?) - - M.P. XXXV.
VIII. DVROBRIVIS CAVSENNAS (Ancaster?) - - M.P. XXX.
IX. CAVSENNIS LINDO (Lincoln) - • - M.P. XXVI.

From Lincoln the route continues viâ Doncaster (Danum), York (Eboracum), Catterick (Cataractonis), and Penrith, to Carlisle.

It will be seen that the only way of identifying any given station with a modern site is by the distance here given (the letters M.P., *i.e.*, *millia passuum*, referring to the Roman miles, of which ten are equivalent to eight English miles, between each station) from some known locality, such as London or Lincoln—a not wholly satisfactory process when the considerable probability of error in MS. numbers is considered. The exceeding indirectness of the route traced out is another element of difficulty; it is hard to see why Antoninus takes us from London to Lincoln viâ Colchester, when the Ermine Street led directly from one to the other. And this particular Iter is less circuitous than many given by him.

§ 12. Questionable, however, as this evidence is, it is that on which almost all Romano-British sites are established, and by it Cambridge appears to correspond to the Roman Camboritum. The name is seemingly derived from that of the river, with the Celtic affix *rhyd, i.e.*, ford, the word Cam being also of Celtic origin, and signifying "crooked," in allusion to the markedly tortuous course of the stream. Some antiquaries have located Camboritum at Grantchester, seeing that Nennius calls the town Caer Grant ; but local investigation shows that at the latter village there was only a small fort, while at Cambridge we find the remains of a considerable station. It is evident, indeed, that Cambridge must always have been the crossing-place of the river, as there, and there alone for many miles, the higher ground approaches the water at both sides. Elsewhere one bank or the other is always low, and must of old have been marshy.

§ 13. On this higher ground, then, and on the highest part of it, that on the west side of the Cam, the Romans fixed their station, possibly on the site of a pre-existing British town. The site is of some natural strength, the projecting extremity of a low range of hills, so that there was a rapid descent from the north and south ramparts, and a perceptible slope from the west side, while the river defended the eastern approaches. The lofty mound commanding the ford (in Roman times doubtless a bridge), which is now the most prominent feature of the site, and is commonly supposed to be of Roman or British origin, has been shown by Professor Hughes to be almost certainly of later date. But even without it the conquerors were quite sufficiently secure. Indeed, after a very few years no fortifications at all were probably needed. The first outburst of native resistance having been crushed, the peculiar power of assimilating her conquests which marked Imperial Rome, even more than Republican, came into full play, and brought about in Cambridgeshire, as elsewhere throughout the Empire, that wonderful *Pax Romana* which forms so absolutely unique a phenomenon in the history of the world. For nearly four centuries the county was as wholly peaceful as it has been for the last two, and, to judge by the remains of the period, fully as populous. All along the valley of the Cam, in particular, such remains have been unearthed in extraordinary abundance, remains indicating the presence not of soldiers, nor of the great landlords who dwelt in villas, so much as of a teeming swarm of small agriculturists, whose ashpits, filled with the rubbish of their humble households, have been found by the fossil-diggers of our century in field after field.

§ 14. The most characteristic feature of this rubbish is, naturally, broken pottery, of coarse and common type for the most part, with an occasional fragment of more delicate " Samian " ware. This ware was not, so far as we know, manufactured anywhere in Britain; it was imported from abroad, and almost invariably bears the stamp of the maker, *e.g.*, CISTIO. TITI. The common home-made ware is never thus stamped.

§ 15. Of Roman arms, offensive or defensive, Cambridgeshire has supplied few examples, nor yet many distinctively Roman ornaments. One brooch, however, found near Barrington, deserves notice as being an exact replica of that discovered in the bed of the Thames on the building of the present London Bridge, and now in the British Museum. It is of bronze, in the form of a swan, once richly gilded, and with a *spring* pin (held by archæologists to prove its Romano-British origin). The Roman ashpits have also provided specimens of horseshoes—thin, broad soles of iron, without heels, and fastened by the traditional three nails. Thimbles, too, have been found in them, formed of bronze, closed at the end, and pitted, like ours, for the needle, but made to wear upon the thumb, as the name, indeed, shows to have been the original practice, "thimble" being equivalent to "thumb bell."

§ 16. But, next to pottery, the commonest objects by far are the Roman coins, which have been, in Cambridgeshire, turned up literally by the thousand. No great hoards have been discovered—at least, of late years; but the individual coins are everywhere. They are rarely of precious metal, and for the most part of common type and in poor preservation; but their number is astonishing, and proves how vast an amount of petty traffic then went on in the district year after year and century after century. It would be hard to name a single Emperor, from Augustus to Honorius, whose currency does not occur amongst them, while the list also includes Republican coins and those of Julius Cæsar at the one end, and the name of Valentinian III. at the other. The most plentiful are those of the especially British emperors, Carausius, Allectus and Constantine; and amongst the most interesting are specimens of the commemorative issue struck on the capture of Jerusalem, A.D. 70, bearing the head of Vespasian on the obverse, and on the reverse "the daughter of Jerusalem" weeping beneath a palm-tree, with the inscription IVDAEA . CAPTA.

§ 17. Britain continued in connection with the Roman Empire long enough to be included in that magnificent system of administrative division evolved by the genius of Diocletian, and embodied in the Notitia. Heretofore the Empire had been divided only into provinces, governed, some by Senatorial, some by Imperial officials, each responsible only and directly to the supreme central authority at Rome. Constant collisions and abuses were the natural outcome of so inconvenient an arrangement, till Diocletian introduced a new and abiding element of order by his creation of an official hierarchy rising grade above grade, and his corresponding reapportionment of the Roman dominions. By his scheme the whole of those dominions were distributed into four "Prefectures," each containing on an average some three "Dioceses," and each of these again from five to fifteen "Provinces." Thus, Britain formed a "Diocese" under a "Vicar" or "Count" of "respectable" rank (the second in point of dignity), himself subject to the "Illustrious Prefect of the Gauls," whose authority extended also over France, the Iberian Peninsula, and even Morocco. The diocese comprised five provinces, Cambridgeshire being in that denominated *Flavia Cæsariensis*, corresponding to the later kingdoms of Mercia and East Anglia. This province was governed by one of the thirty-two "Presidents" of the Empire, under the "Vicar of Britain"; while its military affairs were directed partly by the Vicar of the Diocese, partly by the "Respectable Duke of the Britains," whose headquarters were at York, partly by the "Count of the Saxon[1] Shore," whose duty it was to guard the coast against pirate raids, and whose jurisdiction extended over the whole sea-board from Yarmouth to Shoreham.

§ 18. The troops assigned to these functionaries by the central War Office at Rome were not, however, those recruited in the country. It was the constant policy of the Roman Government to discourage local association and local loyalty in its subjects, and to impress them with the solidarity of the Empire by quartering the levies of each province in divers and distant districts. Thus, amongst the thirty-five several bodies of soldiers enumerated in the Notitia as on service in Britain, one alone, the "Victores Juniores Britanniciani," bears a local designation; whilst amongst the others we find not only men of the same prefecture, Gauls, Spaniards, and Moors, but troops from such far-away regions as Dalmatia, Dacia, Thrace, Lybia, and Syria. Even barbarian prisoners taken in war were utilized for the insular service; the

---

[1] See Chapter III., § 1. The name is first found in Eutropius, ix. 21.

energetic Emperor Probus, in 277 A.D., thus adding to his forces in Britain a horde of Vandals discomfited by him on the Rhine, shortly after their great defeat by Aurelian on the Danube. Zozimus mentions that they successfully repressed some local disturbances in our island, and the name Vandlebury, given (on the authority of Gervase) to the great camp on the Gog Magog Hills above Cambridge, not improbably records this remarkable method of recruiting. So may also the many coins of Probus scattered about the district.

§ 19. In spite of such precaution, however, a certain amount of local solidarity could not but grow up in the British army, heterogeneous as its elements were—more especially as those elements seem rarely to have been changed, inscriptions showing, for example, that the Second, Sixth, and Twentieth Legions were permanently quartered, from year's end to year's end, at Dover, York, and Chester respectively. The army of Britain, accordingly, always acted as a whole throughout the various civil commotions which convulsed the Empire in the third, fourth, and fifth centuries, and is described by Zozimus as specially distinguished $ἀυθαδείᾳ$ $καὶ$ $θυμῷ$. Here, in 286 A.D., the pretender Carausius assumed the diadem, and the island remained severed from the rest of the Empire till his murderer and successor, Allectus, was overthrown ten years later by Constantius; the reign of these two usurpers being signalized by the first appearance in history of the British fleet, which, under Carausius, developed into so important a factor in politics as even to include a Mediterranean squadron.[1] Coins of Allectus, found in the Cam valley, bearing on the reverse a British warship cleared for action, attest the patriotic interest there taken in Britannia's first ruling of the waves.

§ 20. The name of Constantius brings again to our notice the Diocletian system of government, under which

[1] See Gibbon's " Decline and Fall," chap. xiii.

two joint-emperors, "Augusti," each with a "Cæsar" as coadjutor, swayed the four prefectures of the Empire, Diocletian himself taking "the East"; his "Cæsar," Galerius, Illyricum; Maximian, Italy; and his Cæsar, Constantius, "the Gauls." As each Augustus retired, his Cæsar was to take his place and appoint a fresh coadjutor in his own. The plan was ingenious, but, unlike most of Diocletian's ideas, proved unequal to the stress of practical politics, strained as these were by the last mortal struggle between heathenism and Christianity.

§ 21. That final persecution, which has branded beyond his deserts the name of Diocletian, gave to Britain the martyr St. Alban; but Constantius himself was a suspected, and his wife Helena an avowed and ardent Christian, so that, when their son Constantine of York made his successful bid for the Empire, it was under the banner of Christ that he led the British army to victory at the Milvian Bridge, A.D. 312. The device on that banner, the well-known Labarum—consisting of the initial letters of the word Christ in Greek, between Alpha and Omega, the first and last letters of the Greek alphabet, the whole forming the word $APX\Omega$, "I reign"—is seen on coins of this date found in Cambridgeshire, and marks the era at which our country became an avowedly Christian land. The Faith had, indeed, maintained a foothold on our shores since its early preaching in the Apostolic age, if not by St. Paul himself; but now for the first time it received a regular ecclesiastical organization under the three archbishops of London, York, and Caerleon, Cambridgeshire being within the jurisdiction of the first-named. What were the sites and extent of the suffragan sees is matter of conjecture; but rural churches around Cambridge can scarcely have been less numerous than now, during the century of peace and prosperity which succeeded Constantine's departure from the island. Coins of the usurpers Magnentius and Decentius found in the district remind us of the only political convulsion which for a moment disturbed that peace, in their rebellion (350 A.D.) against the house of Constantine, and of the cruelties attending its suppression by Constantius II.[1]

§ 22. This rebellion, though but momentary in its immediate consequences, had most important results in hastening the break-up of the Roman Empire throughout the West. The legions never recovered the awful slaughter by which Magnentius was checked at Mursa, on the Drave, when 24,000 of his adherents fell, and of the victorious army of Constantius a yet larger number.[2] From this time forward the Western army corps were grievously depleted, and those of Britain, in particular, sent their best levies with the British pretender Maximus[3] against Gratian—(Cambridgeshire furnishes coins of both these rivals)—never to return. This was in the year 383. Two decades later, the fatal year 406 saw the Rhine frontier absolutely denuded of its troops by Stilicho, for the life and death effort which crushed the barbarian hordes of Radagaisus on the hills of Florence, and saved Italy and Rome—for the moment. Then across the undefended stream poured a great flood of Vandals and other German invaders, who overflowed the peaceful and fertile provinces of Gaul, never again to be expelled.

§ 23. Of the troops in Britain a smaller proportion was withdrawn by Stilicho, and what was left of the British army now made one last effort to save the West for Rome. A local *pronunciamento* declared the despicable Honorius to be unworthy of the purple, and once more proclaimed a British Constantine Augustus.[4] Though only a private soldier of low birth, this pretender showed an energy worthy of his great namesake. Within a year, not only Britain, but Gaul and Spain also, acknowledged his sway; and Honorius himself was fain to negotiate

[1] Zozimus, ii. [2] *Ibid.*, xiii. [3] *Ibid.*, vi. ; Orosius, ii. 34.
[4] *Ibid.*, vi. ; Orosius, vii. 40.

with him a division of the Empire, and to recognise him as a legitimate Augustus. For four years he thus held his own, till treachery brought about his overthrow and impaled his head above the gate of Carthagena. And for long centuries the fame of his valour alike against the heathen barbarians and the unworthy Emperor, echoed down the lays of Cymric harpers, till it found a place amongst the deeds of Arthur; amid whose champions we may even read the name of this Constantine's chief British General, Gerontius or Geraint.

§ 24. But his action was fatal to Roman Britain. What Stilicho had done for Gaul, Constantine did for our island. Of the three "British" legions, one, the Twentieth, had been withdrawn by the former, and every available soldier between the four seas would seem to have followed the fortunes of the latter.[1] The same consequences ensued as in Gaul. The unhappy civilians, almost unarmed and wholly untrained to war, were at the mercy of barbarian invaders, and barbarians far more savage than those beyond the Channel. The naked Picts of Caledonia, in their blue war-paint, burst over the Roman wall; the wild Scots crossed from Ireland in their wicker boats, with their war-cry of "Hoity Toity"; and no Count of the Saxon Shore remained to repel the pirate raiders of the North Sea. Sometimes as allies, oftener as rivals, these terrible foes swept the land from end to end, Cambridgeshire coming in for its full share of their ravages. Once and again, if Bede is to be trusted,[2] did the Britons appeal for aid to Rome, but in vain. Rome itself was now in its death-agony, and could do nothing for such distant dependencies. Their last piteous missive, "The Groans of the Britons," was to "Aetius, thrice Consul," in the thickest of his mortal struggle with Attila

---

[1] Procopius, "De Bello Vandalico," i. 2.
[2] "Ecclesiastical History," chaps. xii., xiii.

(A.D. 423). "The barbarians," they sigh, "drive us to the sea; the sea drives us back to the barbarians." Finally, in despair, they proposed to the fiercest[1] and most formidable of the invaders a permanent settlement within their borders—a settlement which has changed Britain into England.

[1] The special ferocity of the Saxons is enlarged on by Sidonius Apollinaris (viii. 6).

CHAPTER III.

ANGLO-SAXON PERIOD—I.

§ 1—4. Origin of Saxon name—English march through Cambridgeshire—Picts defeated at Stamford—Romano-British civilization stamped out.

§ 5—10. Existing villages founded—Common fields—Eorl and churl—Marks—Anglo-Saxon cemeteries—Ornaments—Weapons—Currency—Spindle-whorls.

§ 11—13. Fate of Britons—The Fens still British—Girvii—British names surviving—Basket-work.

§ 14—17. Southern Cambridgeshire—Mercia and East Anglia—Local dialect—Bretwaldas—Conversion of East Anglia—Bishop Felix.

§ 18—32. Last struggle of heathenism—Penda—King Anna and his family—St. Etheldred—Foundation of Ely and Thorney—St. Wilfrid—Burial of St. Etheldred—Her rule of the Isle—"Families" and "hides"—Theodore of Tarsus—Parishes formed—The cross of Ovinus—The Heptarchy.

§ 1. IN the year 1890 there was found in South Cambridgeshire a beautifully-preserved specimen of the weapon which has given its special name to the next period of our history—the *seaxe*, or short sword of the North Sea rovers. Etymologically the word is connected with the Latin *seco* and the English *hack;* while the weapon itself was a narrow blade of steel, single-edged, and with the same murderous-looking, peculiarly-shaped point found to this day in Scandinavian clasp-knives, which, moreover, are still known by almost the identical name. Florence of Worcester (Chron. 1138) relates how the existing district of Saxony derives it name from " the long and victorious knives" with which "a foreign and savage race from the north" overcame the previous Thuringian inhabitants. In the Song of Beowulf (perhaps the earliest extant example of Anglo-Saxon poetry) the special keenness of this weapon is insisted upon. The hero having found his sword unable to wound a dragon, draws a "wæl-seaxe biter and beada scearp," which at once cleaves "the worm" in twain.

§ 2. Such were the weapons which our Teutonic forefathers wielded in their deeds of valour and of carnage; with such terrible effect upon the minds of their enemies that the name Saxon—men of the seaxe—became from their first onset, and has remained to this day, the epithet which the ancient tongue of Britain has applied not only to the tribes who knew themselves by that name, but to the kindred Angles, or English, whose designation, on Teutonic lips, very early began to include the whole body of Low German hordes which in the fifth century poured into Britain.

§ 3. Of the details of that savage conquest history tells us unfortunately little; but there seems no reason to reject the tradition that an English tribe originally obtained a settlement in Kent as allies of the Britons against the Picts, and that at Stamford, on the Welland, the Pictish spears were routed by the English swords—as the Macedonian spears had been by the swords of the Romans, and as the Swiss spears were to be by the swords of the Spaniards. Their march to the scene of battle must have led the English along the Icknield Street through Cambridgeshire; and when the inevitable war broke out between English and Britons over the terms of their bargain, when every inlet on the Eastern and Southern coasts gave entrance to fresh swarms of pirates, flocking to their new home with such impetuosity that their old quarters by the Elbe mouth were still desert three centuries later,[1] the Ouse and the Cam must have admitted their black keels into the very heart of our county. Cambridge itself undoubtedly shared the same fate of utter destruction which befell almost every British town in the land; for the invaders, like the kindred Boers of to-day in South Africa, were a race of warrior husbandmen, holding city life in contemptuous loathing, and counting each city they met with as a mere shelter for enemies, to be swept away, not as a coveted dwelling-place for themselves.

§ 4. Thus, as Mr. Freeman points out, we find in many places throughout Britain the old Roman site lying waste, and around it villages with English names. Thus it is still, for example, at Anderida, where the English villages of Pevensey and Westham on either side of the deserted site bear abiding witness to the ferocity with which (as the Anglo-Saxon Chronicle for 491 A.D. tells us) the South Saxons under "Ælle and Cissa beset Anderida and slew all that dwelt therein, neither was one Briton left there any more." Thus for centuries it was at Chester, where the name of the city yet records the fact that, after being destroyed, in 603, by Ethelfrith of Mercia, "it remained," according to Florence of Worcester, "a waste chester" even to the days of Alfred. And, in like manner, thus for centuries it was at Cambridge. English villages arose north and south of the Roman ruins, their names of Grantchester[2] and Chesterton derived from the intervening "chester"; but that "chester" itself, the "chester" of Camboritum, remained desolate for generations. As the English advanced in civilization, this feeling neces-

---

[1] Bede, "Eccl. Hist.," xv.
[2] The original use of this name is, however, uncertain. In Bede it seems to stand for Cambridge itself (see § 27). In Doomsday, and in the "Placita" of Edward I., the village is called *Grantsete*. But in the Patent Rolls (1371) it is *Grauncestre*.

sarily changed; but only a very few British cities held out long enough to reap the benefit of the change. London, York, and Lincoln may possibly have preserved a continuous existence from Roman and British days; no Cambridgeshire town did so. Except in the case of Cambridge itself, their very names are gone, and everywhere we find villages of purely English nomenclature. The swarming population to which the Romano-British remains in the Cam Valley testify, were remorselessly massacred, and their place occupied by the new-comers, fewer probably in number, yet numerous enough fairly to fill the land.

§ 5. For the existing villages date almost certainly from this earliest settlement of our race; and they stand thickly dotting the face of the ground like knots in network, at an average distance of about a mile and a half from each other. There have never existed in Cambridgeshire those many isolated farms and cottages which are so marked a feature in the landscapes of Wessex or Northumbria. The few that are to be seen are of exceedingly recent erection; the whole life of the county has always been drawn together in its villages, which, within living memory, rose, with their trees and their surrounding enclosures, like islands amid the unenclosed and virgin prairie, even as they rose when first settled. And within living memory every village had, as then, its "common field," divided into three or four portions for the rude rotation of crops then practised (one portion being always fallow); and with one or more strips in each portion for every household, each strip theoretically ten chains (a furlong or furrow-long) in length by one in breadth (*i.e.* an acre).

§ 6. And in each village would be found the Squire, or Eorl, holding his position purely by birth, and not, as the later Thanes, by royal appointment; beneath whom ranked the great body of small land-holders—the yeomen, or churls ("ceorls.") These, almost universally, tilled their fields with their own hands, only the wealthiest amongst them being able to boast of that rare possession, a personal slave or thrall. Moreover, every such village community, when first settled, tended to form a self-governing, self-supporting area, or Mark, feeding and clothing itself from its own fields and flocks, settling its own affairs in its own Parish Meetings, and jealously guarding its borders against intrusion from without. From the beginning, however, the tendency of these Marks to coalesce into larger political entities is perceptible, and, with the advance of civilization, speedily becomes rapid.

§ 7. Thus did our English forefathers make their homes in Cambridgeshire: supporting themselves by their husbandry; ploughing the common fields with their oxen; sowing, reaping, and gathering into barns; while the unenclosed prairie provided pasture for their cattle, and, to a certain extent (for it can never have been rich in game), a hunting-ground for themselves.

§ 8. The fossil-diggings of our own day have thrown something of light upon the life of those ancient days, by disinterring sundry cemeteries, known to be approximately of this date, because at once English and heathen. The relics thus recovered show us that men and women alike were buried with many of their choicest possessions, scarcely a grave being found barren. We find that bronze brooches, commonly showing traces of rich gilding, and sometimes inlaid with enamel, were in general use; that bead necklaces, of glass, crystal, pottery and amber, were worn by both sexes; that ladies knew the use of powder-boxes and of chatelaines (a small mirror of silvered bronze being one of the attachments); that warriors used spears, swords, daggers, and shields of wood (the "war-linden" of the poets), with an iron boss in the centre to protect the hand, but apparently not helmets; at least, none have been found. Very rarely the deceased warrior is equipped with that peculiarly English weapon, the bill, which (as found at this date in Cambridgeshire) is a short stout blade, about nine inches long and three wide, single-edged, and curved like an eagle's beak (whence its name). This weapon is specially mentioned as being used on the English side in the Song of Maldon.

§ 9. The tombs have also yielded a few, but very few comparatively, of the bronze rings which formed the original Anglo-Saxon currency, and made "ring-giving" the ordinary poetical equivalent for generosity. Still more rarely are found specimens of the "scætta," the earliest Anglo-Saxon coin, the name of which still survives in the phrases "to pay your shot" and "to get off scot-free." These interesting little coins are thin flat discs of silver, very rudely minted with what are evidently intended for imitations of the later Roman coins. The Capitoline wolf, for example, copied from the bronze mites of the city of Rome (which are plentiful in this district), develops into as extraordinary a congeries of dots and scratches as the Macedonian horse on the British coinage,[1] and, like that, often ultimately assumes a wholly different shape. It is striking to contrast the wealth of local currency under the Romans with the extreme lack of anything equivalent in Saxon times. One wonders whether business was almost wholly transacted by barter, or whether the Roman coins continued in circulation.

§ 10. But the articles by far most frequently found in the sepultures are the spindle-whorls, without one of which, apparently, no respectable woman could be decently buried. These whorls are small, roughly-spherical objects of stone or of bone, about an inch or more in diameter, and pierced with a hole for the spindle. Their function was to act as a fly-wheel and keep the spindle in constant motion; and they continued in use at

---

[1] See Chapter I., § 22.

least as late as the sixteenth century, for they are mentioned by Sir Thomas More as being in the hands of every maid-servant.

The passage is so humorous as to be worth quoting. More is telling of a prototype of Crabbe's "Preceptor Husband," who would fain have taught his wife "The Treatise of the Sphere" (*i.e.*, the Ptolemaic system of the universe), and, to show her that "the Earth hangeth in the midst of the Universe by its own weight, 'You must,' said he, 'mark well that in the Universe *higher* and *lower* mean simply *outer* and *inner*; so that, all the Spheres being each in a round compass over the other, the Earth lieth in the very midst, and is the innermost place of the Universe. Being therefore in the lowest place, its own weight keeps it there, because no heavy thing can of itself ascend upwards, and to fall out of its place on any side would be to fall from a lower place to a higher. Imagine therefore that a hole were bored through the earth, and a millstone thrown down here on this side from our feet: it would finally remain in the Centre of the Earth. It could not go further, for then it would be falling outwards or upwards.'

"Now, while he was telling her this tale, she nothing went about to consider his words, but, as she was wont in all other things, studied all the while nothing else but what she might say to the contrary. And when he had, with much work and oft interrupting, brought at last his tale to an end: 'Well,' quoth she, 'I will argue like, and make you a like sample. My maid yonder hath a spinning whorl, because all your reason resteth in the roundness of the world. Come hither, thou girl; take out thy spindle, and bring me hither the whorl. Lo, sir, ye make imaginations; I cannot tell you what. But here is a whorl, and it is round as the world is; and ye shall not need imagine a hole bored through, for it hath a hole bored through indeed. But yet, because ye go by imaginations,

I will imagine you. Imagine me now that this whorl were ten miles thick on every side ; and this hole through it still, and so great that a millstone might well go through. Now if the whorl stood on one end, and a millstone were thrown through it from the other end, would it go no further than the midst, trow you ? By God, if one threw in a stone no bigger than an egg, I ween if ye stood at the nether end of the hole, five mile beneath the midst, it would give you a pat upon the pate that it would make you claw your head, and yet should ye feel none itch at all.'

"It were long to tell you of all their disputations, for words would she none have lacked, though they should have disputed the space of seven years. Her husband was fain to put up his sphere, and leave his wife with her whorl."[1]

§ 11. Thus did Cambridgeshire become an English district. And meanwhile death, exile, or personal slavery, were the only alternatives open to the unhappy Britons ; so that by the middle of the sixth century not a free " Welshman " (a name which, on English lips, included all Britons alike) was left in the county, save, perchance, in the recesses of the Fens.

§ 12. For by this time the Fens, that great morass which was to be distinctive of the northern part of Cambridgeshire for the next thirteen hundred years, had fairly come into existence. Either by the destruction of the Roman dykes, or by the subsidence of the land, or, more probably, by both these causes combined, the floor of the great forest surrounding the Wash became submerged, the rivers which had flowed lazily through it could no longer flow at all, their waters were backed up and spread over all their banks at every level spot, so that half the county grew waterlogged, and was transformed into an impenetrable waste of trackless bogs and reedy meres;

[1] Bridgett's " Life of Sir Thomas More," p. 449.

where a few very small and low and inconspicuous islets might well provide a refuge for the hunted survivors of the conquered people.

§ 13. Thus, as late as the tenth century we find "*British* thieves" mentioned as haunting the district,[1] and a warrior, bearing the distinctively Celtic name of Maccus, one of the prominent heroes at the battle of Maldon; while in the Tabula Eliensis (1078) we meet with Donald, Evan, Constantine and David. The name *Girvii*, by which the inhabitants of this district became known after the English conquest, may well be connected with the Welsh *gwryw*, manly,[2] a title likely enough to be adopted by the heroic few who there stood at bay. Their Alderman under Queen Etheldred was, moreover, one Owen;—while their country contains various local designations quite capable of a Welsh derivation, that of Ely itself being very probably the word which meets us in the Glamorganshire river Ely and in the Denbighshire Elwy. The existence, in English, of the Welsh word "basket" points in the same direction; for, until the final draining of the Fens, this district was the special seat of the basket-making industry, for which the infinite abundance of osiers and rushes amongst its sluggish watercourses afforded exceptional facilities. British baskets were known by that name in Rome as early as the days of Martial, whose "Epigrams" (xiv. 99) introduce us to one of these articles:

"Barbara de pictis veni *bascauda* Britannis."

§ 14. Nor was it only along their lower course that the rivers were affected. For miles above the Fenland proper—indeed, to within half a dozen miles of its source—the meadows adjoining the Cam became marshes suffi-

---

[1] See Freeman, "Norman Conquest," vol. iv., p. 470; also "Hist. Ramsey," § 86.
[2] The word *grw* is also found, with the meaning of "chieftain."

ciently inconvenient of passage to form a decided barrier between the populations on either bank. The river accordingly formed throughout almost its entire length the boundary between the East Anglian and Mercian districts of the English Name; the remarkable difference even yet observable in dialect and local custom between adjoining parishes, separated only by so narrow a stream, bearing testimony to this day of their several origin. But the East Anglian portion of the county was so far the more important that, when at length the shire was formed, the whole of it was counted to the East English and was under the East English Alderman or Earl. And meanwhile its history is almost wholly dependent on that of the East Anglian monarchy. The dialect, however, is almost wholly Mercian, and is thus devoid of the charm of provinciality. For, as Freeman points out, it is this very speech of South-Eastern Mercia which (through the influence of the great abbeys, so thick hereabouts) has developed into "classical" English, leaving the once more important tongues of Wessex and Northumbria as localisms. A few special words are, nevertheless, still current amongst the peasantry: "stunt" for steep, "fleet" for shallow, "frorn" for frozen, "meese" for mice, "horkey" for harvest-home, and "to-year" for this year (as "to-day" is ordinarily used). The thrush is known as the "maywish" (the "mavis" of old English ballads), and cowslips are "paigles," a word said to be derived from Pega, the sister of St. Guthlac of Crowland (673), whose name is also to be found in Peakirk Drove, the road between Wisbech and Thorney.

§ 15. After upwards of a century of Christianity, Cambridgeshire thus became once more a land of heathens. The Romano-British churches (as the contemporary British historian, Gildas, tells) were everywhere razed to the ground, and their places taken by the sacred groves in which the sanguinary rites of Anglo-Saxon worship were celebrated. In some instances there is reason to believe that the very site of the ancient religion was thus dedicated to the service of the idols, and re-dedicated to Christ when the Christian faith was once more solidly established.

§ 16. But, before that happy consummation, many religious and political convulsions tore and devastated the land. Amongst the earliest converts brought into the fold by the Mission to the English, sent, under Augustine, from Pope Gregory the Great, in 599, was Redwald, King of East Anglia; the two divisions of which, inhabited respectively by the North-folk and the South-folk, had been for the first time brought under one sceptre by his grandfather Uffa (from whom the dynasty, down to the time of its extinction by the Danes, continued to be denominated Uffing). Redwald was converted in Kent, by Augustine himself, and succeeded its first Christian monarch in the vague hegemony amongst the Princes of Britain implied in the title "Bretwalda." By a play upon the first syllable, which originally implied mere extent of dominion (Bret = broad), this title gained the meaning of "Wielder of *Britain*"; and the popular voice bestowed it on various local rulers who made their influence felt beyond the limits of their own immediate kingdom.

These successive Bretwaldas, as given by Bede,[1] are:

1. Ella of Sussex, A.D. 477.
2. Ceawlin of Wessex, A.D. 560.
3. Ethelbert of Kent, A.D. 593.
4. Redwald of East Anglia, A.D. 616.
5. Edwin of Northumbria, A.D. 617.
6. Oswald of Northumbria, A.D. 634.
7. Oswy of Northumbria, A.D. 642.

The Anglo-Saxon Chronicle[2] adds an eighth, Egbert

[1] "Eccl. Hist.," Book II., chap. v.   [2] Anno 827.

of Wessex. In this addition we may probably trace the hand of his grandson, Alfred the Great, who re-edited the Chronicle, with large additions from Bede, and thus raised it from being a mere record of dates to the dignity of a history. That the Bretwaldaship was not a mere name we may see from the respect paid to Ethelbert's authority, even by the Welsh, whose bishops, in obedience to his summons, assembled to meet Augustine in Gloucestershire.[1]

§ 17. Puffed up by his elevation to this lofty dignity, Redwald, on his return home, endeavoured, at the instigation of his wife, to combine his ancestral with his new faith. "In the same temple," says Bede,[2] "he had an altar for the sacrifice of Christ, and another small one to offer victims to devils." Such compromise was utterly opposed to the spirit in which the Gospel was preached; and Redwald's system died with him. His son and successor, Earpwald, came to the throne in 617 as an unmixed heathen, but before the termination of his reign, in 628, had been persuaded by the great Edwin of Northumbria, himself a royal convert, to accept Christianity as the religion of his people.[3]

§ 18. The assassination of Earpwald by a certain pagan points to a heathen reaction in the land, which, in fact, remained in a state of anarchy for three years, till the crown finally fell to a truly zealous Christian—Sigbert, the brother of Earpwald, long banished to France, and there converted.[4] On ascending the throne, he made special efforts to instruct his people in the truth, and, "being desirous to imitate the good institutions which he had seen in France, set up a school for boys to be taught in Letters." It is doubtless more than a mere coincidence that, in this introduction of Continental methods, his special assistant was a Bishop of Continental birth,

[1] Bede, "Eccl. Hist.," Book II., chap. ii.
[2] *Ibid.*, Book II., chap. xv.   [3] *Ibid.*   [4] *Ibid.*

Felix of Burgundy, whose landing is recorded by the name of Felixstowe, on the coast of Suffolk, and who was consecrated by Honorius, Archbishop of Canterbury, as the first Bishop of the East English. The burial-place of this prelate at Soham, in our county, became the site of a famous monastery, which endured till swept away by the great Danish invasion of 870.[1]

§ 19. This dawn of Gospel light was, however, soon to be whelmed in one last terrible tempest of heathenism. Whilst the northern and eastern parts of England were becoming Christian, the great central kingdom of Mercia remained obstinately pagan. And just at this juncture Mercia, possibly because still religiously united, rose to be the most powerful monarchy in England. Its King, Penda, though excluded from the list of the Bretwaldas, was beyond comparison the most influential sovereign seen within the four seas since Roman days. And he made it the great object of his life to uproot Christianity throughout the land. Turning his arms first against Northumbria, he successively stamped out the Roman mission of Paulinus[2] and the Celtic mission of Aidan,[3] crushing and slaying in turn King Edwin,[4] the convert of the former preacher, and King Oswald,[5] the disciple of the latter. Next he drove out Kenwalk,[6] King of Wessex (who in his East Anglian exile learnt to be a Christian indeed), and finally, in 654, burst with his whole force upon East Anglia itself.[7]

§ 20. Sigbert was by this time dead, slain in an earlier Mercian raid, which called him from the monastery

---

[1] Bentham, "Hist. of Ely," p. 68.
[2] Bede, "Eccl. Hist.," Book II., chap. xiv.
[3] *Ibid.*, Book III., chap. iii.
[4] *Ibid.*, Book II., chap. xx. Anno 633.
[5] *Ibid.*, Book III., chap. ix. Anno 642.
[6] *Ibid.*, Book III., chap. vii. Anno 643.
[7] Anglo-Saxon Chronicle. Anno 654.

whither he had retired, to aid his successor Egric against the heathen foe. Like the great Christian hero of our own day, General Gordon, he led on his soldiers unarmed save with a wand, and, like him also, held his post to the death. Egric died with him, and the crown devolved on Anna, "a good man, and the father of an excellent family," almost every member of which attained the honours of canonization. Amongst these were Erkenwald, the great Bishop of London, and Etheldred, the foundress of Ely. This truly Christian household was brought up practically in Cambridgeshire; for, in order to be ready against the danger from Mercia, Anna fixed his royal residence at the strategic position of Exning, near Newmarket, whence he could speedily man the lines of the great dykes—now once more important for defence, as in the old days of the Iceni—and where he could best join hands with his son-in-law, Tonbert, the tributary ruler of the Fenland Girvii, the first husband of St. Etheldred, in resisting invasion from the West.

§ 21. All proved in vain. Neither fen nor dyke, nor the devoted valour of Anna, who, like his predecessor, died upon the field of battle, could check the overwhelming onset of Penda. He fell upon the Christian host "like a wolf, so that Anna and his folk were devoured in a moment," and scarcely a man escaped to tell the tale. The scene of this tragedy is not given by the historian, but it was almost certainly somewhere in the southeast of Cambridgeshire, on the threshold of Anna's realm.

§ 22. This was Penda's last victory. The next year he was himself slain, and the tide of Christian progress ran the stronger for its momentary check. Anna was gone; but throughout the whole of England the scattered members of his family proved each a centre of spiritual life. His son Erkenwald became Bishop of London;[1] of

[1] Bede, "Eccl. Hist.," Book IV., chap. iii.

his daughters, one, Etheldred, as Queen Consort of Northumbria,[1] worked along with her aunt, St. Hilda, the foundress of Whitby,[2] in restoring the Faith throughout that wide realm, ere she returned to Ely; another became Abbess of Brie,[3] in France, setting up there a school to which, for many decades, English girls were sent in large numbers for education; another of Barking;[4] another of Dereham.[5] Yet another, Sexburga, wedded the King of Kent,[5] and not only herself did great deeds there for the Church, but left two daughters who carried on the family zeal, one being described by Bede as "the golden coin of Kent,"[6] and the other, Ermenilda, aiding, as the Queen of Wulfhere, Penda's son, in St. Chad's work of converting Mercia.[7] Seldom, indeed, has any district sent forth so fruitful a mission, or bred such a band of saints.

§ 23. And though the district was as yet without a name, yet it evidently had no small local solidarity; for amongst these saintly women there was a marked tendency to drift back to the neighbourhood of their birthplace—a tendency which has given that neighbourhood a memorial worthy of their father's house, in the glorious minster of Ely. Renouncing the pomps of Northumbrian royalty,[8] Etheldred returned to the scenes of her early life, and there, within sight of her native Exning uplands, on the Girvian isle amid the fens which had been the seat of her first husband's power[9] and which was now her own by dowry,[10] she founded one of those religious houses conducted on the system taught by St. Benedict, which met the great need of the age in affording a haven where

---

[1] Bede, "Eccl. Hist.," Book IV., chap. xix.
[2] *Ibid.*, Book III., chap. xxv.   [3] *Ibid.*, Book III., chap. viii.
[4] *Ibid.*, Book III., chap. vi.   [5] *Ibid.*, Book IV., chap. xix.
[6] *Ibid.*, Book III., chap. viii.   [7] *Ibid.*, Book IV., chap. iii.
[8] *Ibid.*, Book IV., chap. xix.   [9] *Ibid.*
[10] "Liber Eliensis," i. 4.

peacefully-minded souls might work out their lives in peace, sheltered from the everlasting din of arms and violence which filled the world around, and able to devote themselves to keeping alive not only the light of Religion, but that of Literature, Art, and Science also. How entirely such Houses were felt to be what the times required is shown by the number which everywhere sprang, as if by one impulse, into existence. Simultaneously with Ely, and almost within sight, there rose the four great foundations of Peterborough, Thorney, Ramsey, and Crowland, all just upon the borders of Cambridgeshire.

§ 24. Thorney, indeed, is actually within those borders; and the lands given to Peterborough (which are minutely specified in the Anglo-Saxon Chronicle), at its foundation in 657, by King Wulfhere of Mercia (son-in-law to Anna of East Anglia), comprised Whittlesea and the adjoining fens in our county. The Abbot Sexwulf took advantage of the King's "giving mood" to procure the foundation of Thorney Abbey also. The chronicler thus describes the scene:

"Then said the King: 'This gift is little. But it is my will they hold it so royally and so freely that neither geld nor fee be taken from it. . . . And thus free will I make this Minster, that it be under Rome alone: and my will it is that all we who may not go to Rome visit St. Peter here.'

"While thus he spake, the Abbot prayed of him that he would give him whatsoever he should ask. And the King granted him. Then said the Abbot: 'Here have I God-fearing monks, who would fain live as anchorites [*i.e.*, hermits], knew they but where. And here is an island which is called Ancarig [Thorney]. And my boon is that we might there build a Minster, to the glory of St. Mary, so that they who would lead the life of peace and rest may dwell therein.'

"Then the King answered and said: 'Beloved Sexwulf, lo! not only that which thou hast asked, but all else on our Lord's behalf I thus approve and grant.' ... And King Wulfhere first confirmed it by word, and after subscribed it with his fingers on the Cross of Christ," *i.e.*, he signed his name with a Cross, on which he laid his finger, saying, "I deliver this as my act and deed," as with the seal on a deed at present. Seals did not come in till the Norman Conquest. Amongst the witnesses to his signature we find " Wilfrid the Priest, who was afterwards Bishop," *i.e.*, the great St. Wilfrid of Ripon.

§ 25. And the idea of Ely itself, with its church on the highest available ground, towering over the waste around, as a standing testimony to the higher life, was drawn by Etheldred from the like situation of her aunt Hilda's Abbey at Whitby, on its cliff over the North Sea. How deeply both these saintly women impressed their personality on the popular mind is shown by their names being the only relics of old English feminine nomenclature to survive the Norman Conquest and come down even to our own times. Etheldred, indeed, has given us two distinct forms—Ethel and Audrey, the latter being the more plebeian vocalization, a fact which has also impressed itself upon our tongue in the derived adjective "tawdry" (*i.e.*, St. Audrey), in allusion to the cheap and showy character of the articles forming the staple of the merchandise which found so ready a sale amongst the low-born multitudes who thronged each October to St. Etheldred's Fair at Ely.

§ 26. Etheldred was instituted as Abbess of Ely by the great Northumbrian Bishop, Wilfrid,[1] the founder of Ripon,[2] and the special champion of the Roman as against the Scottish form of Christianity in England.[3]

---

[1] Bede, "Eccl. Hist.," Book IV., chap. xix.
[2] *Ibid.*, Book III., chap. xxv.   [3] *Ibid.*

From him she had already received the veil[1] in the convent of her aunt Ebba[2] at Coldingham ; and he now followed her from York, to give her the benefit of his counsel in organizing her foundation, and of his eminent architectural skill in the construction of its church and other buildings.[3] Under his influence this original minster of Ely was doubtless of the same Romanesque style that we see in the contemporary churches set up by Benedict Biscop at Jarrow and Wearmouth.[4] The cost was mainly borne by Etheldred's brother Adwulf, now seated upon their father's East Anglian throne.[5]

§ 27. The foundress continued to govern the house for six years. At her death (of tumour, still specially prevalent in this county) in 679, she was succeeded by her sister Sexburga, Queen-Dowager of Kent,[6] who, some years later, in 695, desired to "translate" her remains to the church. "She ordered some of the Brothers[7] to provide stone for a coffin: they accordingly went on board ship (because the country of Ely is on every side encompassed with the sea or marshes, and had no large stones), and came to a small waste city not far from thence, which in the language of the English is called Grantchester, and . . . found a white marble coffin, most beautifully wrought, with a lid of the same stone."[8]

---

[1] Bede, "Eccl. Hist.," Book IV., chap. xix.
[2] *Ibid.* Ebba was her aunt by marriage.
[3] See Bentham, "Hist. of Ely," pp. 53, 54.
[4] Bede, Book IV., chap. xviii. Jarrow was built 682, Wearmouth 674.
[5] See Bentham, p. 54.
[6] Sexburga, while Queen of Kent, had founded an abbey at Sheppey for seventy-seven nuns, the first Abbess being her daughter Ermenilda, Queen-Dowager of Mercia (see § 22), who had received her conventual training at Ely from St. Etheldred.
[7] Etheldred's abbey, like all the earliest foundations, was for both sexes.
[8] Bede, "Eccl. Hist.," Book IV., chap. xix.

Bede here presumably means Camboritum. The site now called Grantchester has no traces of Roman remains such as provided this marble coffin.[1]

§ 28. In connection with this same story, we also learn incidentally that the "country of Ely," like the present "Isle," extended far beyond the actual island on which Etheldred placed her minster, for Bede calls it "a country of six hundred families." Now, the word "family" was in his day strictly a measure of land, a signification which it probably acquired from the fact that a certain recognised amount of land was considered sufficient for the support of the household of an Eorl. This amount appears to have been something like half a square mile, for, in describing the island of Iona (which is actually not quite three miles long, and not quite one mile in average breadth), Bede says: "The island is not very large, but contains about five families according to our English measure." "Six hundred families" would thus be equivalent to three hundred square miles, about the area of the present "Isle."

§ 29. That the name should have had this purely artificial value shows that we are now entering upon that period of local organization which so strikingly marks the history of the latter half of the seventh century. The existing Hundreds (actual administrative entities within our own century) may very probably be of this date. The name is derived from the number of "hides" of land contained in the division, a "hide" being, as it would seem, half a "family." These ancient measures of land are a notorious crux to historians and archæologists, for they are used with no great accuracy by our earliest authorities. But the conjecture here hazarded is supported by the fact that the hundreds do very generally contain about twenty-five square miles (*i.e.*, fifty "families"), and by an entry in the Ramsey Cartulary, which incidentally mentions

See above, § 4.

Anglo-Saxon Period—I. 53

that eleven hides are equivalent to forty-four virgates of thirty acres apiece.[1]

§ 30. And while Etheldred and Sexburga were ruling Ely, the great Archbishop of Canterbury, Theodore of Tarsus, "the first Archbishop whom the whole Church of England obeyed," was doing his mighty work of organizing that Church, with its provinces and sees and parishes, even as it remains in all essential features to the present day. In our county it was at this time that every village began to have its own parish church, as now; those east of the Cam being under the jurisdiction of the Bishop of East Anglia (whose see was first at Dunwich and finally at Norwich), and those to the west probably forming part of the vast diocese of the Middle English (with its "Bishop-stool" originally at Dorchester in Oxfordshire, and finally at Lincoln), which even up to 1840 still stretched from the Humber to the Thames.

Thus, the foundation of Ely brings us to the dawn of the existing state of things in Cambridgeshire, and it is appropriate that the earliest certainly datable monument of antiquity still existing in the county should be of this period. This is the base and shaft of a stone cross, now in the south aisle of Ely Cathedral, bearing the inscription (apparently intended for a pentameter line):

LVCEM . TVAM . OVINO
. DA . DEVS . ET . REQVIEM
. AMEN .

§ 31. This Ovinus, or Owen, whose name shows his British extraction, is called by Bede Etheldred's Prime Minister, "Primus Ministorum." (in the Anglo-Saxon version, "her Over-Alderman"). To him was doubtless committed the administration of her jurisdiction over the Girvian territory. He is said to have lived at Winford ("Owens-worth"),[2] and ended his days in the monastery

---
[1] Rolls Series, vol. i., p. 120.
[2] Bentham, "Hist. of Ely," p. 51.

attached by St. Chad, the apostle of Mercia, to his newly-founded "Bishop-stool" at Lichfield. Bede tells how he "fully forsook the things of this world, quitting all that he had, clad in a plain garment, and carrying an axe and hatchet in his hand, . . . signifying that he did not enter the monastery to live idle, as some do, but to labour;" and how, while thus employed in handiwork, "as he was less capable of meditating on the Scriptures," he heard the angels' carol which sang to his rest the saintly Bishop.[1] Afterwards he was himself canonized, and his cross, which till lately stood at Haddenham, became an object of veneration to the pilgrims who approached Ely from the South.

§ 32. At this time, indeed, the whole of England seemed fast settling down. The existence of a single English Church, already co-extensive with the English race, and tending more and more to unite the whole of Britain in one and the same ecclesiastical polity, prepared the way for the formation of a single English State. The number of separate kingdoms ever became fewer. It early sank to seven; the "Heptarchy" of Kent, Sussex, Wessex, Essex, East Anglia, Mercia, and Northumbria. Then, of these, Wessex subdued Kent and Sussex, East Anglia absorbed Essex, and both these conquering States became for a while tributaries to Mercia. When, in 731 A.D., Bede concluded his History, Northumbria and Mercia were the only independent monarchies. He dwells upon "the peaceful and calm state of the times," the laying aside of weapons, the cultivation of pacific pursuits which characterized the period. "What will be the end hereof," he adds, "the next age will show."[2]

[1] St. Chad died seven days later, March 2, 669.
[2] "Eccl. Hist.," Book V., chap. xxiii.

CHAPTER IV.

ANGLO-SAXON PERIOD—II.

§ 1—4. Bede's forecast—England under Egbert—Mint at Cambridge —Danish invasion—East Anglia their fastness—Great raid of 870—Ely destroyed—Death of St. Edmund—Vikings at Cambridge.

§ 5—11. Peace of Wedmore—Last Cambridgeshire battle—Cambridgeshire in the Danelagh—Reconquest by Edward—Creation of the county—Hundreds and tithings—Fight at Chesterford (?).

§ 12—26. Edgar the Peaceful—Ethelred the Unready—Danish inroads recommence—Battle of Maldon—Brithnoth at Ely—Refounding of the abbey—Shrines.

§ 27—31. Sweyn's invasion—Ulfcytel the Ready—Battle of Ringmere—Cambridgeshire separate from East Anglia—Ravaged by Danes—Sack of Cambridge—Massacre of Balsham—Barrington Ford—Bracteates.

§ 32—40. Edmund Ironside—Battle of Assandun (Ashdon)—Arguments for its locality—Order of battle—English colours— Edmund's charge—Treason of Edric—Canute's minster.

§ 41—44. Canute first King of England—Earlier royal titles—His favour for Ely—Prosperity of the abbey—Officers—Schools— Royal pupils.

§ 45—46. Alfred the Etheling—Rebuilding and expansion of Cambridge—St. Benet's.

§ 1. LITTLE did Bede think, when he portrayed the peaceful outlook in the last sentence of his History, what that "next age," which seemed dawning so brightly, would indeed bring forth. Instead of witnessing that quiet development of Christian civilization to which, at his writing, everything pointed, it brought upon Britain the most shattering tempest of heathen barbarism that she had known for four hundred years. Even before his century closed there fell the first drops of the gathering storm, when, in 787, three ships of the hitherto unknown Norsemen made a descent upon the East Anglian coast, the forerunners of those innumerable pirate fleets whose incursions filled the next three hundred years with misery and ruin. The Anglo-Saxon Chronicle tells us how in this year "first came there three ships of the Northmen out of Hæretha-land [Norway]. And then the Reeve [*i.e.*, the Sheriff] rode to the place, and would have driven them to the King's town, because he knew not what men they were. And then and there did they slay him. These were the first ships of Danish men that sought the land of Angle-kin ";[1] and thus characteristically did they begin the long series of massacres which reddened each successive wave of their inroads upon English soil.

§ 2. Just before the full tempest burst, England at last became one united kingdom under Egbert of Wessex, the last "Bretwalda,"[2] the first "King of the English,"[3] who stood forward as the champion of Southern and Eastern England against the Mercian yoke, first freeing his own Wessex, then, in 825, driving the midlanders from Kent. "And the Kentish-men, and the men of Surrey, and the South-Saxons, and the East-Saxons, came in to him, for erstwhile had they been unrightly forced from his kin. And the same year the King of the East Angles and his folk sought of him help and

[1] This is the earliest instance of the territories occupied by the English races being designated by a common name. "England" is not found till the tenth century.

[2] See Chapter III., § 16. The title is, however, found in charters as late as Athelstane.

[3] Egbert calls himself *Rex Anglorum* in a charter of 828. See also § 41.

wardship for dread of the Mercians,"[1] repulsing an invasion by which Beornwulf, King of Mercia, endeavoured to recover their allegiance, with the slaughter of that monarch himself. Mercia was thus so seriously weakened that Egbert was shortly able, with little resistance, to conquer it; when he assumed the title of Bretwalda, and as such claimed and received (without fighting) the allegiance of Northumbria, thus uniting all England under his sceptre.[2] This was the last of the long intestinal warfare between the various English kingdoms as such; and the decisive battle, in which Beornwulf was slain, probably took place in Cambridgeshire. The town of Cambridge itself was, in all likelihood, now rebuilt, occupying as it did the obvious route from Mercia to East Anglia. Coins of Egbert, there struck, show that in his reign the place was no longer the "waste chester" which it had been in 679, but of sufficient importance to possess a mint.

§ 3. Then the clouds drew down. Year after year brought fresh hordes of heathen Danes and Norsemen across the sea to try every point along the British coast, and wherever they landed to harry, burn and massacre, with that special rollicking delight in destruction for its own sake which was their peculiar national characteristic. They were bitter heathens, and made the churches and the clergy special objects of attack. The great estuary of the Wash afforded one of their easiest anchorages, whence the Ouse and the Cam admitted them to the heart of Cambridgeshire; while the semi-insular character of East Anglia made that district the headquarters,[3] where they could safely leave "their wives, their ships, and their wealth," while they swarmed out to raid throughout the length and breadth of England, and

[1] Anglo-Saxon Chronicle, A.D. 825.
[2] *Ibid.*, A.D. 827.
[3] See Anglo-Saxon Chronicle, A.D. 866, 880, and particularly 894.

whither they retreated with their booty. The example was contagious, and the generation of East Anglians which grew up during this occupation of their land by the "mighty heathen host" which invaded the land in 866 A.D. became as bloodthirsty and faithless as the Danes themselves; so that in 894, though they had given oaths and hostages to King Alfred, "yet, against their plighted troth, as oft as the other [heathen] went forth, then went they forth also," to share in the adventure and the plunder.[1] East Anglia was, moreover, the first district where the Danes "were horsed"[2]—one of the most frequent entries in the chronicles of this period, and one of the most puzzling; for in a land where all fighting was done on foot, and all ploughing by oxen, whence came the large number of horses which the invaders constantly found ready to their hand?

§ 4. Their cruelest harrying of these parts was done in 870, when " they rode back [from York] across Mercia into East Anglia"[3] (a route which would make them cross the river at Cambridge, the only available passage), "and trod down all the land, and brake down all the Minsters that ever they came to"—amongst them Peterborough, Thorney, Ramsey, Crowland, Soham, and, notably, Ely. This was the campaign made memorable by the defeat and martyrdom of St. Edmund, the last King of East Anglia, whom the savage pagans tied to an oak and shot to death with arrows. Five years later three of the Viking leaders chose Cambridge itself as their headquarters, "and sat down there one whole year,"[4] doubtless engaged in the congenial occupation of raiding the neighbourhood, which they seem finally to have made too hot to hold them; at least, they found it

---

[1] See also Florence of Worcester, A.D. 887.
[2] Anglo-Saxon Chronicle, A.D. 866.
[3] *Ibid.*, A.D. 870.
[4] *Ibid.*, A.D. 875.

advisable to "steal away"[1] (Florence adds "by night"), and did not stop till they had intrenched themselves in the distant fortress of Wareham in Dorsetshire.

§ 5. By the Peace of Wedmore, concluded between Alfred and the Danes in 878, Cambridgeshire formed part of the immense district ceded to the invaders, which included more than half England, the boundary being the river Lea, along its whole course, and thence the Watling Street. For nearly half a century our county thus remained part of the Danelagh, subject to Danish law, and to some extent under Danish occupation; though the paucity of Scandinavian names shows that the occupation was far less thorough than in such districts as Leicestershire or Lincolnshire, where the Danish termination "by" (equivalent to the English "borough") meets us at every turn. Still, "the Lords Danes" doubtless appropriated much of the best land, dividing it, after their fashion, "with a rope," *i.e.*, by chain measure, and generally looting any desirable property, especially Church property. Ely they had already burnt in the great raid of 870.

§ 6. During this period the county was the scene of one notable engagement, which is thus described in the Anglo-Saxon Chronicle:

"905. This year Ethelwald the Etheling [cousin to the reigning King Edward, son of Alfred, and pretender to the throne, who the year before had come over sea into Essex "with such ships as he could get"] enticed the [Danish] host in East Anglia to break the peace, so that they ravaged over all the land of Mercia ... and took all they might lay hands on, and then turned homeward again. Then went after them King Edward, as fast as he might gather his force, and overran all their land between the dykes and the Ouse, all as far north as the Fens."

The district thus designated is the southern and

[1] Anglo-Saxon Chronicle, A.D. 876.

eastern portion of Cambridgeshire, "the dykes" being the Devil's Ditch and its companions already described, which now seem to have done their last service as defences against an invader from the southwards.

The narrative continues:

"When, after, he would return thence, then bade he to be cried throughout his whole force, that all should return together. Then did the Kentish men stay their behind, notwithstanding his bode and seven messengers whom he sent after them. Then came the [Danish] host there up to them, and there fought them: and there Siwulf the Alderman . . . and Kenwulf the Abbot . . . were slain, and likewise many with them. And on the Danish side were slain Eric their King, and Ethelwald the Etheling, who had enticed him to break the peace . . . and very many with them. And great was the slaughter there made on either hand; and of the Danish folk were there the more slain, yet held they the battle-stead" [*i.e.* had the victory].

§ 7. Such was the last fight, worthy of being called a battle, on Cambridgeshire soil. Seven years later, in 912, the children of Alfred, Edward the Elder and his sister Ethelfled, "Lady of the Mercians," began that systematic reconquest of the Danelagh which proved so triumphantly successful. District after district was overrun, subjugated, curbed by fortresses at strategic points, dominated by colonies from Wessex, or even, as at St. Ives on the Ouse, from far-off Cornwall, and divided up into shires, each around the county town from which it is called.

§ 8. And thus at length we reach the creation of Cambridgeshire as an administrative entity. The old boundaries and divisions within its borders had been swept away by the Danish inundation; but in 921 "all the [Danish] host among the East Anglians swore to be at one with King Edward, that they would all that he would, and would hold peace toward all to whom the King should grant his peace, both by sea and land. And in especial did the host which owed fealty to Cambridge" —a remarkable expression, indicating that the Danish settlers held their lands by some sort of military tenure— "choose him to father and to lord; and thereto swore oaths, even as he then bade it." It was the district thus specially "commended" to him (to use the phrase of a later date) that Edward formed into his new county of Cambridge, dividing (or re-dividing) it doubtless at the same time into hundreds, according to the current English system of Local Government, which figures so prominently in the legislation of Alfred.

Each hundred was again divided into about ten smaller divisions denominated "tithings," identical, probably, with the "marks" of the original English settlers, and corresponding, with few exceptions, to the existing parishes. (It may be noticed that the boundaries of the hundreds are mostly perpetuated by those of the present Rural Deaneries, some of which correspond to a single hundred, others to two.[1]) By Alfred's "dooms" every Englishman was bound to belong to a certain tithing and hundred, and the whole hundred was held responsible for the good conduct of each of its members, the evil-doer not only being himself punished, but bringing down a fine (varying according to his guilt) upon his hundred. If he had slain, assaulted, or robbed anyone, this fine was payable to the hundred to which the injured man pertained.

§ 9. The new shire began its existence with seventy years of peace, broken possibly in 948 by a momentary invasion from the North. In that year, as the A.-S. Chronicle tells us, King Eadred, brother and successor of the great Edmund, "ravaged all Northumberland," because they had taken a Dane named Eric for their King. A notable feature of this raid was the pillage and burning of St.

[1] See Appendix.

Wilfrid's "great Minster" at Ripon. "And as the King went homewards, then came after the Army of York, and overtook him. The rearguard of the King's host was at Chesterford; and there they made great slaughter. Then was the King so wroth that he would have marched his force in again and wholly wasted the land. When the Northumbrian Witan understood that, then forsook they Eric, and paid bote for the deed to King Eadred." Chesterford is at the boundary between Cambridgeshire and Essex, on the river Granta—a somewhat distant locality for the circumstances, so that Chesterfield in Derbyshire has been suggested as the more probable scene of this "slaughter." If the Chronicle is correct, the "Army of York"—again a noteworthy phrase—must have passed the river at Cambridge in their avenging rush after the royal forces, and again in their hasty retreat after striking their blow.

§ 10. With this doubtful exception, Cambridgeshire remained undisturbed during the succession of able and valiant monarchs who, for nearly a century, showed themselves not unworthy to be the heirs of the Great Alfred. This was the Golden Age of the Anglo-Saxon dynasty. Not only were all the English races united under their immediate rule, but, as Over-lords, they held the whole of Britain under their sway. And this organization of an independent British Empire was a new departure in history, destined to exercise a most potent and permanent influence on the destinies alike of our country and of the world. Hitherto the ancient claims of Rome to the sovereignty of the island, though utterly in abeyance, had never been entirely repudiated. And when the "Holy Roman Empire" was revived by Charlemagne, those claims revived with it, and were actually recognised by (at least) the princes both of Northumbria and Scotland, if not of Kent also, who alike became, by voluntary submission, subjects to the great Emperor; "et eum nunquam," says his biographer, Eginhard,[1] "nisi Dominum, seque subditos et servos ejus pronunciarent." The great power of Offa of Mercia (who ruled all the rest of England, and whose coinage is found in Cambridgeshire) forbade the further extension of this submission; but the current stories of a proposed Roman invasion of Kent on the one hand, and on the other of the recognition of Offa by Charlemagne as in some sort his equal, bear witness to the fact that the idea—wild as it seems to us—was by no means outside the domain of practical politics in the ninth century. The claim was drowned for a while beneath the flood of the Danish invasions, and when that deluge was overpast, not the least proof of the genius of the victorious children of Alfred is to be seen in the sedulous care with which they guarded against this danger also by the assumption of imperial style on their own account, and, in particular, by the adoption of the specially Imperial title *Basileus*.

§ 11. From the days of Augustus (on whose coins it is found) this word had borne with it a claim to empire. The recognition by the ambassadors from Constantinople of Charlemagne's right to bear it had been their recognition of his right to be Cæsar. And from the days of our oldest Edward onwards it became the word on which our English monarchs set the greatest store, as expressing their claim (to use the emphatic language of the Statutes of 1537) "that this realm of England is an Empire . . . governed by one Supreme Head and King, having the dignity and royal estate of the Imperial Crown of the same . . . without restraint or provocation to any foreign prince or potentate of the world." The use of the word "Emperor" by Henry VIII., Mary, Elizabeth, and even as late as Anne, was in assertion of this claim; whilst the world-wide expansion since Anne's day of what is by no mere figure of speech called the British Empire is now

[1] "Life of Charlemagne," cap. xvi.

rightfully remembered in the adoption by our Queen of the ancestral style "Victoria R. et I." We may perhaps be allowed to regret that the more locally characteristic *Basileus* has so entirely become obsolete. It held its ground for many generations, and even in the days of John the acclamation "Chere Basileu" (*i.e.*, χαῖρε βασιλεῦ) was the special English salutation to the sovereign.[1]

§ 12. The culmination of these Imperial assumptions was reached (A.D. 973) in the solemn coronation of Edgar the Peaceful, "the elect of the Anglo-Britons," at the old Roman city of Bath, a ceremony sung in the contemporary lay still extant, and preserved in popular memory by that annual appointment of a "King of Bath" which only died out in the eighteenth century. Edgar had already been fourteen years on the English throne when he thus assumed the British diadem together with the exclusively Imperial title "Pacificus," emphasizing his pretensions shortly afterwards by the well-known ceremony wherein eight vassal princes rowed their Emperor's bark along the Dee.

§ 13. The monarch who was thus honoured was reaping the fruits not only of his ancestors', but of his own energy and forethought. "He got together," says Florence, "a fleet of 360 stout ships. Every year after Easter did he cause 120 of these to gather on the eastern, 120 on the western, and 120 on the northern shore of this island. [These would now be called the Southern, Western, and Eastern shores respectively, for by ancient geographers, as by Cæsar, Britain was thought to be a triangle, with its apex to the South and its base on the North.] He would then sail to the Western with the Eastern fleet, and sending that back would sail with the Western till he found the Northern squadron, in which he would proceed till he once more met the Eastern division; thus every summer encompassing the whole

[1] Richard of Devizes, § 48.

island, thus at once to guard against foes from abroad, and to inure himself and his subjects for the keeping of watch and ward. Each winter and spring would he make a progress throughout every district of England, and diligently look into the work of justice and the law-keeping of the nobles, that the poor might suffer no wrong at the hands of the wealthier."

§ 14. Such a prince deserved to be called "His Pacific Majesty," and whilst he lived peace and prosperity did actually reign within the four seas. But in the rivalry for the throne which followed his death, his precautions were neglected, and when in 979 his child-son, Ethelred, was "hallowed to King at Kingston-on-Thames," the ancient coronation place of West Saxon Royalty, "on the Sunday fourteen nights after Easter," the great Aurora, whose appearance is thought worthy of mention in the A.-S. Chronicle, was felt to be ominous of coming trouble.

§ 15. And not without reason. The very next year the Danish ravages began again; "the seven ships" which raided Southampton being referred to by the chronicler with a sad exactitude, which marks his sense that they were the beginning of sorrows. Kent, Cheshire, Cornwall, Devon, Wales, Dorset, successively furnished the pirates with occupation for the rest of the decade, and then came the turn of East Anglia.

§ 16. That district, though now an integral part of the United Kingdom of England, still retained a certain measure of its old independent national life. The long line of East Anglian royalty had indeed come to an end when the martyrdom of its last representative, Edmund, by the Danes, had gained for him canonization as the patron saint of his kingdom.[1] But though without a separate King, the region still had its own separate Witan,[2] or legislative assembly (in which every free man had a voice), and was treated by the Central Government

---

[1] See § 4.   [2] See Anglo-Saxon Chronicle, A.D. 1004.

as one organic whole, under a local "Alderman"[1] of its own, who at this juncture was a man conspicuous alike for piety and for valour, Brithnoth. There are strong reasons for connecting his name specially with our county, and without doubt a Cambridgeshire contingent took its part in that Battle of Maldon sung with such Homeric vigour and detail by the contemporary minstrel.

§ 17. His lay tells us how Brithnoth came upon the Danish invaders about to pass over the tidal stream of the Panta (now the Blackwater), at whose mouth they had landed with a view to harrying Essex. He had raised the local levies on his march, and hastily gave them such tactical instruction as time permitted. But the backbone of his force was his own "hearth-ward," the band of personal retainers who had marched with him from Cambridgeshire, and who were attached to him by that tie of individual loyalty then regarded as the closest of all bonds between man and man. The Anglo-Saxon Chronicle gives a striking instance of the entire devotion of this loyalty in recording a disputed succession to the West Saxon throne in 755. Cynewulf, the King, having been surprised and slain at night by the pretender, Cyneard, "when the king's thanes who were with him heard the fray, then did each, as he was ready, run with all speed to the place. And to each did Cyneard proffer money and life, and not one would take it, but there did they fight on till every man fell. Then, on the morrow, heard the King's thanes whom he had left behind how that the King was slain; then rode they thither. . . . Then did Cyneard proffer them gold and lands, all they would, so they would yield him the kingdom, and showed them their own kinsmen that held with him, men that

---

[1] This title originally signified the civil head of an Anglo-Saxon clan not yet sufficiently organized to possess a King. At this date it denoted the Governor set by the Crown over a given district.

would never leave him. Then said they that no kinsman was so dear as their lord, and that they would never follow his slayer. And their kinsfolk they bade that they should depart in peace and forsake Cyneard. But they made answer that the same bode had been laid upon 'your mates that were with the King, neither are we more minded to take it than they, who were slain with him.' So stood they fighting until Cyneard and all with him save one were slain." Nor were Brithnoth and his men less mutually devoted. We read how, on his road to the battle, he refused hospitality unless extended to them also, saying, "I cannot fight without my men, neither will I feed without them ";[1] and how, in the fight itself, they fought and fell by his side, till the last desperate rally of the survivors rescued his headless corpse from the victorious heathen.[2] It is interesting to note amongst these retainers one bearing the distinctively Celtic name of Maccus,[3] doubtless a Girvian of the Fens.

§ 18. It was amongst this chosen "comitatus,"

> "His own hearth-ward,
> His liefest and dearest,
> That him lealest held,"

that Brithnoth, after arraying his forces, lighted down from the "mare" which had carried him on the march, and took his stand for the battle. In Anglo-Saxon warfare horses were never used during the actual combat, a national trait which comes out strikingly in the Battle of Hastings, where the Norman force was mainly cavalry, while of the English William of Malmesbury[4] tells us:

[1] Ramsey Chronicle.

[2] They are called "the heathen host" in the lay. The conversion of Norway was shortly afterwards effected by King Olaf, who seems to have fought as a heathen in this very battle (Freeman, "Norman Conquest," vol. i., p. 268).

[3] One of the Welsh princes who rowed Edgar on the Dee is named Maccus.

[4] "Hist.," iii., §§241.

"Rex ipse *pedes* juxta Vexillum stabat cum fratribus." As he did so, a herald from the Vikings, "the Seamen bold," as these pirate rovers called themselves, appeared with a suggestion that they should be bought off:

> " Thy realm mayst thou ransom
> By sending the Seamen,
> To their own full doom,
> Gear and gift.
> Then back with our booty
> To ship will we get us,
> Fare forth on the flood
> And pass you in peace."

In this proposition we see the foreshadowing of that fatal system of Danegeld to which this very year, 991, the English Government first stooped. Well would it have been for the country if the King and his Witan had had the courage to repudiate the demand for ransom as promptly and indignantly as did Brithnoth:

> "Hear thou, sailor,
> What saith this people.
> For ransom we give you
> Full freely our weapons,
> Spear-edge and sword-edge
> Of old renown.[1]

> "This bode in return
> Bear back to thy shipmates,
> This word of high warning,
> That here stand undaunted

---

[1] A.-S.: "Ættrene ord
And ealde sword."

Rhyme has no recognised place in Anglo-Saxon poetry, but in this song is very occasionally found. At this period the idea was just dawning. It was already in use in Latin hymns and in French chansons, and speedily became universal in English ballads. But the rough rhythm and alliteration, which I have endeavoured to reproduce, were the essential features of our earliest minstrelsy.

A chief with his chosen :
This land will we fight for,
For Ethelred's realm,
For our King, folk, and country."

§ 19. The same chivalrous courage which prompted this reply led Brithnoth, all too boldly,[1] to forgo the advantage of defending the passage of the river, and to suffer the Danes, "those loathly guests," to cross unmolested, so soon as the tide fell.

"Then waded the water
Those wolves of the slaughter,[2]
Nor stayed them the stream :
Pressed over Panta
The Vikings' war :
O'er the wan water-way
Weapons they waved,
Their shields to shore
The shipmen bore.

"Then drave from each hand
Full stoutly the spear,
Showered the sharp arrows,
Busy were bows,
Shield met shaft,
Bitter the battle."

The deeds of various heroes are commemorated. Brithnoth himself slays the pirate leader with the cast of a "franca," the missile axe used with such terrible effect by the Frankish warriors of the fifth century.[3]

[1] A.-S. "for his ofermōde." The minstrel clearly feels it a grievously "overbold" act of chivalry. An interesting historical parallel is to be found in the like inaction of King James at Flodden. Despite all remonstrance, he insisted on letting the English pass the difficult ford of the Till unscathed, ere he would join battle with them.

[2] A.-S. wæl-wulfas.

[3] Procopius describes the Franks as "having neither bow nor spear, but each a sword, a shield, and one axe. The iron of this axe is stout, sharp, and two-edged ; the handle, made of wood, is exceedingly short. At a given signal they all throw these axes, and thus, at the first onset, are wont to break the shields of the enemy and slay his men."

> "Then blithe was the chief,
> Out-laughed the stern soldier;
> His Maker he thankèd
> For that day's work
> That the Lord him gave."

Almost immediately, however, he is himself mortally wounded by a javelin, which his page withdraws and hurls back, with fatal effect, against its sender. Brithnoth can fight no more :

> "Yet gave he the war-word,
> The hoar-headed hero.
> The warrior youths,
> His comrades brave,
> He bade charge on."

He sinks dying to the ground, and commends his soul to God :

> "To Thee give I thanks,
> Thou Lord of all living,
> For all good hap
> In this life here.
> Sore need I now,
> O Maker mild,
> That Thou shouldst grant
> My spirit grace,
> That my soul to Thee
> May depart in peace,
> And flee to Thy keeping,
> Thou King of Angels.
> To Thee do I pray
> That the gates of hell
> Prevail not against me."

§ 20. Few finer examples of epic poetry than this Song of Maldon are to be found in any language, and Cambridgeshire may well be proud of her special connection with the hero so gloriously sung. Brithnoth may not improbably have been a native of the county; that he was a large landowner within it is certain. The manors with which he requited the hospitality of the Abbot of Ely on his road to the battle are situated almost wholly in Cambridgeshire, comprising those of Trumpington, Soham, Fulbourn, Teversham, Impington, Papworth, Croxton, Triplow and Hardwicke. It was from Cambridgeshire that he set forth on his march to Maldon, and when he had fallen, amid the desperate fight which so crippled the victorious rovers that they were fain to put to sea at once without either plunder or ransom, it was to Cambridgeshire that his headless corpse was brought back. There it was laid to rest, in the newly-restored Minster of Ely, to which he had been a signal benefactor; and there, within the last century, it was recognised (in the course of some repairs) by the ball of wax with which the Abbot Ælfsige replaced the missing head, and was reinterred, where it now lies, beneath the exquisite canopy of Bishop West's chapel, in the south aisle of the presbytery. The statement made in the commemorative tablet above his grave, that he was Duke of Northumbria, is obviously mistaken, as is also that of the Ramsey chronicler, that the fight at Maldon lasted a whole fortnight.

§ 21. The above-mentioned restoration of Ely is an event of the very first importance in the history of Cambridgeshire. Cambridge itself has scarcely exercised a greater influence on the development of the county than this islet amid the Fens; nay, Cambridge itself would probably, but for Ely, have remained an obscure provincial town instead of one of the great intellectual centres of the world. For from Ely, as we shall see, came almost certainly the earliest germs of our University life.

§ 22. Like all other ecclesiastical foundations within their reach, the original monastery of St. Etheldred at Ely was utterly swept away by the Danes in the ninth century. The fatal year 870, which witnessed the martyrdom of St. Edmund, saw also the overthrow of

Crowland, Peterborough, and Ely. The "Liber Eliensis" tells us that the extremely defensible position of the site enabled it to hold out for some time, repulsing the first attempts of the heathen, and proving an asylum for the neighbourhood,[1] as it had proved of old in the sixth century, and as it was to prove again in the eleventh and thirteenth. Even so late, indeed, as the nineteenth, it was still looked upon as a refuge in case of invasion. During the Napoleonic scare of 1805, when a French landing was dreaded (and with reason, until Trafalgar ended the hideous nightmare) on every English seaboard, it was to Ely that the East Anglian districts turned their eyes. Even so far off as Earlham, in Norfolk, Mr. Gurney kept a carriage and four in constant readiness, night and day, to convey his family, at the first alarm, to this fastness.

§ 23. But, save in the case of the British Girvii, Ely has never, throughout history, proved itself capable of more than a temporary defence, and it did not succeed in keeping the Danes at bay for many months. Then followed the usual wholesale massacre and destruction by which the Danes made their mark: the monks and nuns were slaughtered, the abbey buildings burnt, and the site remained desolate. Some years later, after the Peace of Wedmore, Alfred (though Ely lay within the Danish boundary) procured the settlement there of a small clerical college.[2] This college consisted of eight priests, who, repairing as best they could one aisle of the ruined church, preserved the relics of the foundress till better times.[3] A distant echo of this foundation is still to be recognised in the existing designation of the Cathedral precincts, which at Ely are called, not, as usual, "the Close," but "the College." A very doubtful legend

[1] "Liber Eliensis," i. 40.
[2] William of Malmesbury, "De Gest. Pont.," § 293.
[3] "Liber Eliensis," i. 41.

makes Alfred take this special interest in Ely as having been himself a scholar in the earlier abbey school. It is, however, certain that, though Cambridgeshire lay outside his boundary, it was not beyond his influence, and his coins are found in the county.

§ 24. But not until the pacific reign of the great Edgar did his Chancellor, Bishop Ethelwold of Winchester, again make Ely the great religious centre which it has remained continuously ever since. On the ruined site of Etheldred's convent he planted an abbey of Benedictine monks, and induced the King to re-endow it with that peculiar jurisdiction over the Isle of Ely which she had possessed as Queen of the Girvii, and which the Bishops of Ely retained up to the present century. After the sack of 870 the revenues and jurisdiction of the isle had been annexed to the crown of Mercia, by Burgraed, the last King of that district. They were now restored to the Church, and the ancient limits most accurately marked out afresh by Edgar, after consultation with the leading men of the whole neighbourhood. The western boundary was marked by a still existing ditch, now called Bishop's-Delf, whence the "Isle" extended to the Nen at Peterborough, twenty-five miles in breadth, with a length (from "the middle of Tydd bridge" to the Ouse near Upware) of twenty-eight miles. Within these limits it was not "the King's peace," but the peace of the Abbot (afterwards of the Bishop), against which malefactors were held to offend, and the courts of justice were held in the name of the latter. And the Isle, though for some civil purposes regarded as a part of Cambridgeshire, has at this day its own County Council, within these same limits, and ecclesiastically is exempt from archidiaconal jurisdiction, being immediately under the Bishop, as representing the Abbot of Ely.

§ 25. By the benefactions of such as Brithnoth, the re-founded abbey was, from the first, richly endowed. We have seen on how princely a scale he paid for his entertainment there during his life; and at his burial his widow presented to the newly-restored minster his golden Collar of Office, as well as a curtain ("cortinam") whereon she had embroidered his heroic deeds.[1] It is very possible that this work of art may have suggested to the Norman conquerors, a century later, the idea of the famous Bayeux tapestry, attributed, in like manner, to conjugal devotion.[2]

§ 26. But the chief treasure of the abbey was the possession of no fewer than four shrines of canonized queens—the foundress, St. Etheldred, her sister Sexburga, her niece Ermenilda, and yet another sister, Witburgha. The body of the last was acquired by a pious fraud, committed (after duly obtaining the royal license) by the Abbot upon the inhabitants of Dereham in Norfolk. The story is characteristic of the age. In friendly guise, but attended by a well-armed band of servants, the Abbot came to Dereham, held a court of justice, and liberally feasted the inhabitants. Having thus buried them in deep and unsuspecting slumber, he disinterred the remains of the saint at midnight, and hurriedly conveyed them in a horse-litter to Brandon. Thence a navigable waterway ran to Ely, by which the rest of the journey was made, thus baffling the pursuit of the men of Dereham, who ran along both banks of the river casting missiles, but unable to stop the "conveyance"—which seems to have been made without any thought of wrongdoing, and is recorded by the "Liber Eliensis" with unmixed satisfaction.

§ 27. The Battle of Maldon took place in 991. It was counted as a victory for the Danes. In the usual phrase

[1] "Liber Eliensis," ii. 63.
[2] Whether this tapestry is actually the work of Matilda, Queen of William the Conqueror, is doubtful. See Freeman's excursus on the subject.

of the period, they "held the battle-stead" at the close of the fray. But it was a check so serious that they at once took to their ships, and made no further attempt on East Anglia for fifteen years to come. And when they did appear, it was again to meet with heroic resistance, such as they were greeted with in no other part of Britain. During the intervening years they had harried without much difficulty every other seaboard of England. Northumbria, Lincolnshire, Kent, Sussex, Devon, Cornwall, Wales, were ravaged again and again. Bamborough, Southampton, Exeter, and Salisbury were sacked; London itself barely repelled the foe; while year after year an ever-larger Danegeld was demanded as the price of a momentary armistice.[1] But not till the massacre of St. Bryce brought King Sweyn "Forkbeard" of Denmark on his errand of vengeance did any Danish fleet invade East Anglia. And when he did appear—"with his three wonted comrades, fire, pillage and slaughter, while all England shook before him as a reed-bed rustling before the wind"[2]—he found here, and here alone, men ready to meet him with undaunted hearts.

§ 28. The command of the district was once more in heroic hands. The place of Brithnoth was now filled by Ulfcytel, a gallant soldier, at whose hands the invaders, in their first attempt, so narrowly escaped destruction, despite the smallness of his force, that "they themselves said that never worse handplay had they met in England than Ulfcytel brought on them."[3] His generalship, indeed,

[1] This disgraceful tribute rose by leaps and bounds. In 991 the Danes were contented with £10,000; in 994 they asked (and got) £16,000; in 1002, £24,000; in 1012, £48,000. Besides this, separate counties and districts also bought them off (as they had proposed to Brithnoth) for the moment. Thus, in 1009, East Kent gave them £3,000. These sums must be multiplied twenty or thirty fold to give their equivalent value at the present day.

[2] Henry of Huntingdon, 1004.
[3] Anglo-Saxon Chronicle, 1004.

made so deep an impression on his foes that they gave him the cognomen of "Snelling,"[1] "the Ready," and their sagas speak of all East Anglia as "Ultkel's Land."[2] His gallantry turned back one invasion, in 1004; but six years later, during which, "after their old wont, they lighted their war-beacons as they went"[3] throughout the length and breadth of England, the Danish hosts once more poured in. With the whole force of East Anglia, Ulfcytel, on Ascension Day,[4] 1010, met them at Ringmere, but this time in vain. As usual in the defeats of this period, treason is alleged as the cause of his overthrow. Probably his men were demoralized by the long tale of Danish success all over England. Any way, the battle was speedily decided. "Soon fled the East English. Then stood fast Grantabryg-shire alone."[5]

§ 29. In such honourable fashion do we meet with the earliest mention of our county by name in history. And the manner in which it is introduced shows that it was already beginning to have a corporate life of its own, not wholly identified with that of East Anglia, though its militia formed part of the general East Anglian levy. In the following year, 1011, the chronicler, in his long list of the districts wasted by the Danes, yet more markedly names it apart from East Anglia, with a separate number of its own. Henry of Huntingdon adds that, as a result of the conspicuous valour here exhibited, Cambridgeshire gained a lasting renown throughout the nation: "Dum

[1] "Snell" was the epithet which the Danes were fond of applying to themselves. Thus, in the Song of Maldon their envoy shouts to Brithnoth:
"Me sendon to þe Sæmenn snelle."

[2] See Freeman's "Norman Conquest," vol. i., note HH.
[3] Anglo-Saxon Chronicle, 1006.
[4] The Danes were by this time nominal Christians, and had abstained from their raids during Lent, employing that season in repairing their ships by the Medway.
[5] Anglo-Saxon Chronicle, 1010.

Angli regnaverunt, laus Grantabrigiensis Provinciæ splendide floruit."

§ 30. The gallant stand made at Ringmere was, however, dearly paid for, and drew down upon the county the special vengeance of the conquerors. After the battle the Danes "were horsed," as in 866,[1] and then rode about the district for three months on end, devastating with even more than their usual ferocity.[2] "And they even went into the wild fens, and there they destroyed men and cattle, and burned throughout the fens"[3] the little hamlets then, as now, clustered on each tiny plot of ground elevated above sea-level. "What could be moved that did they lift, what they might not carry that did they burn . . . and so marched they up and down the land."[4] Peterborough was destroyed, Crowland held to heavy ransom; but Ely itself, which again served as a refuge for the district,[5] seems to have escaped—thanks to an unusually wet season, which rendered the marshes around it impassable to the marauders, and drove them to the higher-lying parts of the county to the southward. Here Cambridge was sacked and burnt, and the neighbouring villages ravaged with the utmost ferocity; Balsham, in particular, forming the scene of a wholesale massacre, from which, out of the entire population, only one man is said to have escaped, by defending the narrow and winding stairway of the church steeple.[6]

§ 31. This legend points to the Danes having met with a certain amount of local resistance here and there, as doubtless they did. Ulfcytel the Ready had escaped from the slaughter at Ringmere (he died six years later

[1] See § 3.
[2] Florence of Worcester, 1010; also Henry of Huntingdon, 1010.
[3] Anglo-Saxon Chronicle, 1010.
[4] Ingulf, "Hist. of Croyland."
[5] *Ibid.* The Prior of Peterborough, with twenty monks, fled to Ely, bringing the sacred arm of St. Oswald.
[6] Henry of Huntingdon.

in the yet more fatal defeat of Assandun), and was not the man to let them ravage unharassed. A like inference may perhaps be drawn from a remarkable "find" made in 1875. At an ancient ford through the Cam near the village of Barrington there were then discovered a number of skeletons of men who had apparently fallen in the act of disputing the passage of the river. Swords, spear-heads, daggers, and shield-bosses, were intermingled with the bones, which lay about at random, obviously forming part of no regular interment, intermixed with the skeletons of horses. Associated with these was a circular brooch of green glass, bearing the well-known Danish emblem, the snake-headed raven, while near by there lay one of those curious "bracteates" (small plates of bronze engraved with imitation Saracenic characters) which the Norsemen of this period wore as charms. The whole position would be best explained by supposing that a band of horsemen from the east had forced, or attempted, the ford, in the face of a vigorous defence by the villagers. And at no other period is such a state of things so likely to have been brought about as in the dark days which followed Ringmere.

§ 32. During the remainder of the miserable reign of Ethelred we hear no more of Cambridgeshire. But it is probable that the final act in the tragedy of the Danish wars took place almost within its borders. With the death of Ethelred and the accession of his heroic son, Edmund Ironside, England awoke from the long stupor of terror, and rose against her invaders with a desperate effort which but a few years earlier would have annihilated them, and which, even at this last hour, proved all but successful. The wonderful year 1016 was marked by no fewer than six pitched battles between Edmund and Canute (now, by the death of his father Sweyn, the Danish monarch). In five of these, at Pen in Somerset, at Sherstone in Wiltshire, at London, at Brentford, and at Otford in Kent, the English had the advantage, though gaining no very decisive victory.

§ 33. Very different was the sixth battle. Penned up by Edmund in the Isle of Sheppey, the Danes took ship across the Thames estuary into Essex, and then marched through East Anglia into Mercia, " and harried whithersoever they went."[1] " Laden with spoil, they were returning toward their ships,"[2] when Edmund once more came upon them. For the fifth time he had gathered " all the English nation[3] from all parts of England,"[4] and, following the Danes in their retreat, overtook them " in Essex, at the down which is called Assandun."[5]

§ 34. The exact locality of this famous battle has long been a matter of dispute. Most recent historians, following the high authority of Mr. Freeman, hold it to be Ashington, near the estuary of the Crouch. But there is much to be said for the earlier view, which found it at Ashdon, on the south-eastern border of Cambridgeshire. The Danes, falling back from Mercia with their plunder, would find their most direct line of retreat along the Via Devana, which would enable them to cross the Cam at Cambridge and thence lead them straight to Ashdon. Edmund, in his hasty pursuit (it is to be observed that he was *following*, not trying to intercept them), would come by the same road on their track. We find, moreover, that he was accompanied to the field of battle by a body of monks from Ely,[6] whose presence would seem to favour the theory that the fight was not so very far from that monastery. Ashdon is less than thirty miles from Ely, Ashington nearly a hundred. The lie of the ground at the former agrees as well with the very meagre notice (in Florence of Worcester), which is all we have to guide us, as at the latter; while the name Ashdon is as probable a

[1] Anglo-Saxon Chronicle.
[2] Florence.
[3] Anglo-Saxon Chronicle.
[4] Florence.
[5] *Ibid.*
[6] "Liber Eliensis."

later variant of Assandun (or Esesdun, as Henry of
Huntingdon calls it) as is Ashington.

§ 35. That name is probably derived neither from
"ashes" nor "asses" (though Florence does speak of
"mons asini"), but rather embodies that Celtic word for
"water" which meets us as Axe, Exe, Esk, and Usk, in
so many parts of England. Ashdon is on the watershed
between the valleys of the Cam and the Stour, and beneath
the village, at Water End, rises one of the tributaries
of the former, the Bourne. In the meadows beside the
infant stream may well be the "locus æquus,"[1] whither
Canute led out his host to await the English charge.

§ 36. On the higher ground hard by Edmund had
drawn up his soldiers, after the pattern of the Roman
legionaries, in three lines, himself occupying the centre
of the foremost, the royal post, between the colours, as
we should now call them—the National Ensign, and the
Royal Standard bearing the personal cognizance of the
sovereign. Even at that early date this double system of
war-flags, which is still distinctive of the English army,
already existed, differing only from the present time in the
blazoning of the banners—the National flag being then
the Golden Dragon of Wessex (which remained the
Ensign of England even as late as Henry III.),[2] and
the Royal Standard varying with each reign, as the royal
supporters did until the time of James I.

§ 37. From that post the King now swept down in
person upon the foe, in a charge so brilliant that it awakes
the historians to enthusiasm. "Brandishing his good
sword" ("gladium electum," seemingly a weapon with a
special reputation of its own, like those which meet us in
the romances—Durandal, or Excalibur, or Colada), "he
clove like a thunderbolt the Danish battle-line" ("ictu

[1] Florence.
[2] Mr. Freeman is wrong in speaking of Hastings as "its last field."
See Richard of Devizes, § 1925, and Robert of Gloucester, § 1772.

fulmineo fidit aciem ")¹. But it is probable that this impetuosity lost him the fight. The English, missing him from the royal station, were seized with panic. The blame is, as usual, laid upon the *âme damnée* of the period, the Alderman Edric, whose utterly incomprehensible and repeated treasons form an only less strange episode than the fact that he was as repeatedly and incomprehensibly trusted and re-trusted by those whom he betrayed.² Here he is said to have taken advantage of the King's charge to raise the cry (doubtless the very wail which echoed over the field), "Flet Engle! Flet Engle! Dead is Edmund!"³ and to have set the example of flight, at the head of his own Herefordshire contingent. "And thus did he betray his King and Lord and the whole people of Angle-kin '"⁴ (*i.e.*, England, for which this form is the oldest equivalent).

§ 38. For all England was at stake upon this battle. It was a supreme national effort. "There did the whole English nation fight against him; and there had Canute the victory"⁵—a victory crushing in its completeness. The slaughter was fearful, especially of the higher leaders. There fell "the flower of the English nobility,"⁶ "who never in battle met with greater loss than then."⁷ Amongst them is particularly named the gallant Ulfcytel, who gave his life to cover the retreat of his King,⁸ and Ednoth, Bishop of Lincoln, whose body was brought back to Ely for burial.

§ 39. The names of the neighbouring villages, Castle

[1] Henry of Huntingdon.
[2] Freeman, "Norman Conquest," vol. i., p. 261.
[3] Henry of Huntingdon.
[4] Anglo-Saxon Chronicle.   [5] *Ibid.*
[6] *Ibid.*, and William of Malmesbury, § 165.   [7] Florence.
[8] Thus I interpret the words of Florence, "Regi proprio sanguine spem novam reddidit." How entirely in old English warfare all hope depended upon the life of the monarch is evident both in this campaign and that of Hastings.

Camps and Shudy Camps, and four very remarkable tumuli, which adjoin the churchyard of Bartlow in Cambridgeshire (though themselves in Essex and in the parish of Ashdon), may well be connected with this great battle, and the traces of "Saxon" work in the tower of Bartlow Church may carry back its origin to the little "minster of stone and lime"[1] which Canute afterwards erected to pray for the souls of those who were there slain, and of which the first priest was no less a personage than Stigand,[2] who fifty years later, as Archbishop of Canterbury, placed the crown upon the brow of Harold.

§ 40. Canute, we are told, built like "basilicas"[3] on the fields of all the other battles whereby he had fought his way to the English throne. This was doubtless done with the intention (the same which led the next conqueror of England to follow the precedent after the Battle of Hastings) of showing that he identified himself with the land he had conquered. His treatment of the traitor Edric exhibits a like motive. When the caitiff pleaded his treason as a ground for royal favour, Canute is said to have replied: "You say well; I will lift up your head, as is meet, above all the nobility of England." The head was accordingly impaled on the highest battlement of the Tower of London.[4]

§ 41. Canute, indeed, proved himself a much better King of England than might have been expected in a foreign conqueror. When the "tontine" arrangement,[5] which finally concluded his desperate struggle with Edmund, terminated in his favour,[6] he became one of the most loyal of English sovereigns, and wreaked no grudge

---

[1] Canterbury Chronicle.   [2] *Ibid.*
[3] William of Malmesbury.
[4] This is Henry of Huntingdon's version of the tale, which had many variants. See Freeman, "Norman Conquest," vol. i., note DDD.
[5] Florence.   [6] Anglo-Saxon Chronicle, 1017.

whatsoever on those who had so sturdily resisted him. And it is noteworthy that he is the first of our monarchs to call himself by this title, " King of England." The previous occupants of the throne had been kings " of the English " or " of the Anglo-Saxons," and derived their only territorial title from their hegemony over the whole island. The charters describe them as " Ongol-Saxna Cyning " and " Brytænwalda eallæs ðyses iglandæs " ; " Anglo-Saxonum necnon et totius Britanniæ Rex " ; " Basileus Anglorum, et Imperator Regum intra fines Britanniæ"; "Monarchus totius Brytanniæ"; " Rex totius Albionis"; "Cyning " and " Casere totius Britanniæ"; " Gentis Angligenæ Rex "; " Totius Albionis Archons " ; " Rex totius insulæ." We even find the familiar form " Britanniarum Rex," but only once does even the great Edgar adopt the style " Imperator . . . totius Angliæ." Canute first is " Ænglelandes Kyning."[1]

§ 42. To the monks of Ely in particular, the first "King of England," despite their presence against him at Assandun, became a signal benefactor. The relics, indeed, which they brought to that field he confiscated and bestowed upon Canterbury;[2] but he took the abbey into special favour, and in popular legend his name is particularly connected with it. The story of his being drawn to land there by the singing of the monks at their service is one of the most currently repeated tales in English history; and only less well known is that of his sledging over the doubtful ice from Ely to Soham, with the heaviest man of the neighbourhood going before him as a pilot. Both episodes are derived from the "Liber Eliensis,"[3] which adds that both took place on occasions of his yearly visit to the abbey for the Feast of the Purification. On that day the Abbot of Ely annually entered upon his four months' tenure of office as Chancellor

---

[1] See Freeman, " Norman Conquest," vol. i., note B.
[2] " Liber Eliensis," ii. 21.   [3] *Ibid.*, ii. 85.

of the kingdom, a dignity which passed on for a like term to the Abbot of Canterbury and the Abbot of Glastonbury in succession. These visits were always marked by splendid gifts to the Church, both from himself and from his Queen, Emma, once wife of his unhappy rival, Ethelred the Unready. The latter in particular presented " a purple cloth wrought with gold and set with jewels, such as there was none like it for richness in the kingdom . . . also a large pall of green set with plates of gold, to be placed on the front of the altar on the chief festivals."[1] Canute, moreover, founded, with a draft of monks from Ely, his famous abbey of Bury St. Edmund's.[2]

§ 43. Thanks to this royal patronage, Ely became one of the most flourishing foundations in the realm; and the monastery gained so great a name that it was able to be exceedingly strict in choosing its members, none being admitted to the society but such as were known men of learning and of the best family.[3]

The number of these aristocratic monks (whose social position may be best realized by considering them as Fellows of a college) regularly amounted to seventy; and, as in a college, the Institution involved an educational establishment (for boys), attached to the abbey, as well as a host of lay brethren discharging the menial offices of the house. The scholastic arrangements were under the charge of the Precentor,[4] who was also librarian and director of the scriptorium, to which he had to supply vellum, parchment, paper, ink, colours, gums, and all else needful for transcribing and binding books, on the reproduction of which much time was spent in every Benedictine house. Other chief officers were the Sacrist, who was responsible

[1] "Liber Eliensis," ii. 79.   [2] *Ibid.*, ii. 86.
[3] Bentham, "Hist. of Ely," p. 92.
[4] A complete list of the officers of the abbey is given by Bentham, "Hist. of Ely," p. 127.

for the due maintenance of the fabric, furniture, and services of the church; the Almoner, who distributed the doles; the Chamberlain, who provided all needful clothing and bedding; the Treasurer, or Bursar; and the Cellarer, to whom fell the duty of provisioning the whole vast establishment. This was chiefly accomplished by distributing the burden amongst the various "manors" belonging to the abbey; thus, Cottenham furnished provisions for one week in each year, as did also Hauxton, Newton, Toft, Stapleford, and others; while larger villages, such as Balsham, Horningsea, Shelford, and Triplow, were assessed at two weeks apiece.[1] The other offices were financed in like manner, the revenues arising from particular manors being annexed to them. Those of Foxton, for example, provided the candles for the High Altar. These arrangements, begun at this early period, continued, with little alteration, until the suppression of the abbey by Henry VIII.

§ 44. Such was Ely in the last days before the Conquest. So great was the reputation of the house as a seminary for high-born youth that it was chosen by Queen Emma as the place where her son Edward, afterwards the Confessor, should receive his education. He had indeed been "presented" there at the altar in infancy,[2] the mantle in which he was wrapped being long preserved as a memorial of the event. A very similar ceremony had taken place in the case of his father before him. The special aptitude shown by the future saint for the psalms and hymns which he learnt "in the cloister, amongst the children of his own age,"[3] was also a constant tradition amongst the brethren.

§ 45. It was perhaps on account of this hereditary connection of the House of Ethelred with the abbey

---

[1] Bentham, "Hist. of Ely," p. 94.
[2] "Liber Eliensis," ii. 80.
[3] *Ibid.*, ii. 78.

that Ely was chosen as the scene of the horrible deed which shortly stained our annals. Amongst the various pretensions set up, on the death of Canute, to the various crowns of his great empire, the sons of Ethelred seem to have made some kind of bid for their father's throne.[1] These two young Ethelings, Edward and Alfred, who for some years had lived in Normandy (where their cousin Robert was Duke), came, in A.D. 1036, to plead their claims. with their mother Emma, now Regent of Wessex for their stepbrother Harthacnut, King of Denmark (her son by Canute), between whom and Harold Harefoot (Canute's elder and illegitimate offspring) England had been divided for the moment. Emma's chief Minister, the great Earl Godwin, whose house played so prominent a part in the next half-century of English politics, seems at first to have favoured their pretensions, but shortly to have chosen another line of action. Any way, it is on him that the contemporary authorities throw the blame for the cruel tragedy which followed. Edward escaped, to reign ere long as "the Confessor"; but Alfred, "the innocent Etheling," was treacherously seized at Guildford, and, after witnessing the tortures inflicted on his supporters, was taken in bonds "to Elybury." There, before being set on shore, he was blinded with such brutality that he shortly died of the shock, and was buried in the conventual church,

> "As he worthy was,
> At the west end,
> The steeple well nigh
> In the south aisle."

The pathetic ballad, preserved in the Anglo-Saxon Chronicle, which tells us this, adds that all the horrors which had marked the Danish invasions of England for three hundred years had shown no cruelty more ghastly:

[1] See Freeman, "Norman Conquest," vol. i., p. 484.

> "Nor was drearier[1] deed
> Done in this land
> Since Danes have come."

§ 46. We have now reached the conclusion of this period of our history. Since Assandun it has been concerned with Ely alone. But incidentally we have seen that the good government of Canute had brought prosperity to the county at large. The various parishes must have recovered from the ravages which followed Ringmere, to have been able to discharge their obligations to the great abbey. Even the name of Balsham itself is found amongst them.[2] And there is reason to believe that not only was Cambridge speedily rebuilt after the destruction of 1010, but that this century saw the first settlement of the townsmen on that bank of the river where they now mainly dwell. The "Saxon" tower of St. Benet's Church must have been built about this date, and shows that at least a certain number of the inhabitants of Cambridge were to be found around it, the first beginning of that great expansion of the town which has since carried the name itself to the eastern side of the river, leaving the original "borough" on the western as "Castle End." How it came to be called by this name our next chapter will relate.

[1] A.-S. "dreorlicre."   [2] See § 30.

CHAPTER V.

NORMAN PERIOD.

§ 1—8. Cambridgeshire specially ruined by Conquest—Doomsday—No Thanes in county—No English landholders—Destruction and oppression of Cambridge.
§ 9—12. Reasons for this—William's theoretical position—Wholesale confiscation of land.
§ 13—25. Revolt of Fenland—Danes at Ely—Camp of Refuge—Hereward—Capture of Ely—Tabula Eliensis—Nomenclature—English stamped out.
§ 26—30. Good results of Conquest—Extinction of slavery—Revival of religion—William of Malmesbury.
§ 31—37. Norman churches—Ely a bishopric—New cathedral—Royston—Thomas à Becket.
§ 38—47. Anarchy under Stephen—Galfrid de Maundeville—Bishop Nigel—Rise of existing Cambridge.

§ 1. "DUM Angli regnaverunt laus Grantabrigiensis provinciæ splendide floruit." Writing thus, early in the twelfth century, Henry of Huntingdon evidently implies that the glory of Cambridgeshire was then a thing of the past, fallen with the fall of the native English monarchy.

§ 2. And when we turn to the pages of Doomsday[1] we

[1] I prefer this spelling of the word. The name is less probably derived from Domus Dei (though such official documents were usually deposited for reference in churches) than from Dooms' Day, the occasions on which it would be used for the settlement of disputes by legal authority.

see that this was so indeed. In no county of England does its dry, passionless record present us with a more vivid picture of the wholesale break-up of the earlier social fabric than here. The squires and country gentlemen who had led their tenants so valiantly at Ringmere and Ashdon have disappeared altogether. In the whole survey of the county we do not find a single "King's Thane." This fact alone shows how widespread had been the ruin wrought.

§ 3. These "King's Thanes" were the small local aristocracy, who had stepped into the place of the original Anglo-Saxon "Eorls"—some of them, perhaps, actual descendants of those Eorls, some, of lower lineage, raised to the Thanehood by their own or their forefathers' merits and claims to royal favour. From very early times this process had been in operation. The leading Thanes (or servants, the name being akin to the German *Dienen*) of each local ruler tended inevitably to form a minor local aristocracy in each district; while, as the various districts became welded into a single monarchy, these local aristocracies became, in like manner, merged in the general body of "King's Thanes," who formed the squirearchy throughout the whole realm. And a place in this aristocracy was attainable by any able and forward man, whatever might be his birth. Eorls and Ceorls were divided by an impassable bar of lineage, but any Ceorl might become a Thane, and thus be the social equal of an Eorl. In process of time the use of the latter word died out altogether, and "Thane" became practically equivalent to "gentleman," as, by an almost identical process, the word "Esquire" has become since. The regulation of Alfred, which decrees that all parish priests shall be held King's Thanes, at once illustrates this, and in a striking manner sets forth that social status of the parochial clergy which is still the distinctive mark of the Anglican Church.

§ 4. Now, of these local gentry, not one still held his estate when the Doomsday Commissioners made their inquisition in 1086; nor, indeed, do we find throughout the length and breadth of the county a single proprietor, small or great, bearing an English name. The entire county (outside the "Terra Ecclesiæ" possessed by the parish clergy and the various monastic bodies, and the "Terra Regis," held directly by the King) is seen to have been wholly divided up amongst men of French and Flemish nomenclature. There are only thirty-one private landholders in all, and, of these, only eight possess property in one parish alone. The domains of the remainder are widely scattered; thus, Picot, the Sheriff of the county, holds in forty-two parishes; Herduin de Scalers in fifty-six; Count Alan in sixty-eight. We also find the historic names of Eustace of Boulogne, Gilbert of Ghent, Alberic de Vere, and Judith, wife of the last Englishman of rank who for a while survived, Waltheof; besides several more whom we know to have been mainly provided for in other counties. Universal indeed must have been the confiscation to produce so stupendous a change from the days, but little back, when each village had its Thane. The county, indeed, never recovered from the shock. From that day to this it has been singularly lacking in "county" families.

§ 5. Nor is this all that Doomsday shows us. From it we learn also that not only the squires, but the yeomen, the free landholding "churls," had also ceased to exist in Cambridgeshire within twenty years of the Conquest. In their place we find "tenants," with "villains" and "cottars," tied to the soil and passing along with it to its foreign appropriators. These cold statistics of the Great Survey enable us to enter into the pathetic lament of William of Malmesbury over Hastings—"dies fatalis Angliæ, triste excidium dulcis patriæ "[1]—and to appreciate

[1] "De Gest. Mon. Ang.," § 245.

his impassioned plaint: "Now is England become the home of foreigners, the hold of strangers; not one Englishman is there now left who is either Earl, Bishop, or Abbot; strangers be they all, preying upon the wealth and the vitals of England; nor for this wretchedness is there hope of end."[1]

§ 6. And when we turn from the country districts to Cambridge itself, Doomsday tells us the same tale of misery and overthrow. A fifth part of the place lay in ruins. In the time of Edward the Confessor it had consisted of 400 dwelling-houses ("masuræ"), and was divided into ten wards, each under its "Lawman" or Town Councillor, a name which shows that the organization of the town was of Danish origin. By 1086 two of these wards had been thrown into one, owing to the destruction of twenty-seven houses "pro castro"—on account of the building of the castle; and in the remaining wards no fewer than fifty-three more dwellings are entered as "waste." If we assume the usual urban proportion of six or seven inhabitants to a house, the population must have gone down from nearly 3,000 to little over 2,000. And on this remnant taxation pressed far more heavily than on the former burghers. The customs of the town were assessed at £7, the land-tax at £7 2s. 2d. Both these seem to have been new impositions, payable to the royal treasury. Moreover, T. R. E. ("tempore regis Edwardi") each burgher "accommodated" the Sheriff with the cost of three days' ploughing, a duty now increased threefold—"modo novem vicibus exigunt." King Edward's Sheriff ("vicecomes") had exacted no further "accommodation." His Norman successor required the townsmen to find him, not only ploughing, but carting—" Nec averas nec currus T. R. E. inveniebant, quæ nunc faciunt pro consuetudine impositâ." Finally, the "heriot," or duty payable by the Lawmen to

[1] "De Gest. Mon. Ang.," § 227.

each new Governor on entering office, had risen from twenty shillings to "eight pounds, a palfrey, and a complete suit of knightly armour." The Sheriff, moreover (that same Roger Picot who held so much land about the county), had built himself three mills upon the river, to the destruction of many dwelling-houses and the confiscation of much "common pasture."

§ 7. In all this we see evidence of those changes of old-established custom which were felt so special a grievance of the Norman invasion. Ingulf bitterly complains that the French despised the ancient English method of knighting a man by a special ecclesiastical service; that they changed the Anglican method of attesting writings by signature, and required each deed, "as they called it," to be sealed; that "they held even the very tongue of the English in abhorrence, so that the laws of the land and the dooms of the old English kings were rendered into French, and the very boys at school were forced to learn the rudiments of [Latin] grammar in French instead of English; while the English method of writing was also given up and the French introduced."[1]

§ 8. It would doubtless be unfair to lay, as the contemporary authorities are disposed to do, the whole blame of every deterioration on the Conquest. The extinction of the county squirearchy must have been largely due to the awful slaughter in the Danish wars, and especially after Ringmere; while the tendency of the yeoman class of churls to disappear (either by rising to Thanehood, or by sinking to mere tenants and cottars) had doubtless been going on for many years. But even when all allowance has been made, enough remains to show us that Cambridgeshire suffered excessively and exceptionally in this dismal period.

§ 9. And how came our county to be so specially affected by the Conquest? With the stirring events of the year 1066, Cambridgeshire would seem to have been

[1] "Hist. of Croyland," 1066.

comparatively little concerned. Harold and his army must have passed through it along the Ermine Street in his rapid march to the Battle of Stamford Bridge, and his yet swifter counter-march to meet William at Hastings. Probably (in accordance with the military reputation of the county) a Cambridgeshire contingent accompanied him to either field, but it is not likely to have been a large one. For both in the Yorkshire and in the Sussex battle the English force consisted mainly of local levies, stiffened by the array of Harold's own splendid "house-carls," the Guards of the period, of whom every man was said to be a match for any two foreigners.[1]

§ 10. But while the county escaped with comparatively small loss from the campaign which lost Harold his throne, it was far otherwise with that great national uprising against the invader, the issue of which made William indeed "the Conqueror" of England. Of that struggle it was the chief theatre, the district whose resistance lasted longest and came nearest to being successful, and it suffered accordingly.

§ 11. The occupation, by the French army, of London, the objective of the Hastings campaign, and the consequent recognition and coronation of William as King of England, carried with it the submission of East Anglia and Cambridgeshire. Their local ruler, Earl Gyrth, had fallen at the side of his brother, King Harold, by the hand of William himself, in the assault upon the English breastwork on the hill of Senlac; and with the chief, as usual, fell all thought of local resistance, till another leader should arise. And with Gyrth had doubtless fallen all the best and bravest of such local levies—probably not numerous, but the pick of the land—as had followed him from his earldom to the Sussex downs.

[1] Snorro, in his Saga of Harold Hardrada, says of them: "Their voro menn sva fræknir at betra var lid eins theirra enn II Harald's manna hinna besto" (Laing, iii. 80).

§ 12. Cambridgeshire thus took no part in the belated patriotism which successively attempted to withstand the mighty Conqueror in the West and the North during the campaigns of 1068 and 1069. Possibly, indeed, the levies of the county may even have been called out in support of the ill-used monarch, whose entry into his lawful kingdom was so wantonly delayed by ungracious traitors. For such was William's own reading of his position, carefully insisted upon in every legal act of his reign. He himself seems to have held this fiction in good faith, and would have repudiated as an insult the title by which he is known to history. But fact was too strong for him, and forced him to act as the Conqueror he was, rather than as the constitutional English King he called himself. He had to reward his foreign soldiers, and to establish them everywhere as a garrison against his vanquished subjects. And this his assumption of being, from the day of Edward's death, the legitimate King of England enabled him to do under colour of legality. All who had resisted their lawful Sovereign were active traitors; all who had not risen in his support against the "usurper" Harold were constructively traitors; and in one of these two classes was comprised every Englishman alive. But the law declared the lands of traitors forfeited to the Crown, and, as so forfeited, William dealt with the whole land of England (except the "Terra Ecclesiæ") at his pleasure. Some estates he kept for himself, some he granted to his foreign friends, some he permitted the owners to buy back for money.[1] And it was this wholesale confiscation and impoverishment of the native population which at last roused our county to a despairing effort against him.

§ 13. The final touch which kindled the conflagration was given from without. Amongst the many adventurers who sought to make something for themselves out of the

[1] See Freeman, "Norman Conquest," vol. iv., pp. 22 *et seq.*

existing confusion in English affairs, the Danes once more made, for the last time, a tentative invasion, which might possibly place their King Sweyn on the throne of his uncle Canute, and would at least bring in the wonted plunder, now untasted for two generations. Making first for the Humber, they aroused throughout the North that desperate revolt against William which involved the destruction of York and was stamped out by the awful harrying of Northumberland. The following year, 1070, they shifted their quarters from the Yorkshire Ouse to the Cambridgeshire stream of that name, and suddenly appeared in Ely. There the leaders, "Christian the Bishop, and Osbiorn the Earl, and the Danish house-carls (Royal Guards) with them," took up their abode, in such formidable force as to inspire in the down-trodden English a wild hope of holding the district against their foe, as the Britons had held it of old. "The English folk of all the Fenland came in" to them—in particular a noted "gang" under the command of the famous outlaw Hereward.[1]

§ 14. With his name legend has been so busy, from the days of the false Ingulf in the twelfth century to those of Kingsley in the nineteenth, that it is hard to realize that the above-mentioned facts—that he was an outlaw and led a gang—are absolutely all we know authentically of the origin of this famous man; beyond the record in Doomsday that he was (in 1086) a land-holder both in Lincolnshire and in Warwick. The whole long tale of his early adventures, in Scotland and Cornwall and Ireland and Flanders, is, no less than his mythical connection with the great Earl Leofric, pure romance. But that romancers should have thought it worth while thus to occupy themselves with his career shows how deep a hold his exploits took on the popular imagination, and how his name lived on as that of the last Englishman

[1] Anglo-Saxon Chronicle.

who dared to resist the irresistible Conqueror. The chronicler introduces him to us quite abruptly as leading the Danish fleet to the sack of Peterborough, "out of faithfulness to that Minster," which had been granted to a French Abbot, Thorold. To save the place from such degrading occupancy, Hereward caused it to be first systematically plundered, and then burnt to the ground; after which, while the Danes sailed away with their loot, he succeeded them in their quarters at Ely, whence he defied the Normans to eject him.

§ 15. A more defensible position could scarcely be found. The island of Ely (which must be distinguished from the political district called "the Isle") is about ten miles long by five broad, and was then wholly surrounded by morasses, practically impassable from a military point of view. These morasses, moreover, furnished the island not only with defence, but with so abundant a food-supply, in fish and wild-fowl, that it was able to sustain a large number of inhabitants.

§ 16. The "Liber Eliensis" puts into the mouth of a French knight, for a while captive in Ely, the following encomium on its resources at this crisis: "The island is within itself plenteously endowed; it is supplied with various kinds of herbage, and in richness of soil surpasses the rest of England. Most delightful for charming fields and pastures, it is also remarkable for beasts of chase, and is in no ordinary way fertile in flocks and herds. Its woods and vineyards are not worthy of equal praise; but it is begirt by great meres and fens as though by a strong wall. In this island there is an abundance of domestic cattle, and a multitude of wild animals ; stags, roes, goats, and hares, are found in its groves and by those fens. Moreover, there is a fair sufficiency of otters, weasels, and polecats, which in a hard winter are caught by traps, snares, or by any other device.

* * * * *

" In the eddies at the sluices of these meres are netted innumerable eels, large water-wolves, with pickerels, perches, roaches, burbots, and lampreys, which we call water-snakes. It is indeed said by many that sometimes salmon are taken there, together with the royal fish, the sturgeon.

* * * * *

"There you find geese, teal, coot, didappers, water-crows, herons and ducks, more than man can number, especially in winter or at moulting time. I have seen a hundred—nay, even three hundred—taken at once; sometimes by bird-lime, sometimes in nets or snares."

§ 17. The Fen-men, moreover, knowing by heart all the intricacies of the morass, could, with their long leaping-poles, swarm in and out through many a pass where no Norman horseman would dare to follow. Thus, we have more than once in our history seen Ely made a Camp of Refuge during foreign invasion. Now the name was definitely applied to it, and before many months were past it was crowded with daring fugitives from all parts of England. Morcar, the Northumbrian Earl, who had submitted to William, fled thither from his state captivity at Winchester; the brave Bishop Ethelwine of Durham left his asylum at the Scotch Court to share the struggle; Siward Barn, another Northumbrian leader, of royal blood, came also, " with many a hundred more."[1] The abbey was crowded with these incomers; for the monks, willing or unwilling, could do no other than go with the stream; and legend is doubtless right in assigning the leaders a place at the Abbot's table, while monks and soldiers sat side by side in the refectory.[2] Whether the former as well as the latter were ready to spring to arms at a moment's notice, is much more doubtful, though we know by the presence of the Winchester

[1] Anglo-Saxon Chronicle, 1071 ; also Florence.
[2] Gesta Herewardi, § 64.

monks at Hastings that such irregularities were not unheard of in this crisis, as in others.

§ 18. But it is clear that the soul of the defence was the valiant Hereward. Outlawed as he was (and excommunicated also since the sack of Peterborough),[1] his skill and daring caused him to be universally accepted as leader. And well did he vindicate his right to the position. Against a foe one degree less endowed with military and political genius than William, his defence of Ely would probably have been successful, and have kindled a general rebellion which might have driven the invader from the land. And even William found it no easy task to subdue this hitherto unknown outlaw.

§ 19. The King plainly felt the matter one of extreme urgency, needing his own presence, with all his warcraft and statecraft, to deal with it. On receiving the tidings, he at once hurried down from London to Cambridge, where two years previously he had built the Castle on his return march from the North through Lincoln and Huntingdon. From Cambridge the Akeman Street ran straight to Ely, but William preferred to make his attacks by unexpected routes. At the head of his "buss-carls,"[2] the English seamen called out on the royal service, he threatened the eastern side of the island, from Brandon and from Reach, thus drawing off the defenders from interference with the great causeway, two miles long, which was being constructed for his land-force at Aldreth, in the extreme south-west. Nevertheless, we may well believe, with the legend, that, when this stupendous work (formed of fascines, hurdles, and bags of rushes and earth) was at last completed, the wit and valour of Hereward more than once foiled the advance along it of the Norman army. The very devices which he used, more especially the firing of the reeds, which is said to have annihilated

[1] Anglo-Saxon Chronicle, 1069.
[2] Florence, 1071. The word is originally "boats-carl."

one column of the invaders, may well be the truth; though it is scarcely probable that the scrupulously pious William ever permitted the presence amongst his soldiers of a witch ("phithonissa"[1]) for their encouragement. But that the story should have arisen shows that they sorely needed encouragement.

§ 20. Finally, indeed, it was by statecraft rather than warcraft that the island was won. Though the hearts of the aristocratic leaders seem to have failed them as weeks passed on and their defence of Ely was not supported by the general rising without which it was obviously hopeless, so that they one by one sought the mercy of William, to find it in lifelong prison,[2] yet the sturdy Hereward (" strenuissimus," as Florence called him) still held out. Not till the King, by threatening to confiscate the entire property of the abbey, brought the monks round to his side could he obtain entrance into the island.

§ 21. By their connivance, however, the French soldiers succeeded at length in marching down the causeway from their camp at Belsar's Hill, near Cottenham (probably an old British stronghold[3]), and surprising the passage of the Ouse at Aldreth, almost unresisted. Never before had Ely been reached otherwise than by water; but the Aldreth causeway was soon followed by others. Half a century later William of Malmesbury writes: " Non enim insula tunc nisi navigio adiri poterat; sed nostra ætas sollertior vicit naturam, aggeribusque in paludem jactis tramitem præbuit, et insulam pedibus accessabilem fecit."[4]

§ 22. Thus was Ely at last won by William, and he

[1] Gesta Herewardi, § 75.
[2] See Freeman, "Norman Conquest," vol. iv., p. 477.
[3] The name, however, is traditionally derived from that Belasius who figures in the Tabula Eliensis as "Præses Militum versus Elye."
[4] De Gest. Pont., § 293.

was not long in letting those whom he found there feel the effects of his wrath at their resistance. Hereward, indeed, escaped,[1] to gain the King's peace within a while, and therewith his Lincolnshire and Warwickshire lands. But such of his "gang" as fell into William's hands were treated with that monarch's usual cold-blooded cruelty. No life was taken, for William had a conscientious objection to capital punishment; but, after his wont, the most ghastly mutilations were inflicted upon the rebels, whose eyes, hands, and feet were deemed forfeit for their rebellion.[2]

§ 23. Even upon the monks who had let him in to the island the royal hand was heavily laid.[3] They awaited with fear and trembling the arrival of William, that by personal impetration they might win his pardon and peace; till one day, as they sat at meat, they were startled by the sudden entrance into the refectory of Gilbert de Clare, a Norman knight who, for some reason, desired to stand their friend. "Ye wretched fools (*miseri et vecordes*)!" he exclaimed, "can you choose no better time for feeding than now, when the King is here, actually in your church?" With one accord the monks sprang from table and rushed to the church. But it was too late: William was gone. He had been there indeed, and had cast upon the altar a single mark of gold, for which he repaid himself with interest by fining the luckless monks, who hastened after him to Witchford (three miles along the road towards Aldreth), no less than 700 marks of silver. To meet this crushing imposition, they were forced to melt down almost all the ornaments of the church, especially one particularly famous and venerated image—"imaginem Sanctæ Mariæ cum Puero sedentem in throno, mirabiliter fabricatam, quam Ælfrinus

[1] Gesta Herewardi, § 95.
[2] Florence, 1072.
[3] The following story is from the "Liber Eliensis," p. 245.

Abbas fecerat in auro et argento." And after all, when this mass of silver came to be minted and paid to the King's officers at Cambridge, the "handful" ("dragma") was found to have been fraudulently dealt with by the moneyers employed, and to be deficient in weight. An additional fine of 300 marks was imposed for this offence by William, reducing the abbey to the verge of ruin.

§ 24. A mark, we may here mention, was not a coin, but a certain weight (8 oz. Troy) of coined money—always silver unless otherwise specified. The mark of silver was worth 13s. 4d.; that of gold varied with the varying ratio of the precious metals. In the Ramsey Cartulary we find that in 1088 the land of Over (11 hides = 44 virgates = 1,320 acres) is granted to Will. Peche at an annual rent of 6 lb. of pennies (= 8 marks). He is also granted "brotherhood" of the convent (*i.e.*, a seat in hall, and a grave in the church), paying for each of these privileges a mark of gold, or 100 shillings. Gold, therefore, stood to silver at this date in the ratio of $100 : 13\frac{1}{3}$. The value of money appears to have been at least twenty-fold greater than at the present day, so that William's mark was equivalent to £100, and the sum in which he mulcted the abbey to something like £20,000.

§ 25. Nor was this all. The brethren of the abbey were further required to find free quarters for the garrison of the new castle "intra septa monachorum" (on Chèrry Hill, doubtless), which William raised (at the expense of the county) and entrusted "fidelibus Gallis," so that once again monks and knights were to be seen side by side in the abbey refectory, only that the knights were now not English patriots but foreign oppressors. This state of things is commemorated in the Tabula Eliensis, a painting (in its present form of much later date, but probably a genuine reproduction of some such original representation, showing the names, arms and likenesses of forty knights, each beside the monk on whom he was quartered, thus:

1. Opsalus Miles, Ballistarum Dux, cum Godfrido Monacho.
2. Walterus de Lacey, Scutifer Conquestoris, cum Occha Monacho.
3. Pervelus, trecentum peditum Præses, cum Ednotto Monacho.
4. Guido de S^{to} Leodergario, cum Aldemero pio Monacho.
5. Hastingus, Miles Nauttic Exercitus, cum Nigello Monacho.
6. Hugo de Monte forti, Equitum Dux, cum Odone Monacho.
7. Adamus, exercitus Capitalys Magnificalis, cum Sed Monacho.
8. Blundus, Navium Militarium Dux, cum Wylnoto Monacho.
9. Bryan de Clare, veteranus, cum Clitone Monacho.
10. Tuchet, Dux Architenentum, cum Osberico Monacho.
11. Fides de Furnivallo Lombardo, cum Osulpho Monacho.
12. Ricardo de Ponte Fulconis, cum Leofrico Juniore Monacho.
13. Newmundus, Equorum Magister, cum . . . othe Monacho.
14. Eneas de Novo Burgo, cum . . . lano cenobii Sachrista M.
15. Robertus, Normannus Mauscatis, cum Ranulpho Monacho.
16. Mali, ducentorum peditum Dux, cum Ederico Monacho.
17. Bigotus, tertius filius Bigot, cum Edmund Monacho.
18. Lucey, Normannus Admiralis, cum Constantino Monacho.
19. Alexander de Monte Viginte, cum Davide Monacho.

20. Lucamassus, dux omnium bipennorum, cum Oswaldo Monacho.
21. Antoninus de Longa Spata, cum Alfredo Monacho.
22. Johannes Malamannus, Peditum Signifer, cum Otto.
23. Johannes de Eboraco, Anglo, cum Felice Monacho.
24. Ranulphus, Miles Germanicus, cum Ulfketel Monacho.
25. Eustachius le Blanke, Speculator, cum Sebanno Monacho.
26. Eustachius le Noyer, cum Edwino Monacho.
27. Nigellus de Fontaundore, cum Donaldo Monacho.
28. Dunstanus le Grosse Manchus, cum Egberto Monacho.
29. Bigotus, equitum trecentorum dux, cum Condulpho Monacho.
30. Sewardus Anglus, annonæ prefectus, cum Leofino Monacho.
31. Paganus le Grape, Equitum Signifer, cum Athelgal Monacho.
32. Bardolphus, Operatibus præerat, cum Ricardo Monacho.
33. Abraham de Pechs, cum Ethelberto Eweni Monacho.
34. Aimundus filius Alani, cum Barthredo Monacho.
35. Talbotus, sœpius in legatis missus, cum Duffo Monacho.
36. Argentien, curam vulneratorum habet, cum Helfrico Monacho.
37. Gerardus de Longo Champo, cum Hulfketel Monacho.
38. Pigotus, pontium procurator, cum Witstano Monacho.
39. Belasius, Præses Militum versus Elye, cum Utwaldo Monacho.
40. Ivo, Willm Comitis Warren frater, cum Leofrico Monacho.

This interesting list shows us how thoroughly Ely was made a place of arms for the invader. We find mention of cavalry, infantry, artillery (No. 1), sappers (No. 20), archers (No. 10), commissariat (No. 30), ambulance (No. 36), scouts (No. 25), engineers (Nos. 32 and 38), and even marines (No. 5). (The Admiral, however, had at that date nothing to do with naval forces; it was a title taken from the Spanish Saracens, and constantly found in the contemporary Song of Roland, merely denoting military command.)

§ 26. The names, too, are instructive. Amongst the forty leaders we find only two Englishmen, the rest being French, with one German and one Lombard. The titles of Lacy, Bigot, De Montfort, etc., show that we are on the threshold of a new period of English history. Amongst the monks, on the other hand, we find almost purely English nomenclature, though such names as Constantine, David, Nigel, Evan, and Donald, bear witness to the Celtic survival in the Fenland. Godfrey, the only Frenchman, had been put in charge of the abbey by William, on the death of the last English Abbot, Thurstan. It may be noticed that, up to this date, a man's name is an almost certain guide to his nationality. Not until the next generation did Englishmen begin to christen their children by French designations—a practice which spread so rapidly and generally that ere long our native nomenclature was utterly wiped out, surviving only, as now, in the names of our greatest kings and saints: Alfred, Edward, Edgar, Edmund, and Ethel.

§ 27. That this should have been so is the most striking proof of the thoroughness of the Conquest, an abiding echo from the dark days when "it was shame even to be called an Englishman," a shame from which English parents strove in some degree to shield their children by thus endeavouring to hide, so far as might be, their nationality. A William, a Robert, or a Eustace was at least not branded by his very name as belonging to the despised race; he was not one of the "Godrics and Godgifus," as the Normans in mockery designated the Anglophile Henry Beauclerk and his English Queen. And in thus realizing how low our forefathers were brought, how utterly their national pride—then, as now, the strongest of all sentiments in the English breast—was trampled in the dust, our sympathies cannot but be with those who so bravely upheld the English cause, and whose last hopes were shattered for ever by the fall of Ely.

§ 28. Yet, in the light of later history, we know how great a blessing the new blood infused by the Conquest actually proved to our race; how what seemed to William of Malmesbury to be "the sad wreck and ruin of our dear country" ("triste excidium dulcis patriæ") was indeed the grafting upon its stem of a new stock destined to endow it with far richer fruit than of old. Nor were there wanting, even from the very first, signs that this was indeed so. William of Malmesbury himself points out how much there was in the old English social system that needed to be swept away, and how much the Norman zeal and energy leavened for good our national character. And in particular he refers to one blessing incidentally brought about by the Conquest, which historians as a rule far too much ignore, but which a history of Cambridgeshire should least of all pass over[1]—that it practically abolished in England the curse of personal slavery.

[1] The final abolition throughout the civilized world of this hateful institution is specially connected with our county. The earliest leader of the noble band of abolitionists, whose efforts throughout the first half of the nineteenth century have brought about this result, was a Cambridgeshire man, Thomas Clarkson, a native of Wisbeach. On the road between Cambridge and London, not far from Ware, an obelisk still marks the spot where, as a young man, in 1782, he knelt down by the wayside and vowed to devote his life to this sacred cause. A conspicuous Gothic memorial has also been erected in his honour by his fellow-townsmen of Wisbeach.

How great a curse it was to within his memory, how horribly it degraded the unhappy slaves, while working yet more horrible degradation in the character of their masters, his pages tell us. But he speaks of these horrors as already a thing of the past.[1] Slavery, indeed, was not abolished by statute. No edict of William forbids, or even mentions, it. But none the less did the Conquest bring about the almost immediate overthrow of this hateful institution. We have seen how eloquent a testimony the pages of Doomsday bear to the conversion of the old English free-born "ceorls" (or "churls") into "villains" attached to the soil; but it bears no less eloquent a witness to the fact that, while the churls sank into villenage, the thralls rose to that condition. Very few "servi" are found amongst its entries; and to the thrall it was no small step upwards to become a "villain." He was, indeed, bound to the land he tilled for his lord, and passed with it from master to master; but he could no longer be sold away from it. No longer did he hold his life and his home and his family at the mere pleasure of his owner; no longer was the honour of his wife and daughters at the mercy of each wicked and unscrupulous reprobate who might happen to have bought them; no longer could there be that cruel break-up of households which has always been the worst feature of slavery amongst Aryans; and no longer could he himself be compelled to work in chains, or under the lash till he dropped. As a "villain," his duties towards his lord were fixed, and though their performance may often have pressed hardly upon him, yet he knew what they were, and that when they were duly done no more could be exacted from him. Had the Conquest done nothing else for us, this great result would have been worth all its misery and bloodshed.

§ 29. But it did much more. William of Malmesbury also shows us to how much higher a level of civilization

[1] De Gest. Mon. Ang., § 245.

it at once began to raise the land. His description of the English and Norman characteristics is well worth quoting. After an eloquent panegyric on the earlier development of England, he continues thus:[1] "Nevertheless, in process of time, the desire after letters and religion had decayed for many years before the Normans came. The clergy, content with but slight learning, could scarce stammer over the words of the Sacraments, and a parson who knew grammar [*i.e.*, who was a real Latin scholar] was an object of wonder indeed. The monks mocked the rule of their Order by fine garments and unrestrained feeding. The nobility, given up to luxury, went not in the morning to church, after the Christian use, but merely, in careless fashion, heard Mattins and Masses from a hurrying priest in their own bedchambers. . . . The common folk, left unprotected, became a prey to the more powerful, who heaped up riches by seizing on their goods or selling their persons into foreign lands, though, indeed, this people is noted rather for being given to revelling than to gathering wealth. . . . Drinking in parties was a universal practice, in which they passed whole nights, and days also.[2] Thus they con-

[1] De Gest. Mon. Ang., § 245.
[2] A vivid picture of this propensity is given by Wace in his description of the manner in which the English army spent the night before Hastings:

"Tote nuit mangierent et burent

. . . . .

Bublie crient è *weisseil*
È *laticome* è *drincheheil*
Drinc hindrewart è *drintome*
Drinc helf è *drinc Tome*."

These curious words are doubtless the very sounds which came across to the Norman camp, and seem to signify respectively "bubble it" (*i.e.*, froth it up), "wish health," "let it come" (*i.e.*, pass the cup round), "drink health," "drink hinderwards" (*i.e.*, pass the cup back again), "drink it home" (*i.e.*, toss it off), "drink half," and "drink to me."

sumed their whole substance in mean and sordid houses, unlike the Normans and French, who, in noble and splendid mansions, live with frugality. The vices attendant on drunkenness, which enervate the human mind, followed. . . . In fine, the English at that time wore short garments, reaching to the mid-knee; they had their hair cropped, their beards shaven, their arms laden with golden bracelets, their skin adorned with punctured designs; they were wont to eat even unto surfeiting, and to drink even unto vomiting. These last qualities they have imparted to their conquerors; as to the rest, they have adopted their manners.

§ 30. "I would not, however, have these evil propensities ascribed to the English universally. I know that many of the clergy at that day trod the path of sanctity, by a blameless life; I know that many of the laity, of all sorts and conditions, were well-pleasing to God. Be injustice far from my record! The accusation does not involve the whole indiscriminately. But as, in peace, God's mercy oft-times cherishes together alike bad and good, so no less do His judgments bring both into a like sore captivity.

§ 31. "The Normans . . . were then, and even now, most heedful in dress, and nice in food, yet without excess. A race inured to war, they can scarce live without it; fierce in their onset against the foe, and, when force availeth not, prompt to use craft, or corrupt by bribes. As I have said, they live with frugality while building lavishly; they envy their equals, would fain surpass their superiors, and spoil their subjects, though defending them from all others; they are faithful to their lords, though on but slight offence they will renounce that faith. They weigh treason by its chance of success, and will sell their allegiance for money. The politest of all nations, they deem strangers worthy of like honour with themselves. They also intermarry with their vassals.

§ 32. "They revived, by their coming, the rule of religion, which had everywhere grown deadened in England. You might see churches arise in every village, and monasteries in the towns and cities, built after a style unknown before; you might behold the country blossom out into renovated rites; so that each wealthy man counted that day lost to him which he had neglected to note by some high deed."

§ 33. Much of this, no doubt, is declamation; but there is every reason to take it as substantially true. Our own county records completely agree with it. The Tabula Eliensis itself, though the memorial of a foreign occupation of the abbey, bears witness to the fact that the foreigners proved themselves no unpleasant guests, and that their national "politeness" won the hearts of their unwilling hosts. So much was this the case, that we are told how, at their withdrawal in 1078 (on the occasion of the rebellion of Robert Curthose in Normandy), the monks parted from them with no small regret, accompanying them to the confines of the Isle at Haddenham, and there watching them march out, along the same causeway by which, ten years earlier, they had marched in, with heartfelt farewells and benedictions.

§ 34. And here, as elsewhere throughout England, our ecclesiastical architecture testifies to the Norman revival of religion. The earliest style of church-building of which there is any large survival is known by their name, and was by them introduced into the land. Amongst the local village churches, indeed, there is less Norman work to be seen than in most districts—a further proof of the exceptional depression brought about in Cambridgeshire by the Conquest, from which the land does not seem to have recovered enough for much church-building till over a century had elapsed and the Early English style had developed. But in Cambridge we have still standing the Round Church of the Holy Sepulchre,[1] and we have the records of others built at this period. Picot, whom we have met as the tyrant Norman Sheriff of the county, atoned for his ill deeds by rebuilding the Church of St. Giles, and there founding a secular canonry, which in 1112 was endowed with his own forfeited property (forfeited for treason), and developed into the famous Priory of Barnwell, with its splendid Norman church, the rival of Ely. And at Ely itself there remains to us the most glorious example of what the Norman genius could do, in the stately nave of the cathedral, begun by Abbot Simeon in 1081, and completed by Bishop Ridel in 1189, just after the Norman period of architecture closed.

§ 35. This collocation of names brings us to that event of this period which has left the deepest and most abiding mark on our county history—the advancement of the Abbots of Ely to episcopal dignity. It is this that has saved to us our glorious minster. Had it remained merely the church of a conventual foundation, it would have shared the doom of the yet more glorious buildings at Glastonbury and at Bury St. Edmunds; and a wreck of grass-grown walls and shattered arches would alone have marked for us the site of the soaring nave, the mighty towers, and the exquisite work of choir, lantern, and Lady Chapel. Only because its Abbot was also a Bishop did Ely escape the havoc wrought by the greed of Henry VIII.

§ 36. The change was brought about mainly owing to a series of disputes as to the authority over the abbey of the Bishop of Lincoln, of whose vast diocese Cambridge-

---

[1] Charters Nos. 73 and 75 of the Ramsey Cartulary (vol. i., p. 145, A.D. 1114, 1130) grant to Ralph cum Barba of Cambridge and others of the Fraternity of the Holy Sepulchre the cemetery of St. George and the land adjacent to build there a minster in honour of God and of the Holy Sepulchre.

shire then formed a part. The monks had always claimed
the privilege of choosing any Bishop they pleased to be
their Visitor and to institute their Abbot; but when the
first Norman Abbot, Simeon, a man of the blood royal,
was appointed by the Conqueror, in 1081, Remigius, the
Bishop of Lincoln, insisted that he alone had the right to
institute—a quarrel renewed when Richard of Bec succeeded Simeon as Abbot, in 1101. Finally, to solve the
difficulty, all the authorities concerned—the abbey, the
Bishop of Lincoln, the Archbishop of Canterbury, and
the King—agreed to ask the Pope that Ely might be
created an episcopal see, with the Isle of Ely and the
county of Cambridge for its diocese.[1] And thus, on
Richard's death, Hervey, who was already a Bishop
(having held the See of Bangor), stepped into his place
not only as Abbot, but with the additional dignity of
Bishop of the diocese. Ever after these two offices were
combined in the same person, a development borne
witness to even yet by the position occupied by the
Bishop in Ely Cathedral. Instead of having a throne at
the east end of the southern stalls, as elsewhere, he sits,
as Abbot, in the place occupied in other cathedrals by the
Dean, the westernmost stall on the south side of the
choir, the Dean, in turn, sitting as Prior in the corresponding stall to the north.

§ 37. The Bishop also succeeded to the Abbot's secular
jurisdiction over the Isle, and two-thirds of the abbey
lands were assigned to the see, producing an income of
over £1,000 per annum. The monastery was left with
little more than £300, only sufficient for the support of
forty monks, as they complained. These sums must be
multiplied at least twenty-fold to be expressed in the

[1] Not till 1841 was the diocese enlarged to its present dimensions
by the addition of Bedfordshire and Huntingdonshire (from the
Diocese of Lincoln) on the west, and the archdeaconry of Sudbury
(from that of Norwich) on the east.

present value of money, which gives something like £200 a year as the accepted value of a monk's position, justifying our comparison of that position to the average Fellowship of a college in these days. It must be remembered that a monk, like a Fellow, was supposed to be *ex officio* a gentleman.

§ 38. While the ecclesiastical troubles of the time were producing this happy result, the abbey was also vexed by a series of secular grievances. At the great Assize of Salisbury in 1086, "knight-service" was for the first time imposed upon Church lands, and in place of a mere subsidy, as before, Ely was compelled to keep forty actual knights in readiness for the King's service, a number increased by William Rufus to eighty. This burden was severely felt; and yet more did the abbey suffer when, on the death of Abbot Simeon, Rufus, after his wont, kept the appointment vacant for over seven years, meanwhile letting out the abbey lands. Abbot Richard, moreover, got into trouble at Court (mainly through being related to the too powerful family of Gilbert de Clare), and was deprived by Henry I. Whether the Crown had a right to such jurisdiction over Church dignitaries was the burning question of the day, and, like a stanch ecclesiastic, Richard refused to surrender to the King his pastoral staff, laying it up, rather, in the abbey church, and appealing to the Pope, by whom the dispute was finally adjusted after much litigation.

§ 39. But through it all the minster continued to rise, and on St. Etheldred's Day, October 17, 1106, was opened for Divine Service, and received her relics and those of her sister saints. In all main features it remains to this day as it was on that, a standing token of Norman zeal and Norman genius.

§ 40. And meanwhile a humbler monument of Norman influence was developing itself in another part of the county. On its extreme south-west border, where the Icknield Way crosses the Ermine Street, a Lady Roesia, wife of Eudo Dapifer, the first Norman holder of the manor, set up a wayside cross, which a century later gave its name to the adjoining Priory of St. Thomas of Canterbury, founded, shortly after his martyrdom, by Eustace de Mark, and called "De Cruce Roesiæ." As usual, a little town by degrees clustered round the monastery gate, and, like Peterborough, was named from it. Thus arose the town of Royston, which continued until 1896 to bear traces of its late origin, by being in two counties—Cambridgeshire and Hertfordshire—and in the five distinct older parishes which here meet. At the same period the use of the prehistoric cave beneath the Icknield Street at this point, as a hermitage, was signalized by the execution of the rude carvings which are still to be seen around its walls.[1] The connection of the origin of the town with the martyrdom of Thomas à Becket is still remembered in "Becket's Fair," the great annual event at Royston, held on his festival, July 7;[2] while at the neighbouring village of Hauxton is likewise to be found one of the very few remaining memorials of the devotion to him, so widely spread in mediæval England, and stamped out with such special thoroughness by Henry VIII. In the little Norman church—itself a rare sight in our county—we may yet see depicted on the wall the effigy of the prelate who, beyond all others, was the very embodiment of Norman ecclesiasticism.

§ 41. During the miserable "nineteen winters" of anarchy which marked the reign of Stephen, Cambridgeshire came in for its share of the universal devastation wrought throughout England by his freebooting barons. The particular malefactor who afflicted our county was one Galfrid de Magnaville or Mandeville, a brigand who

[1] See Chapter I., § 19.
[2] This was the day of his "translation."

established himself in the Fens, and thence harried the country far and wide, "plundering, consuming, stripping, and destroying everything." Cambridge itself was surprised and sacked by this desperado, even the churches "there and all around" not being spared. Churches, indeed, being respected by ordinary marauders, were used as sanctuaries by the parishioners, and were thus the special objects of such outrageously godless men as Galfrid, whose death, "excommunicate and unabsolved," is recorded with satisfaction by the writer of the Acta Stephani. "Nor was the earth permitted to give a grave to the sacrilegious offender." He was slain beneath the walls of the castle (now entirely vanished) which Stephen had constructed at Burwell for the express purpose of shutting him into the Fens.

§ 42. Nigel, Bishop of Ely, meanwhile was doing his share of the fighting, mostly against Stephen: now holding out the Castle of Devizes, until forced to surrender on pain of seeing his cousin, the Chancellor, hanged before the walls; now fortifying Ely against the King; now routed out of it by the royal forces, who surprised the entrance at Aldreth; now taken prisoner; now escaping; and finally stripping the shrine of St. Etheldred of its silver plating to pay the fine of 300 marks which purchased for him the King's pardon.

§ 43. The Cambridge sacked by Galfrid de Mandeville was probably even then on the main lines of the present town. From the Via Devana (the street which enters the place as the Huntingdon Road on the north-west, and, running straight through, leaves it as the Hills Road on the south-east), the tracks must already have branched out which, under the names of Trinity Street and Jesus Lane, still lead to the old Church of St. Benet on the one hand, and to the then recently-built Priory of Barnwell on the other. The population ejected from the "Borough" by the Norman occupation would doubtless swarm down, as at Lincoln, to the lower ground beside the river, and build, along the Via Devana, what is now called Bridge Street. It is probable that their habitations extended southwards till they joined those previously built round St. Benet's; for in the midst of this line, in the angle formed by Trinity Street and Bridge Street, was at this period established the Cambridge Jewry.

§ 44. The establishment of the Jews in England was one of the incidental effects of the Conquest. They had followed in the wake of the invading army (as they followed the German hosts into France in 1870), assisting the Normans to dispose of their spoil, finding (at usurious interest) ready money for the impoverished English to meet requisitions withal, and generally meeting so universally felt a need for money-broking of all kinds, that ere long every large town had its Jewry. In a curious diatribe by Richard of Devizes (1190),[1] Canterbury, Rochester, Chichester, Oxford, Exeter, Worcester, Chester, Hereford, York, Ely, Durham, Norwich, Lincoln, Bristol, Winchester, and of course London, are all mentioned as containing Jewish settlements; and doubtless many other places are, like Cambridge, omitted in this list. That its "Judaismus" already existed we know from contemporary documents.

§ 45. Yet the position of the Jew in England was all along highly anomalous. As a member of an alien race, and still more of an alien religion, he could acquire no kind of constitutional recognition within the realm. The common law ignored him; his Jewry, like the royal forest, was outside its domain. Legally he was nothing more than the King's chattel, holding all he had simply at the King's pleasure.[2] But to the Crown the Jew was so great a source of profit that it was careful not to

[1] Chron., § 78.
[2] Green, "Hist. Eng. People," chap. ii., § 5.

oppress him over-much, and to guard him as far as possible from the oppression of others. His bonds were preserved in the royal archives (a fact of which the memory long remained in the name of the "Star" Chamber[1]), and their payment was enforced by royal authority. It was this special protection of the Throne which caused the Jews to be considered instruments of monarchical despotism, and led to the many popular outbreaks against them. Nor were the Jews in mediæval England by any means the tame and cringing beings portrayed by Sir Walter Scott in 'Ivanhoe.' History rather shows them as overweening and insolent, at no pains to conceal their contempt for what they regarded as the superstition of their Christian neighbours, and relying on the royal support to protect them even in outrages against the rites and emblems which those neighbours held sacred, thus giving ground for the "anti-Semitic" feeling which finally brought about their expulsion.

§ 46. In close contiguity with the Jewry rose along with it two noteworthy Christian edifices. On the northeast, across the Via Devana, a confraternity (presumably connected with the newly-established Military Order of the Temple) built one of the round churches which reminded beholders of that Church of the Holy Sepulchre at Jerusalem which it was the special office of the Templars to defend against the infidel, from whom it had just been won (1099) in the First Crusade.[2] On the south-east Bishop Nigel, of Ely, found time, during his busy political and military permutations under Stephen, to erect his Hospital of St. John, on the site with which the name of that Evangelist has ever since been indelibly associated, and which was designed to play so special a part in the coming development of Cambridge.

[1] שְׁטָר being the Hebrew for "bond."
[2] See above § 34. The only other like churches in England are those of the Temple in London, of Maplestead in Essex, and of St. Sepulchre, Northampton.

§ 47. The existence of the Jewry shows that Cambridge was in the twelfth century a place of some importance. Whether that importance was in any degree due to its being already a seat of special learning has yet to be proved. In the above-mentioned list of English cities, "the clerks" of Oxford are specially referred to, and we may perhaps infer that no such were yet to be found at Cambridge. But with the growth of the place would arise a demand for education, which would be met partly by Picot's monks at Barnwell, but chiefly by teachers from the old and famous abbey school at Ely, the training-place of more than one monarch. And early in the next century events occurred which caused this germ to burst into profuse life, and gave to Cambridge its great and lasting renown as a University.

CHAPTER VI.

EARLY ENGLISH PERIOD.

§ 1—4. Burst of progress in the thirteenth century—Church-building —Friars in Cambridge—Educational movement—Literary development of the thirteenth century—English historians—Foreign dialecticians.

§ 5—15. First universities—Bologna, Paris, Oxford, Cambridge— Earliest University organization—Course of study—Trivium and Quadrivium—Proctors—Collegiate system begun—Its advantages —Merton, Peterhouse.

§ 16—19. Bishop Longchamps—Interdicts—Queen Eleanor—Papal ban—Exemption of preceptories—Shingay—" Fairy-cart "—Report of bailiwick.

§ 20—25. Barons' War—Cambridgeshire a national stronghold— Ravaged by Royalists—Recovered by Barons—John's march from Wisbeach—Patriot defence of Ely.

§ 26—33. Historians of the period—Local anecdotes—Eltisley cyclone —Matthew Paris—His notes on the weather and the crops.

§ 34—41. Growth of Cambridge—The King's Ditch—Monastic buildings—Religious Houses throughout the county—Hospitals—Hermitages—Our Lady of Whitehill—Papal Bulla.

§ 42—61. Episcopal registers—Vicarage of Grantchester—The polltax—Wat Tyler—The Black Death—Ashwell inscription—Ely lantern—Lady Chapel.

§ 1. THE thirteenth century opened in our county with a burst of material and intellectual progress. While, as we have seen, but little Norman work is to be found in our parish churches, this is far from being the case with the "Early English" style, which came in with the Plantagenets, before the twelfth century closed. It is scarcely too much to say that the present lines of almost every church in Cambridgeshire date from this time. Windows and arches of later style have been inserted, roofs and clerestories added, but the ground-plan of nearly all our village churches is still as it was then planned out and laid down. Now were built the exquisite chancels of Cherry Hinton and Foxton, and the lovely doorway of Barrington, with many another gem of architecture glorifying many a remote and quiet hamlet. Now, at Cambridge, came into being the beautiful church of St. Rhadegunde's Priory, still remaining to us as the chapel of Jesus College; now, at Ely, rose the Galilee at the western door of the minster, and the lancet-pierced façade which closes it to the east. The former was completed by Bishop Eustace, 1215, the latter by Bishop Northwold, 1252. It may be here mentioned that the accurate record kept at Ely of each addition to the cathedral is the standard which has enabled the dates of the various architectural styles to be known throughout England. Roughly speaking, those styles may be said to begin:

   Norman, 1075.
   Early English, 1175.
   Decorated, 1275.
   Perpendicular, 1375.

§ 2. And along with these surviving remains of this great epoch, the zeal and piety of the age erected other buildings, of which, alas! the greed and rapacity of a later age have robbed us. It was at this time that there was begun in Cambridge (A.D. 1214) that noble church of the Franciscans which the University vainly endeavoured to save for itself on their dissolution; and not long afterwards the town was adorned by yet another famous church, belonging to the rival Order of the Dominicans.

The former stood on the site now occupied by Sidney Sussex College, the latter on that of Emmanuel; and before the century was out the Carmelites had settled at Newnham (whence the winter floods drove them across the river to the site of Queens'), and the Augustinians in Pembroke Street.

§ 3. Friars — gray, black, and white — thus became familiar figures in the streets of Cambridge. That they should have appeared there shows the growing importance of the town. For, unlike the earlier monks, whose abbeys were mostly founded in remote spots, themselves creating the towns which afterwards clustered round them, the friars invariably struck for the great centres of population, there to exercise their special work of preaching and teaching. At this time the "Mendicant" Orders were newly founded, and in the first flush of their zeal, and their presence must have given no small impulse to any educational movement already begun at Cambridge in connection with the famous abbey school of Ely.

§ 4. That movement was a ripple of the great tide of literary development which throughout Europe marked the twelfth century. In England, the strength of that development is seen in the wonderful galaxy of historians which, with that century, suddenly sheds its light upon us. Florence of Worcester, Henry of Huntingdon, William of Malmesbury, Ingulf, Geoffrey Gaimar, William de Monte, John and Richard of Hexham, Jordan Fantosme, Simeon of Durham, Gervase, Giraldus Cambrensis, William of Newburgh, Richard of Devizes, all appear in close succession, as well as several unnamed chroniclers; while Robert of Gloucester, Roger of Wendover, and Matthew Paris carry on the line into our present period. And while the English intellect was thus mostly devoting itself to chronicling the past, theological and metaphysical problems were occupying the attention of Continental students. Two successive Archbishops of

Canterbury, Lanfranc and Anselm (the first foreigners and the first men of letters whom the see had known since Theodore of Tarsus), were amongst the earliest to engage in this arena, the contests in which speedily showed that proficiency in dialectic skill was the weapon most needful for victory.

§ 5. And from this consciousness our University took its rise. For, whatever earlier embryonic schools there may have been here, it is certain that the University of Cambridge owes its existence to Oxford, as Oxford, in turn, owes its existence to Paris. And Paris, as a University, came into being with the famous lectures which drew such crowds of disciples from every quarter to learn the science of logic from the lips of Abelard. Those crowds, at first, of course, a mere unorganized mob, speedily learnt to combine for mutual protection against the dislike and the extortion of the townsmen amongst whom they dwelt. Solidarity of interest developed corporate feeling, and ere long an actual corporation, recognised and privileged by the State, sprang into being; not yet, indeed, called by the name of University (a phrase signifying at first merely a corporation, and only growing to its present use late in the fourteenth century), but having a formal legal existence as a "Studium" or "Studium Generale." So rose Paris, and contemporaneously with Paris, though a few years the older, rose, by precisely the same process, the sister University of Bologna, whose speciality was civil and canon law, as that of Paris was logic.

§ 6. From these two sources the University movement spread rapidly over Europe; one of the first places to follow in their steps being Oxford, at that time (after London and Winchester) the third city in England, and already, accordingly, possessing something of a scholastic reputation. Hither is said to have come, in 1149, the famous Professor Vacarius of Bologna, to lecture on civil law, and here, certainly, about the same date the influence of Paris developed that special instruction in logic which has been so constant a feature of Oxford intellectual life. The University grew rapidly. As we have seen, Richard of Devizes, in 1190, mentions "its clerks" as the distinguishing feature of Oxford, in his descriptive list of English cities[1]; and Matthew Paris tells us that in 1209 the number of University men in the place was even larger than at the present day; the teachers and scholars together amounting to no fewer than 3,000. He also tells us that when, owing to an unusually serious town and gown riot, the whole number were that year "sent down" by royal mandate, many of both teachers and scholars migrated to pursue their studies in Cambridge.

§ 7. That so undistinguished a place should have been selected for this purpose has been usually supposed to argue that it must have been already an educational centre. Cambridge was not, like Oxford, Paris, or Bologna, one of the leading cities of the land; it had no such royal charter as put Oxford on an equality with London and Winchester; it had no great political associations; why, then, should this Oxford colony have chosen it for their place of settlement unless its schools were the attraction? This may well have been so. Schools there undoubtedly were at Cambridge before this, and some unknown teacher may have proved so influential as to draw from without those extraneous crowds of students from whom Universities, as we have seen, had their birth. But this is purely conjectural; Cambridge may have been chosen, as Northampton and Stamford were afterwards successively chosen by like seceders from Oxford, from no such motive, but for wholly accidental reasons.

§ 8. Anyhow, there is no doubt of the fact that at this time the schools of Cambridge were largely colonized by

[1] Chronicle of Richard of Devizes, § 84.

scholars from Oxford, nor that twenty years later the place had a European reputation as a "Studium," for in 1229 a great disturbance between citizens and students in Paris caused a very large migration thence also to our lecture-rooms. Yet another swarm made its way over from Oxford in 1240, and the University of Cambridge had fairly sprung into existence.[1]

§ 9. By this time the experience gained in the establishment of the older Universities was bearing fruit, and it is probable that from the very first Cambridge organized itself upon the lines which that experience suggested. The Masters associated themselves into "faculties," according to the subjects of their teaching; the scholars gathered themselves into more or less exclusive clubs (such as are found to this day amongst the Burschen of every German University) for mutual companionship, and both teachers and scholars felt themselves one body, the government of which was in the hands of the "faculties," whose members were thence called "regents." Admission to a faculty was attained by a seven years' course of study, the first three of which the wholly unattached student was supposed to devote successively to "grammar" (practically equivalent to the colloquial study of Latin), logic, and rhetoric. His accomplishments in these subjects were solely tested by the manner in which, as a junior or senior "sophister" (a designation which has descended even to our day), he acquitted himself, in his second and third year, in the public disputations open to all undergraduates. If he did his part in these satisfactorily, he would always find

---

[1] The special connection which has always subsisted between Oxford and Cambridge is shown by the fact that, from the first, every inceptor in any faculty at either swore to practise at no English University save his own and the other. It was this exclusive bond which, more than any other cause, brought to naught the attempts to found rival Universities at Northampton and Stamford in 1260 and 1330 respectively.

some Master ready to take him as a "Bachelor" or apprentice, in which capacity he passed from the *trivium* (as the above-mentioned course of study was called) to the *quadrivium*, a four years' curriculum of (1) arithmetic, (2) geometry, (3) harmony, (4) astronomy. After this his master might license him to teach on his own account, by virtue of which the "licentiate" entered the ranks of the Regency in the particular "faculty" which he might choose to select. By this time he would probably be twenty-one or twenty-two years of age, having come up at fourteen or fifteen. His performances at either end of his academic career have enriched our language with words still in use, the elementary nature of his undergraduate *trivium* being enshrined in the word "trivial," and the superficial character of too many of the lectures which, as Master of Arts, he was required to deliver in due course (*cursorie,*) being remembered in "cursory."

§ 10. Such was the earliest condition of Cambridge University. As years went on the organization rapidly developed. The appointment of a Chancellor gave it a head, to whom the power of granting licenses to admit to the M.A. degree was shortly confined; and to the *trivium* and *quadrivium* were added further courses (each of several years' duration) for those who wished to gain the higher degree of Doctor, in Divinity, Law, or Medicine. The public disputations came to be held in special Schools (built in the fourteenth century), and the undergraduate, no less than the Bachelor, was required to be under the instruction of some M.A. before he was allowed to take part in these exercises.

§ 11. Undergraduates being thus, for the first time, formally recognised by the University, proctors, too, were appointed to keep order amongst their hitherto lawless hordes. One of these officers had special jurisdiction over each of the "nations" into which the student body was divided—a system unreasonably borrowed from Paris, where men of various nationalities were actually in residence. For the purposes of the system, both at Oxford and Cambridge, England was conventionally assumed to be divided by the river Trent into two "nations," Northern and Southern, to one or the other of which every undergraduate necessarily belonged by reason of his birthplace. This arrangement obviously gave special encouragement to faction fights, one of which, in 1261, was peculiarly murderous, and all but brought the University to ruin. The two proctors of the present day are a survival from this ancient convention. From the beginning the University officials had been granted, by royal charter in 1231, special privileges with regard to the town; the "taxers," for example, having power to regulate the rent of lodgings for the students, and the proctors being supreme over the weights and measures used in the market. The former authority still survives (vested in the Lodging-house Syndicate), and even the latter has not long been obsolete. Amongst his official insignia there is still handed on to the Senior Proctor of each year the archaic cylinder of sheet iron, a yard in length and an inch in diameter, which was of old the standard test for the dimensions of every roll of butter sold in Cambridge.

§ 12. Before the thirteenth century closed was introduced that system of collegiate education destined to exercise so absorbing an influence on the whole constitution of the University. The earliest students must have been mere casual lodgers in the houses of townsmen; but the idea of starting lodging-houses, or "hostels," for their sole benefit would immediately suggest itself to private enterprise. Such Hostels soon sprang up in large numbers, and continued, though gradually choked to death by the growth of the Colleges, for many years. Even late in the sixteenth century, one of the effects of the Reformation most lamented by Dr. Caius is the extinction (through the decreased numbers of the students) of nearly all these abodes. To this day the name of Garret Hostel (now a court in Trinity College) remains to remind us of these ancient institutions. In our time, indeed, the institutions themselves have once more been revived, such being the formal position of both St. Edmund's Hall and Selwyn College.[1]

§ 13. The position, indeed, of the last-named corporation—the latest-founded of our Cambridge colleges with regard to University recognition—is precisely that of our earliest college at the date of its foundation. The College was then, in respect to the University system, simply a better-organized and permanently-endowed Public Hostel, such as the earlier private lodging-houses of whose existence the authorities were just beginning to take cognizance. Little was it then foreseen that this new idea would carry all before it, until the University itself came to be considered a mere aggregate of colleges, and every University official was required to belong to one or other of these newly engrafted corporations.

§ 14. The collegiate idea, however, was fruitful in such vast practical advantages that it was bound to carry all before it. The unattached student, rioting and starving in his unregulated lodgings, under no sort of discipline or tutorial direction, could not hold his own in the schools against the carefully-trained and comfortably-harboured Scholar of a College, his superior in physical, intellectual, and, above all, moral advantages. Hitherto such advantages had only been attainable by the young Dominican or Franciscan novice in his cloister;[2] their extension to the mere secular undergraduate was due to

---

[1] These are denominational institutions, the former Roman Catholic, the latter Anglican.

[2] Cambridge, Oxford, and Paris were the only Universities in Europe which admitted members of the Mendicant Orders to a degree.

the genius of two remarkable men—Walter de Merton at Oxford, Hugh de Balsham, Bishop of Ely, at Cambridge.

§ 15. As usual, Oxford, "the place of great movements, as Cambridge is the place of great men," took the lead. Merton College was founded in 1265, with a code of statutes so good that when Hugh de Balsham followed at Cambridge, by the creation of Peterhouse, twenty years later, he adopted them bodily. He had, indeed, endeavoured to adopt them in his previous abortive attempt to graft his new College upon the ancient Hospital of St. John—an attempt so fruitful in quarrels between the old and the new members of the foundation that the latter were speedily removed to their present abode, at what was then the extreme southern end of the town.

§ 16. The mention of this great expansion of Cambridge, as a town, recalls us to the course of civil events during this first period of University development. The ravages of Galfrid de Mandeville in the reign of Stephen were succeeded by over half a century of peace, during which the county was only vexed by the proceedings of William Longchamps, the high-handed Chancellor of Richard Cœur de Lion, who was Bishop of Ely 1189-1192. For some not very intelligible reason, in the course of his quarrels with the Archbishop of Rouen, he put under interdict part, at least, of his own diocese, so that no burial of the dead could take place. Strange to say, this outrage was submitted to by all concerned; so that when Queen Eleanor, the widow of Henry II., came, in 1192, to visit her dowry manors in the county, she was shocked to find "human bodies lying everywhere through the fields unburied," and grieved by the tears and wailings of the mourners, who implored her intervention. "Being of a tender-hearted disposition" (as Richard of Devizes tells us, in spite of her dealings with Fair Rosamond), "she forthwith postponed her own affairs" to the task of removing this grievance; which she succeeded in doing, "for who could be so steel-hearted that that woman could not bend him to her wishes?"

§ 17. This episode may remind us that there were a few spots in the county where this peculiar method (so strangely in favour amongst the ecclesiastics of this period) of putting pressure on adversaries by interdicting their dependents from the consolations of religion failed of its effect. The Houses of the Templars and Hospitallers were exempt, even from the ban of the Pope himself. Thus, the Preceptory of the latter Order at Shingay, in the south-western district of our county, was the only place for miles around at which Church services could be attended by the living, or burial secured for the dead, during the six years (1208-1214) when this ghastly spiritual weapon was made use of by the Pope in the dismal days of King John. Local tradition still remembers the "fairy-cart" (*i.e.*, the *feretorium*, or wheeled bier) which, by night, carried to Shingay the bodies of those who were denied funeral rites elsewhere.

§ 18. To the historian this Preceptory is of special interest, owing to the fact that a report of its revenues, made to the Grand Master of the Order in 1338, still exists in the Record Office at Malta. That it should yet be found there, in spite of the straits to which the Order was reduced when driven thither from Rhodes by the Turkish arms, shows with what care the Knights of St. John of Jerusalem preserved their records. We thus learn that the Preceptory or "bailiwick" of Shingay was worth £187 12s. 8d. per annum, being only surpassed in value by three others in England. The total comprised the following items:

610 acres of arable land at 1s. 6d. per acre,
80   „   „   „   1s. 3d.   „
220 „   „   „   1s.   „

(These last were in the adjoining parishes of Arrington and Croydon, where the land is poor, lying on the hillside.)

70 acres of meadow at 2s. per acre,
60 acres of common pasture at 1s. per acre.

(Agricultural rents, as these figures show, were as high in this period as at any time; each shilling in the above list approximately representing £1 in present money.) There was also a watermill (returned as worth 10s. per annum in Doomsday), supplemented by a windmill (at this date a comparatively recent invention), both together bringing in £2 10s. yearly. The manor-house was worth £1 per annum, and its dovecotes 13s. 4d. The Preceptory also held the rectories of Wendy and Sawston, worth £13 6s. 8d. and £33 6s. 8d. respectively. The work of the "customary tenants" (*i.e.*, the "villains" who held their land by payment of certain accustomed services in lieu of rent)[1] is valued at £13 9s. yearly; the fines, etc., levied at the manorial courts at £25; while the "voluntary" fees of those who sought the good offices—spiritual or temporal —of the Knights amounted to no less than £23 6s. 8d.

§ 19. The yearly expenses of the House amounted to £70 18s. 8d., the chief item being food. Of wheat, 80 quarters at 3s. was the annual allowance; of barley (for brewing), 120 quarters at 2s.; of oats (for the stable), 120 quarters at 1s. Meat, fish, etc., came to 3s. 6d. per week. This provided for the regular household and their guests, the doors of the House being open (as the Founder had desired) to all comers. The regular inmates were the Preceptor, two knights, two chaplains, the Vicar of Shingay, and the servants, who, besides their keep, received wages—men getting 13s. 4d. a year, boys 6s. 8d., very nearly equivalent to what are paid now. The Vicar of Shingay received 20s., the Preceptor £12; while each knight was allowed clothing to the value of £1 6s. 8d., and 8s. for pocket-money.

The House was habitually tenanted by Knights; but there was a period when for these were substituted the

[1] See below, § 52.

Sisters of the Order, driven out from their original Hospital at Jerusalem on the capture of that city by Saladin in 1179. Two of these ladies (all Sisters of St. John being necessarily of noble birth), Sisters Amabilia and Amice de Malketon, thus took up their abode here in 1180. A leaden seal (*bulla*) was found on the site of the preceptory in 1876, bearing on one side a representation of the shrine of the Holy Sepulchre, with the inscription IHERVSALEM · HOSPITALIS, and on the other a figure kneeling before a patriarchal cross, with the legend S · GVARINVS · CVSTOS. This Guarin de Montaigu was Grand Master of the Order from 1232-1269.[1]

§ 20. Ere the date (1338) at which the Preceptor of Shingay sent in this exhaustive report, Cambridgeshire had been, for almost the last time, the scene of great events in our national history. During the gallant stand made by the barons of England against the tyrannies of John and of Henry III., this county was amongst the special strongholds of the national party. As such it was ravaged in 1215 by the royal mercenaries, not Englishmen, but the hired scum of Europe, who "sacked towns, churches, and churchyards, sparing neither women nor children ... even the priests at the very altars, with the cross of the Lord in their hands, clad in their sacred robes, were seized, robbed, and tortured "—in various horrible ways, given with much detail by the historian.[2] The following year, again, a band of these ruffians, from Brabant, burst into the Isle of Ely, "laying waste the whole country," sacking the cathedral (where the exquisite Galilee, at the western entrance, had just been completed by Bishop Eustace), and only

[1] This seal is exactly the same size as the Papal bulla mentioned in § 41. The letter S stands for "sigillum" = seal, the strange construction, with the name of the seal-owner in the nominative instead of the genitive, being not unexampled in similar cases.
[2] Roger of Wendover, § 361.

not burning it on payment of heavy ransom. "When the barons heard these things," says Roger of Wendover, "they looked one upon the other and said: 'The Lord gave, and the Lord hath taken away; blessed be the name of the Lord.'"

§ 21. The baronial forces were at this juncture almost confined to London; but a few weeks later (on the arrival, at their invitation, of Louis the Dauphin, to claim the English Crown), one of their first steps was to clear Cambridgeshire of the Royalists, Cambridge Castle itself falling into their hands. The strategic value of this post (as the one point where an army could pass the Cam) all but enabled them to capture John himself in his retreat from Suffolk, and obliged him to adopt that perilous route across the Wash, which ruined his army and led to his own death.[1]

§ 22. And when the long struggle for constitutional liberty in Church and State seemed crushed by the patriot defeat, in 1265, at Evesham, the last stand for English freedom was made in Cambridgeshire. As against the Conqueror, two centuries before, so now again the Isle of Ely served as a camp of refuge for the broken relics of the national forces. "The disinherited," as the historian calls them (their estates being forfeited for "treason"), "on the Eve of St. Laurence" (August 9) established themselves in the island. Thence they raided the country far and wide for provisions and booty (the Jews of Cambridge being named as their special prey), while every expedition sent against them[2] was foiled with a skill and daring once more reminding us of the days of Hereward, one of whose descendants was actually amongst these patriots.

§ 23. History, indeed, seemed strangely to repeat it-

[1] Matthew Paris tells us that it was in crossing the estuary of the Nene at Wisbeach that John suffered this disaster.
[2] Matthew Paris, § 360.

self. As the Papal authority had supported William the Conqueror, so now it supported Henry against the national cause. The Papal Legate summoned the defenders of the Isle "to return to their Faith, and to unity with Holy Mother Church, and to their obedience to the Roman Curia," by submission to the King. In answer to this, the patriots repudiate the insinuation of heresy, protesting "that they believe and keep the Articles of the Faith which are contained in the Creed; that they also believe in the Gospel, and in the Sacraments of the Church, as the Church Catholic believeth, and that they are ready to live and die for this Faith." They add that they do indeed acknowledge "obedience to the Church of Rome, as the Head of all Christendom, but not to the avarice and tyranny of those who misgovern it." They complain that "the land is enslaved by aliens," that the abbeys are being ruined by the extortions of the King and the Legate, that the churches throughout England are given to foreign incumbents, who live abroad on the stipend, and leave the duty to ill-paid hirelings. And, in default of the redress of these grievances, they vow that they will "appeal to the Apostolic See, to a General Council, and, if need be, to the Supreme Judge of all [*i.e.*, to the God of Battles] . . . seeing that they fight for the common weal of Church and Realm."[1]

§ 24. This brave utterance reminds us how entirely the barons' cause was indeed that of the Anglican Church. As in the earliest days of their struggle, so now in its dying effort their chiefest object was that which they had embodied in the very first clause of the Great Charter: " Ecclesia Anglicana libera sit "—" Let the Church of England be free, with her rights entire and her liberties inviolate." Truly did they deserve their own favourite title for themselves, "the Army of the Church."

[1] Matthew Paris, § 367.

§ 25. But neither the goodness of their cause nor their own skill and valour availed the "disinherited," when the consummate generalship of the great Edward, the mightiest warrior of the age, the statesman who took up and gave effect to these very aspirations for whose sake they resisted him, took the field against them. In 1268 he appeared in person upon the scene,[1] forced his way across the morasses (seemingly at more than one point) "on bridges of hurdles," and speedily captured or dispersed all who ventured to oppose him. They had maintained their fastness unsubdued for nearly three years. And so ended the last of the many defences of Ely. Never since that day has the Isle been again the scene of warfare.

Two of the small iron badges which were amongst the special features of this contest have been found in the county, one bearing the well-known Royalist cognizance, the three lions, the other the very unusual emblem of a butterfly, which was possibly some baronial bearing.

§ 26. The historians for this period are Roger of Wendover, who died 1236, and Matthew Paris, who carried on his work till 1273. Both are careful and voluminous writers, whose pages are enlivened by many an anecdote and notice, incidentally throwing light on the condition of the people. Thus, the former tells us that in July, 1234, much famine-stricken folk invaded the ripening harvest-fields and devoured the crops, "for which they may scarcely be blamed. Of the farmers, however (who, from their avarice, ever hold the poor in suspicion), many were greatly angered at this pious theft. And they of a town called Alboldesly [Eltisley], in Cambridgeshire, hied them all on the next Sunday, the 16th of July, to their church, and with tumult demanded of the priest to excommunicate, upon the spot, all those who had thus plucked wheat-ears in their fields. But

[1] His army is said to have consisted chiefly of Scottish troops.

one ... pious man ... adjured him in the name of God to exclude *his* crops from the sentence, adding that he was well content that the poor should take from him in their need, and that what was left he commended to the Lord's care. Now, scarcely had the priest perforce begun to pronounce the sentence, than there suddenly arose a mighty storm of thunder, lightning, whirlwind, rain and hail, and the corn in the fields was lifted as by a blast from hell; and all that grew therein, and the cattle, and the very birds were destroyed, as though trodden down by carts and horses. But ... that honest and just man ... discovered his lands ... to be without any trace of harm. And thus it is clear that, as glory is given to God on high by His angels, so there is peace on earth towards men of good-will. This storm began on the borders of Bedfordshire [where Eltisley stands], and passed to the east through the Isle of Ely. ... And here is a wondrous thing: Such crops as still stood when it was over were found so rotted that neither horse nor ass, bull nor pig, goose nor hen, would eat thereof."[1]

§ 27. Matthew Paris gives almost every year a short summary of its weather, and as he was himself a Cambridgeshire man (born at Hildersham), and wrote no further off than St. Albans, his climatic notes are doubtless applicable to Cambridgeshire. Thus, we learn that in 1237 a tidal wave and storm caused much destruction, especially in the lowlands around Wisbeach, and that quartan ague—a constant disease in the Fens—was worse than ever before.

The seasons of 1238 and 1240 were almost exactly as in 1896: hot, dry weather till the middle of August, succeeded by long-continued rain, so that the farmers who got in their corn early did well, while the rest

[1] A storm of precisely the same character devastated Essex, June 24, 1897.

suffered heavily. In 1241 an extraordinary drought, from March 25 to October 28, was succeeded by a specially bitter winter.

The year 1258 was as disastrous to Cambridgeshire agriculturists as 1879; by the Feast of the Assumption (August 15) the harvest was not yet begun, and much was still uncarried even at All Saints' Day, by which time it was not worth carrying, "but was left as manure to enrich the soil." The previous years had also been bad, 1256 being marked by daily rain from August 15 to February 2 (N.B., the year began March 25), and the fruit harvest in 1257 being completely ruined by autumnal rains, "so that apples, pears, figs, cherries, plums, all sorts of fruit, in fact, that are preserved in jars, were quite spoilt." In that year, too, corn rose to the famine price of 10s. (equivalent to about £10) per quarter. In plentiful seasons, such as 1243, 1248, and 1255, it was only 2s. per quarter.

§ 28. The Calendars of the Patent Rolls and Close Rolls also give us much interesting information about our county. Thus, an entry in the latter tells us how, on August 31, 1213, Roger le Bigod, Robert Picot, and Robert de Barnwell are appointed to inquire into the damages suffered by the church and clergy of Ely during "the recent discord between the King and the clergy."

The following year there is a grant of liberty to the Bishop of Ely when hunting in his forest to pursue the game into the King's forest; and on February 18, 1215, the custodians of the bishopric (the See being vacant) are bidden to support Richard, huntsman to the late Bishop, and his dogs, out of the issues of the bishopric. He is to be allowed three assistants, two horses, and nineteen dogs. A subsequent mandate to the bailiffs of the Isle increases the pack to "fifteen greyhounds and twenty-one hounds *de moto*. . . . And let them hunt in the Bishop's chases for the flesh they are fed upon." Twenty bucks and does out of the King's forest are also granted to "the Bishop's park" at Ely.

On March 18, 1215, these same custodians are bidden to supply 100 live pike to put into the stews of the Count of Salisbury, the King's brother; and in 1220 there is an order to the bailiffs of Cambridge to deliver 5,000 eels at Oxford before the coming Christmas "for the King when there." As this order was only issued December 10, the bailiffs must have found it no easy task to comply with it.

On November 3, 1218, we find an order on the Treasury to account to the bailiffs of Cambridge for £26 3s. for the King's expenses when at Cambridge; and another to pay to Peter Sarcenno, a Roman citizen, 13 marks, lent to the Abbot of Thorney at the Court of Rome by order of King John, "when he was there on the King's business"—*i.e.*, to arrange for the surrender of the Crown of England to the Pope. The Abbot was also paid 30 marks on his own account.

In like manner, on June 25, 1224, we have an order on the Exchequer to pay to the Bishop of Ely 40 marks, "which he paid at Newenham to Walter de Kirkham, the King's clerk, by order, on the Sabbath before the Nativity of John Baptist," for his expenses in going to France with the Bishop of Norwich as the King's messenger on the Feast of All Saints.

On November 23, 1222, the bailiffs of Cambridge are to deposit "at the New Temple in London" moneys collected for the Holy Land; on June 22, 1224, they are to buy and send to the King at Bedford as many good ropes and cables as could be bought in the town. A simultaneous order bids the Prior of Crux Roesiæ (Royston) deliver to the army at Bedford the cords which the King had caused to be stored with him.

On April 4, 1223, the lands of Richard de Mountfitchet are seized because he attended a tournament in spite of the King's prohibition. Like entries of the seizure of lands on various pretexts are constant in these rolls, and show how insecure were the times. First, "the lands of the Normans" are confiscated, a process involving wholesale transference of property in parish after parish; and everywhere we find land taken, given away, and (very rarely) given back to its owner, as in the case of John Coleman, to whom the Sheriff is bidden (on February 28, 1216) "to deliver all his land again, he having been received back into favour." It must have seemed somewhat of a mockery when, on April 17, 1216, a mandate to the Sheriff ordered "a general peace" to be proclaimed.

§ 29. In these rolls we can also trace the development of Cambridge itself.

In March, 1207, comes a writ to the Sheriff to deliver the town of Cambridge to the burgesses to whom the King had granted it, "to hold it at farm according to the King's charter." This charter of incorporation had been purchased by the townsmen for 250 marks, and gave them the privileges of "free burgesses," with a Provost and Bailiffs of their own, and a Merchant Guild. They thus gained the right of regulating their own markets, and of that self-government which they had enjoyed of old and lost at the Conquest.

These privileges were the result of a royal visit to Cambridge, for which, on March 3, 1207, a mandate bids Ramsey Abbey send fish thither "for the King's use on Wednesday next, being Ash Wednesday." Another royal visit, that of Henry III. in 1265, was made the occasion of giving to the Provost the higher title of Mayor, thus completing the incorporation of the borough.

The town was required to supply on demand twenty soldiers for the King's service, while the rest of the county and the Isle were ordered to find 300 axemen and 100 diggers. Rates appear to have been fairly heavy at this period. A house rented at 40s. is mentioned as paying 16s. "to the farm of the town yearly."

§ 30. Before the close of the century we find these newly-regained liberties of the town trenched upon by the privileges granted to the infant University. In 1292 "the Chancellor, Masters, and Scholars" are granted powers to prevent regrating,[1] under which all "forfeited victual" is to go to the Hospital of St. John. And two years later the outgoing and incoming Chancellors are "associated" with Master Hugh de Babington as a Royal Commission to audit the accounts of "the burgesses and good men of the said town of Cambridge"—a system which seems to have been continued for some time.

On September 10, 1299, we find the castle and town of Cambridge assigned as dower to "Margaret, sister of Philip, King of France" (the second wife of Edward I.). Soham Manor also formed part of this dowry, and likewise Chesterton, which by a charter of King John was let to the Prior of Barnwell at a rent of "thirty pound sterling of white money." By this same charter the priory was allowed to hold an annual fair at Barnwell "on the Feast of St. Etheldred [October 17] and three days thereafter."

§ 31. These last entries are in the Calendar of the Patent Rolls, which also tell us that, in 1297, Richard Peytevyn, Preceptor of the House of the Temple at Wylburgham (Wilbraham), is promised payment of 2 marks 10 shillings (=£1 16s. 8d.) for three and a half sacks of wool bought by Geoffrey Hurrell of Cambridge, John Portehors, "and their fellows appointed to buy wool in the County of Cambridge." The trade in wool was at this time a royal monopoly, but the price given seems extraordinary, equivalent to some £16 per sack at the present value of money. From the "Placita de Quo

---

[1] This is the process which is now known as making a "corner" in any article of merchandise.

Warranto" we learn that in 1300 the Templars claimed various rights (including freedom from the jurisdiction of the Hundred and County) not only in Wilbraham, but in Chippenham, Boxworth, Waterbeach, Landbeach, Madingley, Newnham, Grantesete, Impington, Rampton, Knapwell, and Barton, by a charter of Henry III.

§ 32. Complaints against wrong and robbery send us down their far-off echoes in these rolls. Thus, in 1309, Walter Martel of Shepreth complains that William, son of Ralph of Shepreth, and Juliana, his wife, forcibly entered his manor of Shepreth, fished his ponds, wrecked his houses, felled his trees, and carried away the timber. Whereupon a commission is issued to Hervey de Stanton (the founder of Michaelhouse) to investigate the matter.

On July 23, 1327, Thomas Stortford, parson of Barenton (Barrington), complains that John Andrew, Chaplain of Foxton, and others, assaulted him at Barrington. And his brother William complains that the same persons assaulted him at Foxton. Faction fights between these adjoining villages (one being on the Mercian side of the Cam, the other on the East Anglian) were till within the last quarter of the nineteenth century still common at their respective Village Feasts. At the date of this complaint Barrington Feast was on St. Margaret's Day (July 20), and then these assaults were probably committed.

And in 1330 we have a complaint from the Bishop ot Ely that certain purloiners have made away with great part of a whale which had been cast on shore near Wisbeach, at a spot where he claims all *wreccum maris* as his sole property.

§ 33. The "Placita de Quo Warranto" give us some vivid touches as to the village life of those days. The Lord of the Manor claims in many places the right to a very large jurisdiction over local crime, extending even to capital cases. Thus, at Dullingham, Robertus de Bello

Campo claimed by inheritance the right to "a gallows, pillory, and ducking-stool, also infang-thief, and the goods of felons and fugitives." Gallows were also to be found at Bassingbourn, Fowlmere, Litlington, Steeple-Morden, and Swavesey, the two last having pillories as well. By the right of "infang-thief," the local authorities of these places could deal summarily with any robbers caught within their bounds.

§ 34. Before the end of the thirteenth century the town of Cambridge had grown to the dimensions which it barely overpassed till the nineteenth. We have seen that in 1285 it already extended as far south as Peterhouse, thus even overleaping the limits assigned to it twenty years earlier by Henry III. In 1265 that monarch made the town his headquarters against the patriot barons at Ely, bringing with him his brother Richard, Duke of Cornwall, the King of the Romans, who was lodged in Barnwell Priory. He did not gain any success against the barons, but provoked great indignation by executing in Cambridge as a traitor a man of noted courage, Walter Cottenham, whom they had knighted at Ely and who fell into his hands. In revenge for this outrage, as soon as his forces were withdrawn, the patriots made a dash upon the place and sacked both the priory and the town, in spite of the famous "King's Ditch" with which Henry had endeavoured to secure it.

§ 35. This ditch (which is marked as still open so late as Lyson's map of 1808) converted the tract of land lying within the bend of the river on its eastern bank, already the main site of the town, into an island. Leaving the river above Queens' Bridge, it passed along Mill Lane and part of Downing Street, bending round between Great St. Andrew's and the Post Office, proceeding along the line of Hobson Street and an extension of that line through Sidney Gardens to Park Street, and thus finally reaching the river again a little below Magdalen Bridge.

§ 36. The site thus enclosed was even then, though there were as yet no colleges, thick with public buildings. Every parish church now within its limits was already in existence, and the ditch, on either side of its course, was fringed with monastic edifices. The Carmelite House stood hard by Queens', that of the Brethren of Penance, "the Friars of the Sack," hard by Peterhouse, those of the Gilbertine Canons and the Augustinian Friars on either side of Pembroke; while the Black Friars occupied the site of Emmanuel, and the Grey Friars that of Sidney, the line being completed by the spacious precincts of the Nunnery of St. Rhadegunde, now Jesus College.

Somewhat further along the Newmarket Road rose the great Priory of Barnwell, with the little "Abbey" Church of St. Andrew the Less, now alone remaining of all its mass of buildings, and originally erected by the monks for the use of the little nest of houses which, as usual, clustered at the abbey gates. The anomalous position of these houses survives in the attachment of many amongst them, even yet, to the distant churches of St. Edward and St. Benet in the town.

Further yet came the Leper Chapel of St. Mary Magdalene, still standing, built, as it would seem, by the same architect as the Church of the Holy Sepulchre in the town, for both edifices show the remarkable feature of a hooded doorway. This was under the charge of the Friars of Bethlehem, and was naturally the outermost building connected with the town of Cambridge. It thus introduces us to the long list of Religious Houses with which the zeal and liberality of benefactors had already enriched our county.

§ 37. Of the greatest of these, Ely, we have already spoken at length. Within sight of its towers rose another great Benedictine abbey at Thorney, founded, like Ely itself, by Bishop Ethelwold of Winchester, in

972,[1] on the site of an earlier eremitical building[2] destroyed in the Danish invasion of 870.

William of Malmesbury (A.D. 1135) describes it as "a little paradise, delightsome as heaven itself may be deemed, fen-circled, yet rich in loftiest trees, where water-meadows delight the eye with rich green, where streamlets glide unchecked through each field. Scarce a spot of ground lies there waste; here are orchards, there vineyards. . . . Nature vies with culture, and what is unknown to the one is produced by the other. And what of the glorious buildings, whose very size it is a wonder that the ground can support amid such marshes? A vast solitude is here the monks' lot, that they may the more closely cling to things above. . . . If a woman is there seen, she is counted a monster, but strangers, if men, are greeted as angels unawares. Yet there none speaketh, save for the moment; all is holy silence. . . . Truly I may call that island a hostel of chastity, a tavern of honesty, a gymnasium of divine philosophy. From its dense thickets it is called Thorney."

The Abbot of Thorney was "mitred," which gave him authority to confer the four Minor Orders, those of Doorkeeper, Reader, Exorcist, and Acolyte. The value of the house at its dissolution is given as £411 12s. 11d.

§ 38. Benedictine monks also established themselves for a while at Denny, where, however, they were shortly succeeded by the Templars, and these, again, in 1291, by the Minoress Nuns, the ruins of whose buildings (almost the only monastic ruins in the whole county), are still to be seen there. Benedictines had also once been found in the foundations of St. Felix at Soham,[3] and of the Scottish Princess, St. Pandionia, at Eltisley; but these had already been destroyed, the one by the Danes, the other, according to tradition, at the Conquest.

[1] See Chapter IV., § 21. [2] See Chapter III., § 24.
[3] See Chapter III., § 18.

Early English Period. 143

The Augustinian Canons, besides their great House at Barnwell, had dependent establishments ("cells" in monastic language) at Anglesey and Spinney; while the Gilbertines, or "White Canons," were found, not only at Cambridge, but also at Fordham and Upwell. Their three houses were all cells to the mother Abbey of Sempringham in Lincolnshire, where their founder, St. Gilbert, had originally planted them. It may be noticed that these Canons were the only Religious Order of wholly English origin.

The Hospitallers we have already seen at Shingay; and they also inherited from the Templars, at the dissolution of that Order in 1312, the preceptories of Chippenham and Wilbraham.

At Linton the "Crutched Friars" had a House, and here was also an "alien" Priory, a cell of the Abbey of St. Jacutus de Insula in Brittany. On the suppression of this Priory in 1439, its property was made over to Pembroke College, Cambridge, then newly founded. Another alien Priory at Isleham (a cell of the Abbey of St. Sergius in Normandy) was handed over, in 1393, to the Carthusians. Alien Priories were also found at Swavesey, and at Thirling near Upwell.

Benedictine nuns had their principal abode in the Abbey of Chatteris, founded by the Lady Alwyn, niece of Edgar the Peaceful, besides somewhat smaller houses at Ickleton and at Swaffham.

All these twenty-eight foundations were doing public work, in the relief of the poor, and, almost invariably, in education also. The nunneries, in particular, acted as boarding-schools for girls, thus supplying a need which is only at this day beginning to be once more satisfactorily dealt with.

§ 39. And besides these monastic foundations, the county possessed no fewer than eleven endowed Hospitals, four at Cambridge (including that for the lepers at Stourbridge), and others at Ely, Leverington, Longstowe, Thorney, Wisbeach, Wicken, and Whittlesford (where the chapel still remains).[1] These Hospitals were institutions not only for the care of the sick, but also for the aged and infirm, thus fulfilling the functions not only of modern hospitals, but of almshouses and convalescent homes as well.

There was also a College at Newton (in the Isle), with a Warden and several chaplains; and the county was dotted with various minor sacred places, such as the hermitages in Royston Cave and on Shelford Bridge, and the far-seen chapel of " Our Lady of White Hill " on the ridge between Barrington and Haslingfield.

§ 40. This chapel must have been one of the most conspicuous objects in the county. Its site, on the eastern extremity of the long ridge terminating in White Hill,[2] commands one of the most extensive views in England, sweeping round from Ely in the north to the Dunstable Downs in the south-west. No fewer than eighty-four churches are visible. We need not wonder that it became a famous place of pilgrimage, and (before the end of the Plantagenet period) full of votive offerings, the most remarkable being the huge dungeon hinges which had once confined Lord Scales, and which he dedicated on his release. The Pilgrims' Way which formerly led to this chapel from the nearest point of the Ermine Street (not far from the Old North Road railway-station), running along the whole length of the White Hill ridge,[3] and still traceable, though in parts disused, is yet known as the " Mare Way," *i.e.*, the Mary Way.[4]

---

[1] This hospital was under a Prior appointed by the Bishop of Ely. It was endowed with sixty acres of land and a watermill.

[2] White Hill gained its name from the three great "clunch" pits on the north, south and east of the end of the ridge.

[3] So the great Pilgrims' Way, in the South of England, runs along the ridge of the North Downs to Canterbury.

[4] Till 1870 the Orwell Maypole (visible for miles around) marked at once the highest point of this road and the meridian of Greenwich.

Early English Period. 145

The whole place has now utterly disappeared, and the only relics of this once celebrated sanctuary are the name of Chapel Bush, which still clings to the site, and a bulla of Pope Martin V. recently found there.

§ 41. This bulla is a thick disc of lead, 1½ inches in diameter, bearing on one side the name MARTINVS · PAPA · V, and on the other the heads of St. Paul and St. Peter, superscribed SPA and SPE respectively. The former occupies the place of honour, in dexter chief. Both heads exhibit the traditional features of the Apostles (of which Lanciani has collected an unbroken series from the first century onwards), St. Peter being represented with curly beard and hair, St. Paul with a long flowing beard. The workmanship is rude in the extreme, the device having remained unchanged from the time of Pope Paul I. (A.D. 757), when art was at its lowest ebb. At the Renaissance these primitive portraits were disused, and conventional types substituted.

A like bulla, of Gregory XI., was lately found built into the wall of Fen Ditton Church. It seems to have been the practice thus to use them, as under the Roman Empire it was the practice to build into the wall of each new house coins of the reigning Augustus. (This practice may possibly account for the wealth of Roman coins scattered about everywhere in Cambridgeshire.[1])

Gregory XI. (1370-78), was the first Pope to restore the Holy See to Rome, after the exile at Avignon, under the influence of St. Catharine of Siena. Martin V. (1417-24) consecrated Milan Cathedral and was the first generally-acknowledged Pope after the Great Schism.

§ 42. The existence, in so poor a district, of so many monuments of piety and public spirit (and it must be remembered that every one of them, besides the 165 parish churches of the county, was either founded or practically rebuilt during this period) is a striking token

[1] See Chapter II., § 16.

of the extent to which the inhabitants were then under the dominion of religious motives. And this is further testified to by many of the entries in the Ely episcopal registers of the day, which show how minutely the ecclesiastical authorities scrutinized and regulated popular life and devotion.

§ 43. Thus, in 1376, the Bishop writes to "his dear son," John Fowler of Wisbeach : "Since you are not able every day to attend worship in the parish church of Wisbeach, on account of its distance, the very muddy condition of the highroad, and the dangers of other roads, we therefore permit you, your household, and your neighbours, to worship for one year in the chapel of Morrowe, provided that on Festivals and High Days you all go to your parish church." This license was renewed annually.

In like manner John and Geoffrey de Leverington are licensed "to have the Divine Offices celebrated for one year in decent oratories in their houses." They must go to the parish church on Sundays and festivals.

Special license is issued to Sir W. Castelacre to choose for two years his own confessor, who shall have power to absolve him even in the cases canonically reserved to the Bishop, viz., perjury "in assisis," disinheritage, bloodshed, corruption of nuns, and trespass against the church of Ely. This the regular diocesan "penitenciaries" could not do.

§ 44. To the parishioners of Haddenham the following mandate is sent by the Bishop: " We hear that the Dedication Festival of your Church falls on the Vigil of the Nativity of the Blessed Virgin Mary [September 8], and that you, like all other faithful Christians, fast on that Vigil on bread and water; which fast, though laudable, is not becoming to so great a Festival as the Dedication of your Church. We therefore transfer your Dedication Festival to October 20th."

So also the Master and Fellows of Peterhouse are

bidden to change the Dedication Festival of "S. Mary's extra Trumpington gates" from November 3 to July 11, because "the multitude of Festivals" about the former date interfere with its due observance. This church, now Little St. Mary's, was at that time used as a College Chapel by Peterhouse, as St. Benet's was by Corpus, to which the passage joining either College with its respective church still bears witness. The special connection subsisting between this College and its Founder's See is to be seen in the fact that every admission to a Fellowship therein finds a place in the Ely Diocesan Register. The Patent Rolls also refer to its inmates as "the Scholars of Ely dwelling at Cambridge."

§ 45. On June 26, 1377, the Bishop is summoned to the coronation of the King (Richard II.), and a few days later receives a Brief to pray for peace (with France). On July 4, accordingly, he issues a mandate to all his clergy that for six consecutive days solemn processions are to be made around the churches if fine, or within if stormy, "with singing of the Litany" and special prayers for this object. To this act of devotion, for those "confessis ac contritis," forty days' indulgence is attached.

Like indulgences are issued, in 1389, to all who take part in the processions and litanies ordered on Wednesdays and Fridays "for the prosperity of the Anglican Church and the King and Realm of England." Benefactions to churches were also thus encouraged: St. Peter's, Witleseye [sic]; St. Mildred's, Exning; St. Rhadegunde's, Cambridge; and even such remote places as "the Hospital of St. Anthony in the Diocese of Vienne," are aided in this way. Alms-deeds to individuals were likewise held worthy of this privilege. Those who contribute to the support of the "ffayr and good." Dns. Thomas, chaplain of the Holy Trinity, Walsoken; or to the relief of "Philip de Cliston, a poor hermit"; or to the ransom of Brother John Braynok, "who with very many English in the company of Dns. Sir Henry de Percy has been taken prisoner by the Scots" (at Otterburn), are all indulgenced.

These indulgences, it must be remembered, were not licenses to commit sin, but so many days' abrogation of the penance imposed by the confessor as a condition of absolution. As such Luther refused to receive them, and thus began his breach with Catholicism. The system having been found to lead to abuse, indulgences can no longer be pleaded amongst Roman Catholics in abrogation of earthly penances, but are held to avail for the mitigation of the sufferings of purgatory.

§ 46. Wrong-doers are severely denounced in these registers, especially if their offences are against ecclesiastical property.

One John Bernard, being arrested on suspicion of having murdered "the cook of the Austin Friars at Cambridge," and handed over for trial to the Ecclesiastical Courts (his victim being a cleric), the Rural Dean of Cambridge is ordered to proclaim "publicly and in the mother tongue," in all the churches of his deanery, on Sundays and High Days during Mass, that any witnesses in the case are to appear before the Bishop in the cathedral on the Monday after the Feast of St. Dunstan (May 19). The severest penalties of the ecclesiastical courts being stripes and imprisonment, John Bernard, even if guilty, escaped hanging, unless he was handed over to the secular arm.

Certain "iniquitatis filii," unknown, of Chatteris, having detained certain rents due to the Bishop, viz., 9d. from a tenement formerly John Ffithion's,[1] and 16d. from other tenements, the Vicar of Chatteris is ordered to warn the guilty parties on Sundays and High Days during Mass, to pay these rents within fifteen days under pain of excommunication.

[1] *I.e.*, Featherstonhaugh.

Certain miscreants living in Bardney Moor having driven off the Bishop's cattle, the Chaplain of Doddington is ordered to denounce them "cum cruce erecta, pulsatis campanis, candelis accensis et postmodum extinctis ac in eorum vituperationem in terram projectis et pedibus conculcatis."

A like ceremonial is observed in the case of some unknown scoundrels who, one Epiphany night, entered Ely Cathedral, removed the wooden *capsa* covering the *feretrum* of St. Etheldred, and stole therefrom rings, brooches (*firmacula*), and other jewels.

On August 23, 1378, the Bishop is ordered to denounce throughout his diocese certain unknown miscreants who had violated the sanctuary of Westminster, slaying in the Abbey Church a fugitive who had sought refuge there. Accordingly, on Sunday, September 12, "a solemn procession having been made in the Cathedral of Ely by all the priests of Ely, secular and religious, wearing stoles and carrying torches," all who had taken part in this sacrilege were publicly denounced. A subsequent mandate relates that the wrong-doers "Dns Sir Alan de Boxhill, Dns Sir Ralf fferrers," and others, had been thus brought to confession before the Bishop of London, who sent them to Rome to seek absolution from the Pope.

§ 47. Such spiritual censures did not, however, always produce so speedy an effect. Thus, the Master and Fellows of Trinity Hall in 1382 complain to the Chancellor of the University of one Thomas Pond, a priest. Soon afterwards we find the Chancellor passing on the case to the Bishop, inasmuch as Pond "has been under excommunication for forty days, and is still obstinate." This is on September 3, 1382. By-and-by the Bishop in turn has to complain to the King that Thomas Pond, in spite of excommunication, will not obey his monitions. "As he remains obstinate, and the Church can do no more, we pray your Highness to proceed against him."[1] Two years later we find that the secular arm had at length brought the offender to submission; and on January 2, 1385, the Bishop certifies that "dns Thomas atte Pond has returned to the bosom of Holy Mother Church, and humbly sought Absolution."

§ 48. The rights of the parochial clergy are often the subject of mandates. Thus, the parishioners of St. Giles and All Saints' at Cambridge are forbidden to fell the trees in their respective churchyards; and complaints having reached the Bishop that many farmers, having to tithe their sheaves (every tenth sheaf being taken by the tithe-owner), had taken to leaving the larger portion of the corn on the ground, to be collected afterwards with rakes, orders the tithing "omnium bladorum tam rastro congregatorum quam in garbis."

License of three years' non-residence is granted to Robert Gerlthorpe, Rector of Tydd. He may "lease out" his church, but he is to make suitable provision for the duties, and, in compensation for the loss to poor parishioners through his absence, he is to help them each year *juxta vires*.

Similar licenses are granted to the incumbents of Little Gransden, Histon, Kingston, Abington, Elsworth, and Boxworth, mostly for the purpose of keeping their terms in the University. The last-named was not only destitute of a degree, but had not even been ordained. He is to "proceed to the subdiaconate within the time required by law."

§ 49. In 1385 certain lands are assigned to the Rector of Elm, by the Vicar, on condition that he find seven wax

---

[1] The inability of the Church to do more than excommunicate obliged the Civil Power to enforce such of her censures as it desired to see enforced. Amongst these it emphatically numbered those against the Lollard Socialists, and this led to the Act *De Hæretico Comburendo* being passed by Parliament.

candles, weighing seven pounds, "to burn before the High Altar on all Chief Festivals, at High Mass, Mattins, and Vespers, and on other festivals four, three, or two at the least." The candles to be renewed quarterly, and the Rector to pay to the fabric of the church half a mark (6s. 8d.) per month in default of lighting such candles.

In 1389, Simon Romayn, Rector of Fen Ditton, is permitted to enlarge the manse of his rectory by taking over an adjoining house and garden.

The cemetery of Whittlesford having been polluted by blood, the Bishop of Killala ("Aladensis") is commissioned to "reconcile" it (1389).

Two priests of Tydd St. Giles, who, in defending themselves against a highwayman, have cut off his thumb, are to be examined by a commission for "irregularity." But if they are found to have acted only in self-defence, they are to be permitted to resume "the Ministry of the Altar," from which they have voluntarily abstained pending this inquiry.

License of ordination is given in 1388 to William Stuntenyle, a Bishop's *nativus*, or born serf, thus setting him free for life; and another of this class we find temporarily relieved from the accustomed services due to his master, and freed by the Bishop "ab omni jugo servitutis, pro toto tempore nostro," *i.e.*, during the current episcopate. Entire manumission is given in another case.

§ 50. In 1380 we meet with the "ordination" of the vicarage of Grantchester, the rectory being assigned to Corpus Christi College, in whom it is still vested. The "church" (*i.e.*, the rectory) is said to be rated at £21 6s. 8d., and to be actually worth £32 14s. 8d. annually. The ordinary burdens do not exceed half a mark. The Vicar is to take all fees, also tithes of lambs, wool, calves, fowls, pigeons, geese, hemp, flax, fruit, milk, eggs, mills, gardens, and hay. This last item is compounded for at 13s. 4d. annually. Also of the church lands he is to have twenty acres of arable, worth 16s. 8d. (*i.e.*, 10d. per acre), and two of meadow, worth 3s. 4d. per acre. He is also to have £2 per annum from the college, who are to build a Vicarage house of the rateable value of £4 per annum, till the completion of which he and his family are to reside in the Rectory house. The College are to be responsible for the chancel, and to find all needful service books, which, however, the Vicar must keep in due repair, and rebind when needful. He must also find bread, wine, and lights for the services, and exercise due hospitality.

We are thus enabled to form a comparison between the status of the clergy then and now, and find it to be almost exactly the same. The Vicar of Grantchester now receives £240 per annum, having commuted his very complicated tithes for 78 acres of additional land. The glebe thus amounts to 100 acres, bringing in £146, while the College augmentation has risen to £84. Originally it was equivalent to about £40, the land to about £25, and the tithe, presumably, to the rent of some 80 acres, at, say, £1 10s. per acre, making the total income £225, besides the fees, which most probably were very much the same as now, £10. The Vicarage house is now rated at £55.

§ 51. In March, 1377, we meet with the first reference to the famous "poll-tax," destined shortly to stir up the great rebellion which history associates with the name of Wat Tyler. A brief is issued for raising this groat per head "from all priests, deacons, sub-deacons, acolytes, clerics of first tonsure, and all members of hospitals, of both sexes, if over fourteen years of age, and not evidently mendicants." The Bishop deputes the Prior and Chapter of Ely to collect this subsidy throughout the diocese, clerks studying at the University, the four Orders of Mendicants (Franciscans, Dominicans, Carmelites, and Augustinians), and other notoriously poor persons to be exempt. Two days later another mandate orders that the Cambridge students *are* to pay the tax, which, however, the appointed collectors find it impossible to obtain from them. On June 6, accordingly, the Bishop issues a commission to the Chancellor, making *him* responsible for the University quota.

§ 52. We have already seen references to the other great grievance of the peasant revolters in the various entries above given concerning the manumission of *nativi*. These bondsmen had by this time arrived at a stage when the breaking of their bonds became inevitable. It was the Black Death, as we shall see, which finally brought this about; but other causes of much longer standing were working to that end. The *nativus*, or villain, was, as has been already mentioned, far from being a mere slave at any time, and by this date he had reached a fairly high position in the social scale, and was resolved to rise to independence.

A typical case is given by Mr. Powell, in his able monograph on the rising in East Anglia, of one Robert Souter, who, by the advice of his parson, had withdrawn the "customary" services due to his lord. These "services" consisted in finding for the lord two days' ploughing annually, and four half-days' mowing, two half-days' hoeing, six days' reaping, and one day corn-carting. Three hens at Christmas and fifteen eggs at Easter were also exacted from him, besides "fines" on any marriage in his family, and at each succession to his holding. On these terms he held twenty-four acres and two messuages, at the almost nominal rent of 5d. per acre.[1]

He and his neighbours in like case had formed a Land League, and issued a "No Rent" manifesto, for which they were tried (1385), and fined about £3.

The Patent Rolls of 1381 supply a like example. John Reeve, of Sutton, presents to the Bishop's justices

[1] See above, § 18.

that the Prior, as Lord of Sutton, has seized his beasts, and kept them till he paid a hundred shillings. The Prior answers that John Reeve is his villain, and that the goods were seized because he would not submit to the just claims of his lord. And as John Reeve cannot deny his villenage he loses his cause.

§ 53. It was, then, by no means the mere dregs of the population (though Walsingham does call them "discaligati ribaldi") who, in Cambridgeshire at least, joined in the revolt of Wat Tyler. We find that the leaders were in many cases men of good family, that the clergy sympathized with the movement, and that the King himself was currently believed to be behind it. Nor does this belief seem to have been groundless. Richard II., then a brave and enthusiastic boy of fifteen, would appear really to have been carried away by revolutionary sentiment, and to have uttered no feigned words when, on the death of Wat Tyler, he rode in alone amongst the revolters, exclaiming: "I am your Captain." Nor were the charters which he issued to the various counties represented in the peasant army at Mile End intended for the mere frauds they are commonly considered.

§ 54. These charters ran as follows: "Richardus Dei gratia rex Angliæ et Franciæ, et dominus Hiberniæ: omnibus balliuis et fidelibus suis, ad quos præsentes litteræ pervenerint, salutem. Sciatis quod de gratia nostra speciali manumisimus universos ligeos et singulos subditos nostros et alios comitatus Cantabrigii, et ipsos et eorum quemlibet ab omni bondagio exuimus, et quietos facimus per præsentes, ac etiam perdonamus eisdem ligeis ac subditis nostris omnimodas felonias, proditiones, transgressiones, et extortiones, per ipsos vel aliquem eorum qualitercunque factas sive perpetratas, ac etiam utlagariam et utlagarias, si qua vel quæ in ipsos vel aliquem ipsorum fuerit vel fuerint his occasionibus promulgata vel promulgatæ, et summam pacem nostram eis et eorum cuilibet inde concedimus. In cujus rei testimonium, has litteras nostras fieri fecimus patentes. Teste meipso apud London 15 die Junii. Anno regni nostri quarto."

§ 55. But though Richard would fain have supported the popular movement, he almost immediately found that it was a mere flash in the pan. The grievances of villenage were not heavy enough to inspire the peasants with that rooted passion which alone can make a peasant revolt successful. Far stronger proved to be the feeling of the upper classes against them; and in a very few days the young King found himself forced by self-preservation to repudiate any countenance of so feeble an outbreak, to withdraw his charters, and to take the lead in chastising those who had misled him into granting them. His avenging host did not, however, enter Cambridgeshire; where both the revolt and its suppression seem to have taken a milder form than in the neighbouring districts.

§ 56. In our County, indeed, the whole insurrection lasted considerably less than a week. On Saturday, June 15th, the rioting began, and by Tuesday, the 18th, it was over. On that day there appeared upon the scene the Bishop of Ely, who had heard of the disorders in his diocese while with the King in London. "The pious pastor, therefore, left London, and came, as he was bound, to succour his people. And finding certain of the wicked mob at Cambridge, he slew some, imprisoned others, and others he sent back to their homes after taking their oath that they would never turn out for like purpose of mischief."[1]

§ 57. They had certainly succeeded in compressing a large amount of mischief into their three days' outbreak. The rising took place in every part of the county simultaneously, and assumed the form of looting and burning the houses of obnoxious individuals, the Priory of Barnwell and the preceptories of the Knights of Jerusalem at Shingay

[1] Capgrave, "De Illustribus Henricis."

and Chippenham being special objects of attack; while in Cambridge itself there was sacking of colleges and wholesale destruction of the University charters and records. The University chest in Great St. Mary's was broken open, and in every college and hostel the masters and scholars were compelled to surrender every document belonging to them, the whole being finally burnt on Market Hill, where an old woman, Margaret Starre, is said to have voiced the general sentiment by exclaiming, as she scattered the ashes, "Away with the skill of the clerks! Away with it!" And all this was done with the sanction of the Mayor, whom the rioters terrorized into heading them by conjuring with the names of the King and the "Magna Societas"—the great Agricultural Labourers' Union which they were endeavouring to establish. But the wild outburst of anarchy subsided as suddenly as it rose, leaving no abiding trace behind.

§ 58. It was far otherwise with the great social cataclysm, which was, indeed, at the root of this outburst. The peasant revolt was the outcome of the Black Death, that awful visitation which, in the middle of the fourteenth century, swept away so vast a proportion of the human race. Allowing for all exaggeration in the panic-stricken chroniclers of the age, it is evident that the growth of population in England then received a check from which it did not recover for at least four centuries. And the destruction fell especially upon the better-to-do classes, the clergy, and the larger land-holders, thus at once causing a wide-spread dislocation of the labour market and loosening the accustomed bonds of social life throughout the rural districts. Labourers, whose fixed employment was lost with the loss of their masters, wandered away in search of work, and speedily found that the general scarcity of hands enabled them to demand far more than the wonted wages. The ferocious laws passed by Parliament to restrain this tendency, the fixing of the price of labour to that current before the Death began, the making it penal to refuse work at this price, the branding on the forehead of every serf found straying from his parish—all testify to the seething confusion throughout the land, which culminated in the eruption of Wat Tyler's rebellion.

§ 59. A touching testimony is borne to this fearful plague in an inscription still to be seen engraved inside the tower of Ashwell, at the source of the Cam. In rude characters (some of them curiously Greek in shape) a contemporary hand has recorded disjointed fragments of rough Latin verse dealing with the calamity, as follows:

"M . Ct . Xpenta . miseranda . ferox . violenta .
M . CCC . L .
Supest . plebs . pessima . testis . in . fineque . vents .
Validus . oc . anno . maurus . in . orbe . tonat .
M . CCC . LXI."

The opening words are conjectured by Dr. Montagu James to stand for the date: *Ct* being *C ter* or *CCC*, and *Xpenta* being *X* five times repeated, *i.e.*, fifty. Thus the whole would run:

"1350! Wretched, wild, distracted 1350!
The worst and lowest yet live to tell.
And in the end a tempest.
In this year 1361 the Power of Darkness thunders mightily in the world."

The last two lines are probably metaphorical, and refer to the popular commotions already beginning. *Maurus* is a not uncommon mediæval periphrasis for Satan.

§ 60. Just before this fatal year of death the Cathedral of Ely had assumed the form which it still retains, and which is shared by no other church in Christendom. That form was due to a great calamity. In 1322, on February 12, the great Norman tower fell, as so many Norman towers have fallen, ruining the whole central portion of the edifice. Happily, amongst the monks there was found an architect of real genius, Alan de Walsingham, just then holding the office of Sacrist, and thus responsible for the fabric, who proved equal to the occasion.

"For the moment," says the chronicler, "he knew not whither to turn amid such a mass of ruin. But recovering his courage, and confident in the help of God and of His kind Mother Mary, and in the merits of the holy virgin Etheldred, he laid his hand to the work. And first, with great labour, he removed the stones and timber fallen in the ruin . . . and having measured out by architectural art eight positions . . . he caused them to be dug out . . . and with stones and sand firmly made solid. He then, at last, began the eight columns" of his noble Lantern, an absolutely original conception, which was not finally completed till 1348, when the then sacrist, John of Ely, having, as usual, kept a place in his annual account for "the new work," leaves it unfilled, as having at last no expenditure to record.[1]

§ 61. The next year saw the completion of the other great work which has made Ely what it is. The foundation of the Lady Chapel had been laid just before the catastrophe recorded above, and while Alan of Walsingham was himself elaborating the lantern, his subordinate, John of Wisbeach, was carrying out his plans with the adjoining structure. "For twenty-eight years and thirteen weeks did he continue the work with the greatest solicitude," being responsible not only for its structural, but also for its financial, soundness. At one time, we read, the funds came in so slowly as to threaten an entire suspension of the operations. In this strait, John

[1] Part of the expenditure consisted in the repairs of all the bridges around Ely, for the heavy traffic necessitated, and particularly for the transit of the huge trunks of specially chosen oak-trees to form the framing of the lantern.

betook himself to special prayers, and, on the very last day before his cash gave out, found his pick strike against a potter's vessel in the ground. Waiting till his workmen had gone to dinner, he unearthed his find, which proved to be full of gold coins (probably an ancient British hoard), and thus enabled him to carry on his work to a conclusion. He just lived to see it finished, dying three months later in the first sweep of the Black Death.

CHAPTER VII.

"PERPENDICULAR" PERIOD.

§ 1—2. Results of the Black Death—Free labour—Perpendicular architecture—Insularity—John Bull.
§ 3—13. The first colleges—Peterhouse—Michaelhouse—King's Hall—Early collegiate life—Special studies—Pembroke—Clare—Assize of Barnwell—Ely manors—Stock—"Smoke farthings"—Spoliation of the see.
§ 14—27. Foundation of King's College—Henry VI.—Eton—Will of King Henry VI.—Queens' College—Wars of the Roses—Completion of King's College Chapel—Milton's and Wordsworth's descriptions of it.
§ 28—31. Heralds of the Reformation—Reginald Pecocke—Jesus College founded.
§ 32—38. Bassingbourn accounts—Inventory—The Use of Sarum.

§ 1. THE Black Death lies like a dark streak across the line of our annals. After it had passed, and its attendant convulsions with it, we find ourselves, historically, in a new region. Quiet has settled down upon the County, and society is reorganizing itself on fresh and more familiar lines. For the pestilence had done its work, and shattered the old social conceptions of the realm. King, Lords, and Commons might pass laws binding the labourer by the old bonds of villenage; but their decrees were powerless against the yet stronger mandates of Political Economy. Demand would create supply, and draw the now precious labour, however legally attached to the soil, whither it was most sorely needed. Henceforward, therefore, we find the "villain" no more. Almost at a bound he develops into the free hind, tied, as now, only by the current restrictions of the open labour market, and able, whatever the law might say, to sell his work for the best price obtainable.

§ 2. Thus, much that was mediæval and romantic disappeared from our social life, to give place to ideas more prosaic and more modern. The contrast between the new style of architecture which at this time came in, the "Perpendicular," with its scientific but rigid lines, and the flowing grace of the later "Decorated," is a not inapt measure of the difference between the new and the old England after and before the Death. In another respect, too, this contrast helps us to realize the change which at this date took place. The earlier styles had been common to all "Gothic" architecture in every land. "Norman," "Early English," and "Decorated" work is to be found in France and Germany, no less than in England. But "Perpendicular" is a purely English development, and appropriately appears at the time when our insular characteristics began most strongly to develop themselves. It is about this date that we first meet with the familiar "John Bull" as a general term for "Englishman,"[1] and also find the expletive which has unhappily remained as our special national oath already distinctive of English lips.[2]

§ 3. The rural life of our County thus assumed the familiar form which it has exhibited ever since. And along with it the University, too, took upon itself the shape which it has retained to this day. For now came

---

[1] The earliest example I know of is in a Breton ballad of 1347 (Villemarqué).

[2] Joan of Arc, on being pressed to take food before attacking the English at Orleans, is said to have replied, "I will not eat save with a goddam" (*i.e.*, an English prisoner). This was in 1429.

that great development of the College system which transformed ancient into modern Cambridge. Peterhouse, as we have seen, had begun the process two generations earlier. But even Peterhouse did not fully organize itself till 1338, by which time the rival foundation of Michaelhouse (the germ of Trinity College) was over ten years old, and the neighbouring King's Hall, destined also to be absorbed in Trinity, already in being. Simultaneously with these arose Clare Hall. Ten years later, again, in 1347, was founded Pembroke Hall, in 1348 Gonville Hall, in 1350 Trinity Hall, in 1352 Corpus Christi College. This rapid succession of foundations, unparalleled even at Oxford, shows how rapidly the ideal of University life was changing. Henceforward the Fellows of colleges became the recognised aristocracy among the Masters, and their Scholars amongst the students.

§ 4. From the earliest days these two elements formed part of every College system. Nowhere do we find at Cambridge any corporation, like All Souls' at Oxford, consisting of Fellows only; though the number of Fellowships was everywhere much larger in proportion to the Scholarships than it afterwards became. Thus, at Peterhouse there were fourteen Fellows to two or three "Indigent Scholars"; at Michaelhouse eight Fellows to four "Bible Clerks"; at Pembroke twenty-four Fellows to six "Minor Scholars," or "Students." The idea in every case was to keep the College Body exceedingly select, and as far as possible self-contained, association with the promiscuous horde of hostel students outside being rigidly guarded against. As fast as the college finances allowed, buildings were erected, forming an enclave which the younger members, at least, were seldom permitted to pass, save (under escort of some senior) for their exercises in the Schools, or their devotions in the nearest parish church. And as soon as a College was able to build itself a chapel of its own, their seclusion became yet more complete.

§ 5. The early accounts of King's Hall, where as many as thirty-two Scholars had been established by Edward III. (an expansion of his father's sustentation of thirteen "Children of our Chapel" at the University), give us a contemporary picture of this early collegiate life. The foundation provided the Scholars with lodging, food, and clothing. The food was plentiful; the college kitchen supplying meat and fish (mostly salted), its bakery bread, its brewery beer, its garden vegetables, its vineyard vinegar, and its cellar wine (imported annually from Bordeaux). The college laundry, moreover, provided the students with napkins and table-cloths in Hall (a great piece of luxury at that date), and also washed for the Society; which even kept a barber to shave and physic its members, one of his special functions being the "minutio," or periodic blood-letting, which was a regular feature of mediæval community life, submitted to by each inmate in turn. For exercise, archery, tennis and bowls were provided (space permitting) in the college grounds. The Scholars were forbidden to supplement the "robes and furs" provided for their attire by any vain or indecorous apparel, such as red or green shoes, finger-rings, or embroidered girdles. The wearing of arms was strictly prohibited, also that of long hair or beard. Dogs then, as now, were contraband in college, as were hawks. Latin or French only was allowed to be spoken at meals, which, indeed, were mostly consumed in silence, while the Bible or some other edifying book was read aloud (a practice of which the survival may to this day be traced at Eton College). The Master alone had a separate bedchamber of his own, the other rooms mostly accommodating two Fellows apiece, while the young Scholar had to content himself with the moiety of a "trundle-bed"—a couch on low wheels, which lived during the day beneath the senior's standing bedstead, and was drawn out for the night.

In the Patent Rolls we find on September 9, 1377, the confirmation of a grant made by "the late King" (Edward III.) to the Warden and Scholars of King's Hall. The former is to have 4d. per diem (equivalent to about £100 per annum), and each of the thirty-two latter 2d. per diem. The income of the College from this source must thus have represented nearly £2,000 per annum. The Warden (Simon de Nayland) is, moreover, allowed 8 marks yearly for two official robes, the one lined with fur, the other of linen.

§ 6. Such was the earliest collegiate life, when fully developed in its own buildings. This consummation, however, was not reached for a good many years after the foundation of a College, which almost invariably began its existence in some private lodging-house.

§ 7. To deal in detail with the origin and progress of each particular college scarcely falls within the scope of a popular history of Cambridgeshire. The subject has been exhaustively treated in various easily accessible works, notably those of Mr. J. W. Clark and Mr. J. B. Mullinger. While all had the same general object, and were founded on the same general lines, each of these earliest Colleges tended to specialize in some particular branch of study. The "Scholars of Ely," as they were originally called, at Peterhouse, were mostly to devote themselves to "Arts" (*i.e.*, Classics, particularly Aristotle) and Theology. Two, however, of the Fellowships were to be assigned for proficiency in Canon and Civil Law, while one was given to the encouragement of Medicine. Gonville Hall (so called from its founder, Edmund Gonville, Vicar-General of the Diocese of Ely) strictly confined its members to Logic and Theology. Trinity Hall, on the other hand, founded by William Bateson, afterwards Bishop of Norwich, was equally strict in the direction of legal studies. Of its twenty Fellows, ten were required to read Civil, and seven Canon, Law. This was done with the express object of filling up the terrible gap in the ranks of the learned professions made by the Black Death. And it may be noticed that this College alone retains to the present day the stamp impressed upon it by its Founder.

§ 8. The above-mentioned Colleges were all of clerical origin. King's Hall, as we have seen, was a Royal Foundation. Michaelhouse was the creation of a statesman, Hervey de Stanton, Chancellor of the Exchequer under Edward II., and was endowed by him chiefly with Church lands and benefices, such as that of Barrington, which still remain as the heritage of Trinity College; while Corpus Christi (which, like Trinity Hall, was expressly meant to repair the ravages of the Black Death amongst the clergy) was called into being by two Cambridge "guilds," or Friendly Societies, those of Corpus Christi and of the Blessed Virgin, whose names are still recorded in the full designation of the College.

§ 9. The two remaining foundations on the fourteenth-century list were due to the private sorrows of two noble ladies. Marie de Valence ("Maria de Sancto Paulo," as the contemporary deeds call her), a high-born dame, related to the blood royal both of France and England, saw her husband, Amory de Valence, Earl of Pembroke, slain before her eyes in a joust on the very day of their wedding. The cruel shock drove her to seek solace in the practice of benevolence; and, after having established Minor Sisters at Waterbeach and at Denny, she proceeded to commemorate her husband by the College which still bears his name, though originally called by her own, "Domus de Valencemarie." In her statutes she particularly connects her House with the Franciscan Order, to which she had affiliated herself, and with her own native land of France. "Kindness" to the former (and in especial to the nuns of Denny) is solemnly enjoined on her Scholars; while if there could be found, either at Cambridge or Oxford, any duly-qualified Frenchman, he was to have preference in elections to her Fellowships. The qualifications required were that the candidate should be a Bachelor of Arts, freeborn and legitimate, whose private income amounted to less than 6 marks (equivalent, at present rates, to about £80) per annum, and who held no public office of greater value. Things being equal, the Fellowship was to be bestowed on the most orderly and most proficient in his studies—a provision in which we see the first germ of competitive examination for this coveted position. At least half the Fellows were to be in Holy Orders.

§ 10. The less tragic widowhood of Elizabeth de Burgh, who lost three successive husbands, led her to follow the example of Marie de Valence. She was heiress of the great House of Clare, which played so prominent a part in early Plantagenet history, and it was, therefore, by its name that she called her Cambridge foundation, which was, indeed, rather a reconstruction of an earlier house, hitherto called University Hall, which Richard Badew, Chancellor of the University, was vainly striving to establish. Her code is chiefly noticeable for the limit of age it sets up in the case of the junior members of her Society, who, unless elected to Fellowships by the age of twenty, become superannuated and have to leave the College. Clare is supposed, on somewhat vague conjecture, to be the "Solere Hall" of Chaucer, in the Reeve's Tale. The poet himself is also said to have been a student here—as vague a guess. It is more certain that Richard Crookback, both as King and as Duke of Gloucester, held himself of Founder's kin, and took special interest in the College.

§ 11. This great outburst of activity was followed by nearly a century of pause, while the new collegiate system took root and bore fruit in the University. Then succeeded another galaxy of foundations, which practically completed the work. King's College was founded 1441,

Queens' 1448, St. Catharine's 1473, Jesus 1496, Christ's 1505, St. John's 1511, Magdalene 1542, Trinity 1546. Meanwhile, nothing more interesting took place, either in the University or the County, than the successful stand made by the former against the visitatorial jurisdiction claimed over it by the See of Ely. After prolonged contention, the question was finally decided by appeal to Pope Martin V., who appointed the Prior of Barnwell as his delegate. The cause was heard in the chapter-house of Barnwell Abbey, and judgment given for the University—a judgment subsequently confirmed in 1433 by Eugenius IV., the Pope of the Council of Florence, at which representatives of the University were present, not without distinction, as also they had been at Constance.

§ 12. At this period the See of Ely possessed no fewer than ten episcopal residences : six in the diocese, at Ely, Balsham, Ditton, Doddington, Downham, and Wisbeach; and the rest comprising Ely House, Holborn (where was the strawberry-garden referred to in Shakespeare's "Richard III.," Act III., Scene 4), Hatfield House (afterwards the famous seat of the Cecil family), Hadham in Hertfordshire, and Somersham in Huntingdonshire. Appendant to these demesnes was a certain stock (called "implementa episcopatus") of cattle, which every Bishop swore, on enthronement, to leave entire to his successor, viz., 471 oxen, valued (in 1368) at 20s. apiece, 292 stots at 13s. 4d., and 41 draught horses at 20s. Besides the revenue derived from his various manors, the Bishop of Ely levied by ancient custom on every parish in Cambridgeshire "a certaine tribute called 'Elie farthings,' or 'Smoke farthings,' which the Churchwardens do levie according to the number of chimneys that be in the parish."[1]

§ 13. This tax remained a source of income to the

[1] Clay, "History of Waterbeach" (1590), p. 114. This tax is mentioned as already ancient in 1134.

See down to the period of the Civil War, while that from land was grievously curtailed by Elizabeth. On the deprivation of Bishop Thirlby, in 1558, that rapacious Queen seized the entire property of the See, returning but a poor moiety to his Protestant successor, Bishop Cox. From him further surrenders were exacted (notably that of Ely House, Holborn), under threat of deprivation. Strype's history of the Reformation is the authority for the well-known scene in which Elizabeth is said to have replied to his remonstrances: "Proud priest! I made you. And I will unmake you. Obey my pleasure, or I will immediately unfrock you." And this threat she was actually proceeding to carry into effect, when his death forestalled her, in 1580. Not till 1600 did she appoint his successor, meanwhile devoting the whole income of the See to her own benefit.

§ 14. We now reach the crowning point in the architectural history of Cambridge, the erection of

"That immense
And glorious pile of fine intelligence"

which still remains the distinctive glory of the University, overshadowing every earlier and every later building in the town, King's College Chapel. And had the designs of the Founder been carried out, that chapel, instead of standing as an isolated witness to their magnificence, would have formed part of a series of collegiate buildings worthy of itself in grandeur—courts, cloisters, gardens, turreted walls and gateways, and a bell-tower as lofty and as graceful as that of Magdalen at Oxford. "The like colledge," says the historian Stow, "could scarce have been found againe in any Christian land."

§ 15. This truly regal conception seems to have been due almost wholly to the individual initiative of "the royal saint," King Henry VI., and to have been the dream of his life. When only eighteen he began to work out his great ideal by a visit, in July, 1440, to Winchester, there to study in person the system of education established by the genius of William of Wykeham, whereby his scholars, beginning their education there, were passed on for its completion to his New College at Oxford. What William of Wykeham had thus done for Oxford, Henry of Windsor resolved to do for Cambridge. That same year, on October 11, he signed the charter of foundation for Eton, and on February 12 following, that for the sister college at Cambridge, "the Royal College of St. Nicholas," so called from his own birth on December 6, still, to all Etonians, "Founder's Day." Shortly afterwards ("being moved thereto, as we trust, by the inspiration of the Holy Spirit") he somewhat enlarged his plan, changing the name of his Cambridge foundation to "Our College Royal of St. Mary and St. Nicholas," and the title of its head to the distinctively Etonian style "Provost," expressly in order "to weld the two colleges together in an everlasting bond of brotherhood." Seven years more were taken up with the complicated legal transactions necessary for the transfer to the college of its destined site—a site then thick with houses and intersected by streets, clustering around the parish church of St. John Zachary, which stood near the west end of the chapel.

§ 16. Finally, in March, 1448, was signed that marvellous monument of minute elaboration and princely generosity, the "Will of King Henry the Sixth"—not a post-mortem testament, but an expression of purpose to be carried out, as he hoped, beneath the eye of the testator. Already he seems to have visited the college in order to be present on St. James's Day, July 25, 1446, at the laying of the first stone of the chapel, an event recorded in the following lines still preserved in the chapel register of Papal Bulls:

> "Altaris petram quam Rex superedificavit
> Henricus . vj^{tus} hic sacrificando dicavit
> Annis . M.CCCC . sexto quarter . X . d.
> Regis et h. regni quarto iungendo viceno.

"In festo sancti Jacobi sanctam stabiliuit
Hic unctam petram Regia sacra manus.
Ex orientali medio si bis septem pedetimtim
Mensurare velis inuenies Lapidem.
Astiterant Regi tunc pontifices in honorem
Actus solennis Regis et ecclesie."[1]

And in the "Will" he gives the most careful and minute directions, enumerating every dimension of the chapel, the cloister, the bell-tower, the "quadrant" (*i.e.*, court), the library, lecture-rooms, hall, kitchen, and Provost's lodge; so that it is quite possible, from this document alone, to form a ground-plan, and even an elevation, of what was intended. "The Chirch," we read, "shall conteyne in length cciiij^{xx}viij [*i.e.*, 288] fete of assise withoute any yles and alle of the wideness of .xl. fete . . . the walles of the same chirche to be in height iiij^{xx}x [*i.e.*, 90] fete embatelled vauted and chare rofted sufficiently boteraced and euery boterace fined with finialx.

"And in the Est ende of the said chirche shall be a wyndowe of .xj. daies and in the west . . . a windowe of .ix. daies and betwix euery boterace a wyndowe of .v. daies. And betwix euery of the same boteraces in the body of the chirche on bothe sides of the same chirche a closette with an auter therin conteynyng in lengthe .xx. fete and in brede .x. fete vauted and finisshed unther the soil of the yle windowes. And the pament of the chirche to be enhaunced .iiij. fete aboue the groundes without and the heighte of the pament of the quere .j. fote d:' aboue the pament of the chirche and the pament at the high auter .iij. fete aboue that."

§ 17. The bell-tower, 200 feet west of the chapel, and thus nearly on the bank of the river, is directed to be 24 feet square "within the walles," and 120 feet in height

[1] These hitherto unpublished lines were first printed for the service held in commemoration of the 450th anniversary of the laying of the foundation-stone of King's College Chapel, July 25, 1896. The Will of Henry VI. was also then printed in full for the first time.

"vnto the corbel table, and .iiij. small tourettis ouer that, fined with pynacles."[1] The great court, of which the chapel is to form the north side, is to be 200 feet by 230, with the library on the west, 110 feet long, and the hall opposite the chapel 100 feet. "And in the myddel of the said large quadrant shalbe a condute goodly deuised for the ease of the said College."

§ 18. "And I wol that the edificacion of my same College procede in large fourme clene and substancial, settyng a parte superfluitie of too gret curious werkes of entaille and besy moldyng. . . . And I wol that both my seid Colleges be edified of the most substancial and best abidyng stuffe of stone ledde glas and yron that may goodly be had."

§ 19. The expenses are charged upon the revenues of the Duchy of Lancaster, with a yearly endowment (for the two colleges) of £2,000, and a reserve fund of £1,000 "for a Tresour to be kept within them for diuerse grete causes." Even the wages of the workmen are specified. The "Maister of the werkes" is to have £50 per annum, the clerk £48 13s. 4d., the chief mason £16 13s. 4d., the chief carpenter £12 8s., the chief smith £6 13s. 4d. To Eton is assigned £200 "in monee for to puruey theym of bokes to the pleasir of God and wele of my same College." King's is to receive a like special donation of £100 "forto stuf theym with ioialx [jewels] for the seruice of God."

§ 20. In case of his death, the King entrusts the execution of his design to William of Waynfleet, the chosen friend who had worked with him from its beginning, by bringing a colony of Wykehamists to be the first Etonians, "consideryng . . . his high trougth and feruent zele which at alle times he hath hadde and hath vnto my weel and whiche I have founde and proued in hym." And he concludes with a solemn and touching appeal to his executors

---

[1] The original drawing of the design for this tower is in the British Museum, and is reproduced in Lysons' "Cambridgeshire."

and successors, "in the vertue of the aspercion of Christes blessed blode and of his peyneful passion that they hauyng God and myne entent oonly before their eyen ... truely feithfully and diligently execute my same wil and euery part thereof, as they wol answere before the blessed and dredeful visage of oure Lord Jhesu in his most fereful and last dome, when euery man shal most streitly be examined and demed after his demeritees.

§ 21. "And, furthermore, ... I in the most entier and most feruent wise pray my seid heirs and successors, and euery of theym, that they shewe them self welwillyng feithful and tender lovers of my desire in this behalf: And in the bowelles of Christ our alder juste and streit Juge, exorte theym to remember the terrible comminacions and full fearfull imprecacions of holy scripture agayns the brekers of the lawe of god, and the letters of goode and holy werkes. The which imprecacions holy scripture reherseth in the book of Deuteronomy [xxviii. 15-25].

§ 22. "I also in amyable wise exorte my seid heires and successours in Crist Jhesu the liberal rewarder of alle good deedes to remembre the desirable blessing and the most bounteyouse grace promytted to al suche as observe the precepts of the lawes of Crist beyng helpers and promoters of good and vertues desires, Scripture in the same place saying unto such *Venient super te vniuerse benedicciones*," etc. [Deut. xxviii. 2-11].

§ 23. So ends this notable document, which Mr. J. W. Clark rightly calls "one of the most remarkable works in the English language." Its style shows that we are now on the verge of the Augustan period of our national literature, the period when, within a century of this date, our tongue reached its utmost perfection in Cranmer's Bible and the writings of Sir Thomas More. And its matter is full of touching interest when we look at the grievous troubles which maimed the carrying out of its

purport, and darkened the remaining years of its gifted
and devoted author. When he signed it, in March, 1448,
he was still but twenty-six, and when in the following
month his young Queen, Margaret of Anjou, then only
twenty, "restless with holy emulation of her husband's
bounty," founded in her turn the " Queen's College of
St. Bernard and St. Margaret," everything seemed to point
to a long and peaceful reign, during which the royal pair
might tend the carrying out of their pious purposes.

§ 24. But the very next year began those commotions
destined to ruin both. The national discontent engen-
dered by the loss of France, and therewith of the occasions for distinction and plunder which the French
campaigns afforded, broke out in the murder of the Duke
of Suffolk, the rebellion of Jack Cade, and the pretensions
of the Duke of York to the throne. Two years more,
years of ever-increasing turbulence, and the Wars of the
Roses were fairly begun. King and Queen alike had
lavished their means upon their benefactions, and now
had scarcely £5,000 a year between them in personal
estate. Both were ready cheerfully to endure poverty;
but, with the utmost economy, this sum proved utterly
unequal to the strain of a war budget. The loyalty and
devotion, so conspicuous on the Lancastrian side in this
wretched conflict, availed as little as did the like qualities
amongst the Cavaliers two centuries later, against the
overwhelming superiority of the Yorkists in the "sinews
of war."

§ 25. Thus it came to pass that, in the words of Fuller,
"the sound of all bells in the steeples was drowned with
the noise of drums and trumpets," and neither the King's
College nor the Queen's was completed according to the
Founder's design. The latter, indeed, never even got so far
as to receive a charter at all for over twenty-five years; and
when it did so, it was not from the hand of Margaret, but
(just at the date of her tragic death in exile) from that of

her rival, Elizabeth Woodville, wife of Edward IV. The minute but significant change in the name of the college from Queen's to Queens', calls up before the mind of the historian a whole volume of tragedy.

§ 26. The construction of King's College also passed, with the crown, from Henry of Lancaster to the rival House of York, who seem to have felt that the carrying out of so truly royal a work must not be wholly dropped by anyone pretending to be an English monarch. But it went on very slowly, and on a very different scale from that at first contemplated. Still, it did continue. The war (the effects of which, unlike those before it, were almost confined to the armies actually in the field) did not touch Cambridgeshire, nor even prevent the carriage of stone for the chapel from Henry's chosen quarry at Huddlestone in Yorkshire. And though the tidings of his death scattered the workmen for the moment, with such haste that a half-sawn block of stone lay for 250 years on the site as a witness to their despair, yet the work was soon more or less resumed, and lingered on, with many pauses, to be finally completed by the child whose distant royalty the founder was said to have prophesied—Henry Tudor. Under him were raised to their destined height the halffinished walls, with the dream-like harmony of their coloured windows, which caused the chapel to be described as "a house of glass," and under him, at the cost of £100 per span, was spread over all that "high embowéd roof," the appeal of which, both to eye and ear, awoke the enthusiasm alike of Milton and of Wordsworth. For it is of this chapel, with its soaring beauty and its wonderful acoustic properties, that the former writes in the well-known lines of "Il Penseroso ":

> "But let my due feet never fail
> To walk the studious cloister's pale,
> And love the high embowéd roof,
> With antique pillars massy proof,

And storied windows, richly dight,
Casting a dim religious light.
There let the pealing organ blow
To the full-voiced quire below,
In service high and anthems clear,
As may with sweetness, through mine ear,
Dissolve me into ecstasies,
And bring all heaven before mine eyes."

And the sonnet of the latter "To King's College Chapel" echoes the same strain:

"Tax not the Royal Saint with vain expense,
 With ill-matched aims the Architect, who planned
 (Albeit labouring for a scanty band
 Of white-robed scholars only) this immense
 And glorious work of fine intelligence!
 Give all thou canst, High Heaven rejects the lore
 Of nicely-calculated less or more.
 So deemed the man who fashioned for the sense
 These lofty pillars, spread that branching roof,
 Self-poised, and scooped into ten thousand cells,
 Where light and shade repose, where music dwells,
 Lingering and wandering on, as loth to die,
 Like thoughts whose very sweetness yieldeth proof
 That they were born for immortality."

§ 27. So stands King's College Chapel, a worthy memorial even of one so truly great and good as its sainted founder. And it is interesting to note that it was completed distinctly as a memorial to him. Henry Tudor deliberately chose this method of commemorating him, in preference to paying the exorbitant sums demanded by the Roman Curia for his formal canonization.

§ 28. This preference shows that we are now approaching the religious controversies of the next century. Already, while the Wars of the Roses were filling all thoughts, there was pining to death in his secluded cell at Thorney Abbey, in our County, one of the first sufferers in those controversies—Reginald Pecocke, Bishop of St.

Asaph. Protestants have claimed him as a confessor, because he was a translator of Scripture, and on the ground of his condemnation for heresy by the same ecclesiastical tribunals which stamped out the last of Lollardism; but in truth he suffered, not as a Protestant, but as an extreme Papalist. His advocacy of the doctrine of Papal Infallibility, since so famous, was denounced in 1457 as heresy against "the Holy Catholic Church," the Bulls issued by Pope Calixtus II. in his favour were disregarded, and he was sentenced to lifelong imprisonment, under conditions which would now be called those of a "first-class misdemeanant." He was allowed a room "with a chimney" (*i.e.*, a fire), and a window whence he could see the performance of Mass; also food such as that of a Brother of the Abbey. But he was to have no books except the Bible and the Missal, no writing materials, and no companionship save the occasional visits of one "sad" attendant; nor was he ever permitted to cross the threshold of his apartment. And thus, ere long, ennui and heart-break fretted him to death.

§ 29. The foundation, in 1473, of St. Catharine's College by Robert Woodlark (who as Provost of King's extorted the consent of the University to the exceptional privileges which, for 400 years, exempted that body from all University authority) calls for little remark. But in the next in age we meet with yet another foreshadowing of the coming Reformation. Jesus College was set up by Bishop Alcock of Ely (where his beautiful chapel remains at the north-west corner of the cathedral), in place of the ancient Priory of St. Rhadegunde, as the result of a series of transactions showing forcibly how the old was, at that date, giving place to the new.

§ 30. The account books of the priory are still preserved in the College archives, and show that in 1455 the Society was fully solvent, though far from wealthy, on an income of £70 per annum. As we shall shortly see, the value of money at that date was about ten or twelve times what it is at present. This sum, equivalent to some £800 a year, sufficed, with care, for the expenses of the House; but it left no margin, and thus a single extravagant Prioress was enough to reduce the convent to the verge of ruin. In less than twenty years one such Head had run it deeply into debt. In a deed executed March 13, 1478, the unhappy Sisters speak as follows :

"Whereas we and our predecessors, the Prioresse and Nunnes of the Blessed Mary and S. Rhadegunde, at dyvers tymes before-passed whan we were destitute of money for our pore lyffyng had flesshe of R. Wodecock of Cambrydge boucher into the summe of xxi li. of lawful money of England, which he for our ease many day hath forborne," etc.

In payment of this very considerable butcher's bill, they agree to take two of his daughters, free, amongst the *perhendinantes*,[1] or boarders, by whom their necessities now obliged them to eke out their means.

§ 31. Things, however, were too far gone. In spite of the boarders, the income by 1481 had sunk to only £30, and the Bishop of the diocese had to intervene to save the nunnery from immediate collapse. It was in vain. In 1487 a capable manager, Joan Fulbourn, was appointed Prioress by Alcock (who had succeeded to the episcopate of Ely in the previous year)—but too late. The institution continued to dwindle, and the Royal Letter, which in 1496 authorized him to suppress it altogether in favour of his new College, spoke more truth than such documents usually did when it stated, in the ordinary conventional formula, that the revenues had been squandered, that only two nuns remained, and that "Divine Service, hospitality, and other works of mercy and piety, according to the ordinance of the Founders, could not be discharged."

[1] The word is derived from *prandium*.

And one of the earliest scholars of this new College was Thomas Cranmer.

§ 32. Before the bursting of the great "storm of events" with which that name is associated, we may turn to a happy picture of Cambridgeshire rural life at this period, set forth for us in the Churchwardens' account-books of the parish of Bassingbourn, in the extreme south of the County. These books, extending from 1498 to 1534, are kept with most business-like minuteness, and include receipts and expenditure not only for distinctively church purposes, but for roads, bridges, etc., the churchwardens seeming to have acted also as overseers and surveyors.

§ 33. It was evidently a period of great prosperity. Money was from ten to twelve times dearer than now, barley being 3s. per quarter, and the regular charge for a labourer's keep 2d. per day. We see the abiding effect of the Black Death in the very high rate of his wages, 3d. per day if so kept, and 5d. without keep, equivalent to 24s. per week, which is more than twice the current [1896] rate of wages in the district. Masons, carpenters, and other skilled artisans got 7d. or 8d. a day, while an organ-builder could command as much as a shilling. The general prosperity brought about by these high wages is shown in the large profits made at the "Church Ales" (public entertainments corresponding to the concerts, teas, etc., now often held in connection with places of worship), which took place eight or nine times a year, and brought in a clear average gain, "after all charges borne," of at least ten shillings; the most popular occasion being always May Day.

§ 34. The sums thus received were expended upon the current church expenses; for example:

To Agnes Worthyngton ffor washyng off the Chyrche gere
and mendyng—the yere ended att Ascension in the 13th
yer of Kyng har' the vijth . . . . 3s. 4d.
Washing of the ymages of allablaster . . . 4d.

Scouring 4 pr candlesticks 1 year	4d.
for Baner bering about fields on Rogacion Monday	6d.
for strawing church and fulfylling fonte	1d.
For making out of old surplis 5 challis clothes	2d.
To sexteyn ffor keeping of the bellys the yer	1s. 6d.
For a lyne to the Sanctus bell	4d.
Clerkes wages by yer	25s. 8d.
An organ player at Midsomer	4d.
A sexton's shovel	0s. 4d.
To a bookbinder off Cambryg repairing 10 books	22s. 4d.
Ffor binding 3 mass-books	13s. 8d.
Reparacion of one mass-booke clasp	4s. 0d.
For a book to wrytt in our accounse and the Chyrch onoureamentes	1s. 6d.
Ffor writing this Inventorye of ye Chych goodes	1s. 8d.
5 new torches. For 21 lb. wax and 16 lb. Rosyn and 18 lb. of wyke with the colours	17s. 0d.
The Rood Lights for halfe y^r 12 lb wax	6s. 0d.
Half a yer washing surpples, altares clothes and other lynyns off the chirch	1s. 4d.
Mendyng a slewid surpless,[1] with ye cloth, and setting together of 3	0s. 4d.
Vestment maker ffor 2 dayes in Reparacion of Ch. ger	1s. 5d.
To a vest. m. for reparacion of the vestymentes copis and new clothing and redressing of the canopy about the Sacrament	21s. 0d.
Lose of evil money taken at the May ale	4d.
on good fryday for the holy fyer	2d.

§ 35. The cultivation of the "obit" lands (*i.e.*, lands left by benefactors for annual commemoration of their death) is also entered:

5 quarters of seed barley for sowing	14s. 1d.
harrowyng and rolling	8d.
mowing and carting those grains	8s. 2d.
12 lodes of barley carrying	6s.
24 quarter barley comyng of that crop, threshing	5s.
ditto malting	8s.
ditto houseroom	1s. 1d.
A rope 2 shovels and a payer of plow traces	2s.
A horse 4 days work for the warden to ride upon	0s. 8d.

I.e., a surplice with sleeves.

John Cundal and 2 serv^{ts} 1 days wages	9d.
Their 3 boards	5d.
Rob. Cundal 4 days werke, with his board	1s. 5d.
Thomas Ashwell 1 day and halfe, alowed as for his labour mete and drynk	0s. 6d.
Thos Ashwell 6 days werk	1s.
John Creassy 4 days	1s.
3 days bord off 2 men	9d.

§ 36. Travelling seems to have been fully as cheap as at present. Thus, in connection with a certain "sewt off Chyrche goods" the expenses are as follows:

for a journey to London	1s. 8d.
ditto to Oxford	6s. 8d.
3 times to Cambrygg	11s.
expenses 3 days at Cambryg	10s.
To reteyn Mr Burgoyne	3s. 4d.
Reward to the doctor	6s. 8d.
On jorney of a cumpany to Ely:	
At Hadnam fery	9d.
At Ely, ffor soper ffyre and candyll	4s. 0d.
ffor breakffast	2s. 8d.
horsemeyte	1s. 4d.
Journey to Cambridge at visitacion	1s. 0d.
Journey to London, 7 days and 7 nights, man horse and wages	6s. 8d.

§ 37. Much was spent on the "Reparacions" of the church, and in particular on a new peal of bells; in connection with which we may notice that carriage was no dearer then than now:

Cost of refounding Great bell	4li. 5s. 0d.
Makyng clapper according to bell	0li. 2s. 8d.
Carryage of bell to London and backe ye weight being 20 cwt and 10 lb	1li. 3s. 4d.
Carriage of clapper to London and home weighing 60 lb	0li. 0s. 7d.
ffor the new bell called the trebull with the caryage and other charges to London and homeward	14li. 7s. 8d.
for mendyng of the clapper	4s.
ffor taking down and rehang 3rd bell with new whele	16s. 1d.

"Perpendicular" Period.   181

Ward of Ashwell making 3rd bell ageine and he having all olde stuffe and chargyd for 7 yeres after in all maner Reparac'	10s.	4d.
To smith for rep. watch whele of y° clock		4d.
For a new hour whele to the clocke	2s.	8d.
Organ repar', 9 days and board	9s.	
5 shepe skynnes for mending bellows	1s.	8d.
Halfe a hyde of lether	12s.	
To carver for ymag of S. Margar'	10s.	
Bar of yren with 2 staples and 10 rings to hang a clothe before the ymages of S. Marg' and S. Kater' in Lent on -		4d.
Painter for said images with y^r tabernacles	4li. 6s.	8d.
John Glasyer 24 days work in glassyng	12s.	
his board those 24 days	4s.	
Plummer 2 days on roof		10d.
His seruer		5d.
their bord those 2 days		8d.
9 lb sowdir for theyme	3s.	0d.
6 lb sawdre and nails for leds, with wood for to hete his hyerns to mend the vestre	4s.	
Mason for 5 days work	4s.	
Mason and man 8 days at chyrch wall	8s.	
his seruer for 8 days wages	2s.	8d.
his boy for 4 ditto	1s.	
their boarding	7s.	
To pargett or newe overcastyng the stonework of the stepull with a lode of lyme	4s.	4d
1 lode of flynts and gathering		8d.
2 lodes of stone from Ashwell quarry	4s.	
To carriage and gadering one and a half lodes of stone fo y° chirch wall	1s.	3d.
3 lodes of sand, with carriage	3s.	2d.
6 cwt paument tyle at 2s. 8d. per cwt.	16s.	
and laying	5s.	5d.
6 bundles of lathes ffor closing of the stepul windows contaning in a bundell c piece	3s.	4d.

The final completion of the work was celebrated on St. Margaret's Day, July, 1511, by a grand miracle play, entitled "The Holy Martyr Seynt George," to the expenses of which many of the neighbouring villages contributed.

§ 38. The "Inventorye of yᵉ Churche Goodes" referred to on p. 179 shows how very completely the church was provided with everything needful for the decent performance of Divine service. The wealth of books is especially remarkable, including more than one "bibull." Books at this date, though printing had already come in, were a very expensive item in church expenses. An "antiphoner," or anthem-book, is priced at no less than £2. The service-books at Bassingbourn were according to the Use of Sarum, which everywhere throughout England tended more and more to supplant the less generally popular Uses of Lincoln, York, Hereford, and Bangor. Strange to say, this last seems to have had some currency in Cambridgeshire. We find the monks of Royston Priory petitioning their Visitor, the Bishop of London, for leave to change it for that of Sarum. The petitioners set forth that the Bangor Use is imperfect in itself, and in their performance still more imperfect, from the decayed and torn condition of their books, which they are loath to be at the charge of renewing, unless for the more satisfactory Sarum prayer-books. It was this general adoption of a common standard of worship which paved the way for the decision of the Reformers that "henceforth all the whole Realm should have but one use," and led to the issue of the Book of Common Prayer.

CHAPTER VIII.

REFORMATION PERIOD—I.

§ 1—8. Length of Reformation drama—Causes of Reformation—Fall of Constantinople—Renaissance—Bishop West—Fisher—Christ's and St. John's founded—First pensioners—Erasmus—Sir Thomas More—Greek pronunciation.

§ 9—15. Cromwell Chancellor—Change of curriculum—Despoiling of University—Bishop Goodrych—Suppression of Abbeys—Grievances following—Royston Priory—Latimer's protest—Destruction of shrines—Popular revolts—Cambridgeshire Protestants.

§ 16—22. 'Germans' at Cambridge—Magdalene—Trinity—Regius professorships—Bishop Cox—Libraries destroyed.

§ 23—32. Parish guilds suppressed—Church goods confiscated—Barrington Inventory—Overthrow of morality—Peasant risings.

§ 33—38. Mary at Sawston—Proclaimed at Cambridge—Catholic reaction—Dr. Perne—Marian persecutions—Ridley's farewell to Cambridge.

§ 39—44. Elizabethan counter-change—Disastrous effect of unsettlement—March parish accounts—Caius—Emmanuel—Sidney.

§ 1. THE series of events which form the English "Reformation" was far more extended than the current use of the term would lead us to suppose. The name is commonly confined to the period which began when the charms of Anne Boleyn first led Henry VIII. to repudiate the Pope, and ended with the accession of Boleyn's daughter to the throne. But the movement in which these events were prime factors both began earlier, and continued far later than their respective dates. For many years after Elizabeth succeeded to the Crown it remained a most doubtful question whether England would not revert to Catholicism. Even the Gunpowder Plot was not the hopeless insanity it is commonly held; if, as was probably the case, fully half the population were even then Catholics in heart. And when the failure of that plot settled, once for all, the triumph of Protestantism in the land, it took yet another fifty years of struggle to determine the particular kind of Protestantism most favoured by the nation. Not till the Restoration was anything like an abiding settlement arrived at. And it is this whole period of unstable equilibrium in the religion of the realm which ought to be included (as, indeed, it was by the seventeenth-century Puritans) under the name of the Reformation.

§ 2. During this period our county history will introduce us to almost every one of the chief actors in this religious drama. Henry, Mary, Elizabeth, James I., Charles I., both Cromwells, Wolsey, Fisher, Cranmer, Ridley, Latimer, Parker, Erasmus, all play their part in its pages; the fortunes of many amongst them having, indeed, a most special connection with Cambridgeshire.

§ 3. We have already seen the first foreshadowing of the Reformation movement, in the impulse which made Colleges, rather than Abbeys, the objects of pious benefactions during the fourteenth and fifteenth centuries. And this impulse towards extending the field of knowledge, rather than merely cultivating it within time-hallowed limits, received no small quickening by the invention of the printing-press and the fall of Constantinople. These two great events, alike of incalculable importance in human progress, took place almost simultaneously, the date of the latter being 1453. The result of their mutual interaction was at the same time to bring Western thought into contact with the treasures of Byzantine scholarship, and to provide a means whereby this contact could be effected simultaneously at a number of points hitherto impossible. Thus, ere the century closed, had set in the great tide of the Renaissance, destined to overthrow and efface the old traditional channels of culture, and to prepare men's minds for a like break with the past in matters of religion also.

§ 4. Of this Renaissance Ely Cathedral enshrines a notable example. Bishop West, who succeeded to the See in 1515, was in many ways the typical mediæval prelate. Born of humble origin, the son of a baker at Putney, his abilities speedily brought him to the front. An Eton Scholarship, followed by a King's Fellowship, were, as they might be to-day, the fitting prelude to his career of distinction. Not only did he rise to the episcopate, but he was also employed in the highest diplomatic missions; accompanying Henry, for example, to the Field of the Cloth of Gold. No Bishop of Ely ever lived in greater splendour. We read that he had a hundred servants in rich liveries to attend him, and that two hundred poor were fed daily at his palace gates. And he raised for himself a monument of corresponding magnificence, in the memorial chapel, at the south-east corner of the choir of Ely, which bears his name. The structure is of the very richest and most highly-developed Perpendicular Gothic, the mediæval style carried to its utmost pitch of elaboration. Yet every detail of the decoration is absolutely Renaissance in character, from the arabesque scrolls on the ceiling (reminding us of Raffaelle's work in the Sistine Chapel) to the lettering of the Bishop's motto, GRACIA · DEI · SVM · QVOD · SVM.

§ 5. The artistic work of Bishop West at Ely connects itself with the intellectual work of his friend and contemporary, the great Bishop Fisher, at Cambridge. In that work also we see the ancient spirit of mediæval reverence in its furthest development, interwoven with and influenced by the newer impulse of the Renaissance. His position as successively Master of Michaelhouse, President of Queens', and Chancellor of the University, and yet more his Court favour as confessor to Lady Margaret, mother of Henry VII., enabled him to carry out a series of well-planned efforts for the encouragement of the New Learning. He induced his royal patroness to found no fewer than three institutions for this end: the Lady Margaret Professorship of Divinity in 1503, Christ's College in 1505, and St. John's College in 1516. Each of the two latter was a development of an earlier foundation which had outgrown its usefulness: Christ's of an old grammar-school known as "God's House," and St. John's College of that Hospital of St. John which Hugh de Balsham, two hundred and fifty years earlier, had vainly tried to incorporate with his earliest collegiate venture.[1]

§ 6. The distinctive feature of both these colleges was the definite recognition of "pensioners," *i.e.*, students not members of the foundation, neither Scholars nor Fellows, but living in the college at their own expense, subject to its discipline and privileged to share in its instruction, such as now, in every college, form the vast majority of its undergraduates. The introduction of this system was the death-warrant of the earlier Hostels, every one of which, in fact, disappeared within the next fifty years. Their doom was doubtless hastened by the depletion of the University consequent on the changes in religion; but it was the college pensioner who actually killed them. Long before the sixteenth century was over, not a single "unattached" student was to be found in Cambridge. From that time to our own day, to belong to one or other of the colleges was a necessary condition of studying in the University at all.

§ 7. Yet more enduring and important was the next step taken by Fisher: his invitation to Erasmus to come, in 1511, and promote the study of Greek in Cambridge.

[1] See Chapter VI., § 15.

That able but far from thorough-going reformer took up his abode in Queens' College, and introduced into our studies the first Greek Grammar, founded on the treatise which Emmanuel Chrysoloras, a Byzantine refugee, had compiled for his Florentine pupils. This innovation was bitterly opposed by the men of the Old Learning—the "Trojan" party, as the enemies of this Greek invasion were called, and particularly by certain amongst the Religious Orders, to one of whom Sir Thomas More, on behalf of Erasmus, made a pithy and trenchant reply.

"I wonder," he says, "at the unbounded leisure which you find to devote to schismatical and heretical books. Or have you so few good books that you are obliged to consume your short leisure on bad ones? If the books of Erasmus are good, why do you condemn them? If they are bad, why do you read them? As you gave up the care of the world when you shut yourself up in the cloister, you are not one of those to whom leave is given to read bad books for the sake of refuting them. Hence by reading what is perverse you are merely learning it. Not only do you spend good hours on bad books, but you consume much time, as it appears, in talk and gossip worse than bad books; so that I notice there is no kind of rumour or calumny which does not find its way straight to your cell. . . . Whoever enters a [monk's] cell must say an *Our Father* that the conversation may be holy. But where is the use of beginning slanderous gossip with the Lord's Prayer? If that is not taking the Name of God in vain, what is?"[1]

§ 8. Notwithstanding this able championship, the position of Erasmus was made so unpleasant that in less than three years he was driven from Cambridge, leaving, however, behind him two notable traces of his influence —the first fount of Greek type ever used in England, and the theoretical pronunciation (of his own invention) which

[1] Bridgett's "Life of Sir Thomas More," p. 95

to this day cuts off English students from the living language of Hellas. In a very few years, strange to say, this pronunciation became a badge of Protestantism, and as such was made compulsory first by Edward VI., and afterwards by Elizabeth; while Mary was equally insistent on the living vocalization of the language.

§ 9. Bishop West, *felix opportunitate mortis*, was laid to rest in his beautiful chapel in 1534. Had he lived one year longer, he would probably have shared the martyrdom of Fisher; like whom he was a devoted champion of the ill-fated Queen Catharine. Both were succeeded in their respective offices by men of a very different stamp. For now the storm of the Reformation was bursting over the land, and alike at Ely and at Cambridge the chief power fell into the hands of its most active partisans. The new Chancellor of the University was no less a person than Thomas Cromwell, by whom a large portion of its revenues was diverted (under the name of first-fruits and tenths) to the Crown, and a clean sweep made of its old curriculum. His "Injunctions" of 1535 forbid the teaching of Canon Law and of the Schoolmen, and ordain in every college two daily lectures, "one of Greek, the other of Latin." From Cambridge, moreover, he sent forth, all through the County, those "men of fresh and free wit," as Foxe calls them, whose business it was to laugh down the old "superstition," by ridiculing all that had hitherto been held most sacred. This was chiefly done by quasi-theatrical performances in the churches, in which the Mass and other services were parodied, the chrism being called "the Bishop of Rome's butter," the Host "Jack in the box," and the words of consecration travestied as "hocus pocus" (*i.e.*, *Hoc est corpus*).

§ 10. The new Bishop of Ely was Thomas Goodrich, the zealous and unscrupulous agent of the King in that suppression of the ͇Religious Houses which made so stupendous a change in the conditions of English life everywhere, and not least in Cambridgeshire. As usual in such spoliations, the chief sufferers were not those against whom the movement seemed more immediately directed. The dispersed monks and nuns were, for the most part (provided that no difficulties had been made in "surrendering" their abbey, as seems to have been the case throughout our County), allowed small pensions, sufficient to keep them at least from starvation.[1] But the far more numerous dependents of the abbeys, the servants, the purveyors, etc., received no compensation whatever, and were reduced to wander about in search of subsistence, becoming those "sturdy" beggars against whom the horribly cruel legislation of the tyrant (himself responsible for their existence) was shortly directed. No such laws have ever before or since disgraced our Statute-book. By their savage provisions, whosoever lived "idly and loiteringly" for three days together was to be accounted a vagabond, and any justice of the peace might brand him with the letter V, and keep him for two years in servitude, chained by neck, arm, or leg, and put to "any sort of vile work." If he attempted to abscond, his master might brand an S on his "cheek or brow," and keep him as a slave for life. If he ran away again he was hanged. The poor, moreover, received nothing whatever in exchange for their daily dole at the abbey gate; and the ample funds, out of which a wise administration might have provided a truly national system for their relief and education, were diverted into the pockets of private rapacity.

§ 11. The abbey churches were mostly destroyed for the mere value of their stones, timber, and lead, and their services lost to the neighbourhood. The inhabitants of Royston thus complain (in 1541) that "whereas the Town of Royston stands in five Parishes, whereof

[1] Bridgett's "Henry VIII. and the English Monasteries," vol. ii., p. 226.

never a Parish Church is within two miles, through the absence of their Parsons and Curates in cases of necessity, when their presence is most requisite and helpful, the Parishioners cannot have the Sacraments ministered according to the custom of Holy Church, to their great Perils and Jeopardys. That these inconveniences were not so great while the late Priory stood, the Church of which the inhabitants have bought, to their great charges, to the intent to have the same their Parish Church, and therein to have daily Mass and other Divine Services to be celebrated and done." They accordingly petition that "the King's Manor of Royston" be constituted a parish, in the diocese of London, and that the priory church be henceforth called the Parish Church of St. John the Baptist. And so it was accordingly enacted. No provision was made, however, for the maintenance of the new Vicar of Royston, the tithes "of corn, hay, wool, lambs, and calf" being still payable to the clergy of the five parishes. The Vicar therefore had to be supported by a voluntary rate of one shilling in the pound, which was subsequently (in 1662) made compulsory.

§ 12. A further grievance connected with these dissolutions was the general rise in rents to which they led. The tenants of abbey lands had been very leniently treated by their old landlords; ancestral connection and Christian charity alike tending to this result. But the greedy courtiers who now clutched the forfeited property had no such scruples. They rack-rented without mercy, and with results truly disastrous to the social life of our rural districts. The well-known words of Latimer (as brave now in protest against this iniquity of Henry as he was constant to his religious convictions in the reign of Henry's daughter), contrasting the prosperity of his native farmstead in his father's day with its grinding impoverishment under the new régime, paint for us a sadly truthful picture of the state of things in every third tenant-holding throughout the land; for so much of the soil of England had been *Terra Ecclesiæ*. "My father," he tells us, "was a yeoman, and had no lands of his own; only he had a farm of three or four pounds by the year at the uttermost, and hereupon he tilled so much as kept half a dozen men. He had walk for a hundred sheep, and my mother milked thirty kine; he was able and did find the King a harness with himself and his horse, while he came to the place that he should receive the King's wages. I can remember that I buckled his harness when he went to Blackheath Field. He kept me to school; he married my sisters with five pounds apiece, so that he brought them up in godliness and fear of God. He kept hospitality for his poor neighbours, and some alms he gave to the poor, and all this he did off the same farm; where he that now hath it payeth sixteen pounds by year or more, and is not able to do anything for his prince, for himself, nor for his children, or give a cup of drink to the poor."

§ 13. Nor was it only the abbeys which now suffered. Those other institutions which dotted our County, the hospitals, the chapels, the hermitages, fell under the same ban. In 1541 Bishop Goodrich issued injunctions to the clergy, "that all Images, Relics, Shrines, etc., be so totally demolished and obliterated that no remains or memory be found of them." It was doubtless in accordance with this order that the shattered fragments of the lovely alabaster reredos at Toft, with its rich and delicate colouring, were buried beneath the pavement, and that the Hermitage Cave at Royston was not only disused, but absolutely filled up with earth, so that it was actually forgotten for nearly three centuries. It seems also probable that this was the occasion when (apparently under the personal superintendence of the Bishop) every single figure in the exquisite carvings of the Ely Lady Chapel (representing incidents in the life of the Virgin Mary) was deliberately hammered and chipped into shapelessness.

His famous abbey, which for so many centuries had been the centre of the religious life of our County, shared, of course, the fate of all other abbeys, though its church, being a cathedral, happily escaped the general doom.[1]

§ 14. Residents in Cambridge who picture to themselves the widespread local ruin and distress which would follow on the simultaneous annihilation of every college, every hospital, every workhouse, and every elementary school in the town, will be able to form some idea of what the suppression of the Religious Houses meant to St. Albans, to Reading, to Bury St. Edmunds, and to many another town throughout England, and will be able more to enter into the pathetic protest of the townsman of Colchester: "See ye not, my masters, how these abbeys go, *and our living goeth with them?*" It was such practical reasoning, far more than religious sentiment, which prompted the formidable rebellions provoked by the spoliation in Lincolnshire, Yorkshire, and elsewhere. If our County was not so entirely driven to desperation, it was because so many (comparatively) of the old foundations survived. Save at Ely and at Cambridge, there were no Religious Houses of the first rank in the County, and therefore the fewer dependents to suffer at their fall. And both at Ely and at Cambridge the destruction was far less complete than at most places in England. At the former, if the abbey was suppressed, the cathedral and the palace at least remained, and at the latter, while the many convents were done away with, the colleges, though hardly, escaped the greedy covetousness of Henry's unprincipled Court.

§ 15. And there was yet another reason. From the very first, Protestant ideas seem to have found in Cambridgeshire a specially congenial soil. Possibly its connection, through the Wisbeach merchantmen, with the North German trade may have been the reason, but

[1] See Chapter V., § 35.

certain it is that our County was amongst the earliest English homes of Reformation principles, and that it has ever since been distinguished by marked adherence to the Reformation spirit of uncompromising individuality *in sacris*—" the dissidence of Dissent, and the Protestantism of the Protestant religion."

§ 16. Thus, Cambridge itself, though it had embraced far less eagerly than Oxford the New Learning of the Renaissance, speedily went far beyond Oxford in its acceptance of the New Theology. The old orthodox boast, recorded by the historian Lydgate, was that " of heresy bare Cambridge never blame "; for Lollardism, so strong at Oxford, seems to have never affected our University, nor indeed, so far as appears, to have gained an appreciable footing anywhere throughout the County. But in both University and County a very different spirit now manifested itself. In the former was to be found an ever-growing knot of enthusiastic students who made rebellion against the traditional methods of religion the key-note of their lives. These " Germans," as they were nicknamed —amongst them being the famous Tyndall and the more famous Latimer—stealing in by back ways to their clandestine gatherings at the White Horse Inn (now the Bull), gradually grew bolder and stronger, till they became the leading influence in the University.

§ 17. Thus it was that a decision favourable to Henry's " divorce " was forced, according to Cranmer's suggestion, through the Cambridge Senate, long before Oxford gave way on the subject; though even here the iniquitous measure was only carried by a dead-lift effort which taxed the nascent energies of Protestantism to their utmost. Moral and chivalrous sentiment were alike revolted by the King's unprincipled hypocrisy, and when the scheme was first mooted, the very appointment of a syndicate to consider the "divorce" was twice non-placeted in the Senate. And finally it was only carried by inducing

the leading opponents (under threat of Henry's displeasure
—a real and terrible danger) to absent themselves from
the voting. Moreover, even in the packed syndicate thus
appointed the same process had to be repeated before a
decision against Catharine could be extorted from them.
The younger Regents (as at Oxford) were especially
zealous on the side of the injured Queen.

§ 18. And thus, too, it came about that in Cambridge
itself, and throughout the County in general, the suppression
of the Religious Houses was taken far more calmly than in
most parts of England. The University tried in vain to
purchase the splendid church of the Franciscans, the
largest and finest in Cambridge, for itself; failing which,
the colleges vied with each other in demolishing the old
buildings, and carting away the stone for their own new
edifices. The earliest plan of the town (made by Archbishop Parker's direction in 1574) shows only blank spaces
where the great convents had stood; not even ruins are
left. And, save at Denny, the like utter obliteration befell
every Religious House in the County. At Thorney, at
Chatteris, at Shingay, it is almost literally the case that
not one stone is left upon another. Stone, as a building
material, was too precious in Cambridgeshire, and Catholic
sentiment too debilitated.

§ 19. In this way there came into being the two new
colleges whose existence still bears witness to the transformation scene of this period—Magdalene and Trinity.
Both alike were endowed, and to a great extent actually
constructed, with the spoils of the suppressed foundations
around. Magdalene, set up in 1542 by Sir Thomas Audley
(than whom few men were more gorged with monastic
property), stood on the site of an earlier Benedictine establishment, Buckingham College; while Trinity, founded
by Henry in 1546, at the instigation of Queen Katharine
Parr, absorbed not only Michael House and King's Hall,
but no fewer than seven adjoining hostels—one the

Garret Hostel, whose name still survives. The buildings of its Great Court are chiefly formed of stone from the Dominican convent, and the fountain in the midst is supplied by the conduit contrived in the thirteenth century to bring water from a spring near Madingley to the Franciscans. From the confiscated funds were also, in 1540, endowed the five Regius professorships of Divinity, Law, Medicine, Hebrew, and Greek.

§ 20. These new foundations were, however, as nothing to the public institutions lost to national and scholastic interests; and in the reign of Edward VI. a yet more cruel blow was dealt to those interests by the destruction of the University Library. The Bishop of Ely, Richard Cox, born at Whaddon in our County, showed the Cambridgeshire disposition to Protestantism in its extremest form. After running through an extraordinary series of ecclesiastical promotions (being successively Fellow of King's, Head Master of Eton, Archdeacon of Ely, Dean of Westminster, Prior of Oseney, Student of Christchurch —in which last capacity he introduced his wife into the college, "being the first woman who ever lived in any") he became Chancellor of Oxford, and simply annihilated the Library there, on the pretext that the books it contained were Papistical. And this example was followed only too well at Cambridge, where such books as had escaped the sale under Cromwell were now destroyed by the fanaticism of the Reformers. Even the ancient MSS. of the Scriptures did not escape, the illuminations which adorned them being branded as idolatrous.

§ 21. Nor is it the case, as is often said, that the books which thus perished were mostly the endless lucubrations of the schoolmen. The catalogue of 1473 (as Mr. Bradshaw has pointed out) tells us that, out of the eighteen bookcases in the then Library, only one was devoted to such treatises; of the rest, eight were given to Theological works (mostly annotated copies of Scriptural books), four to Law, and one apiece to Moral Philosophy, Natural Philosophy (including Mathematics), Medicine, Logic, and Grammar (*i.e.*, Classics).

§ 22. The college libraries fared no better, and were even more thoroughly done away than those of the abbeys in the preceding decade, which had not been systematically destroyed, but merely sold for waste paper. What a wealth of literature thus perished may be estimated by the reflection that the priceless array of MSS. now in the library of Corpus Christi College does but represent such mere wreck of the abbey library at Canterbury as survived twenty-five years of this waste-paper utilization throughout every shop in the town, to be at last gathered up by the enlightened care of Archbishop Parker, and presented by him to the college of which he had been Master, under the condition that if twelve of his volumes are alienated the donation lapses to Caius College. The disappearance of twelve more there entitles Trinity Hall to claim the remainder. Not one has been yet lost, however, for they are kept most jealously; as well they may be, seeing that amongst them are to be found such works as Alfred's own copy of the Anglo-Saxon Chronicle, and the very MS. of the Gospels brought into England by Augustine.

§ 23. While learning thus suffered amid the confusions of the time, the poorer classes suffered yet more keenly by the suppression of the Parish Guilds. These humble corporations, of immemorial antiquity, and owing their existing form to the legislation of Alfred, were primarily local Benefit Societies, supported partly by endowments and partly by the subscriptions of the members, who were entitled to support in sickness and old age, and to burial with the religious rites supposed to benefit the soul of the deceased. This last proviso was eagerly seized upon by the greedy and unscrupulous Government which bore sway in the name of the young King. Under the pretext of Protestantism they declared all funds devoted to "superstitious" purposes, such as prayers for the departed, forfeited to the Crown, and at one swoop seized, for their own advantage, the lowly provision thus made by the poor for their hours of need.

§ 24. Commissioners were at the same time sent round to confiscate the valuables of the parochial churches; and the inventories drawn up by them still testify both to the wonderful amount of such valuables, even in very poor places, and to the ruthless thoroughness with which they did their work of spoliation. The gain to the Crown from these proceedings was comparatively small, the greater part of the property seized being embezzled by private rapacity; but the loss to the poor, and yet more the demoralization (of which Mr. Froude, in his "History of England," has painted so striking a picture) consequent upon them, was incalculable. Every parish in our County was thus despoiled, the Communion plate, the vestments, and often the very bells, being carried off from the churches.

§ 25. One example will sufficiently illustrate these proceedings. It is taken from the Augmentation Books, Vol. 495, p. 24, and records what was done in the small and unimportant village of Barrington. The account runs as follows:

CHURCH GOODS, CAMBRIDGESHIRE, BARRINGTON PARISH.

This is a true and perfect Inventory indented made and taken the 8th day of August A.D. 6th of King Edward 6th [1552] by us Richard Wylkes, Clerk, John Hudlestone and Thomas Rudston, Esquires, Commissioners amongst others assigned for the survey and view of all manner goods, plate, jewels, bells, and ornaments as yet be remaining forthcoming and belonging to the Parish Church there as hereinafter followeth.

PLATE.— First v Chalices with their Patents [*i.e.*, Patens]; whereof

i is double-gilt weighting   xiii oz.
i other double-gilt   xviii oz.
i other double-gilt   xvi oz.
i other double-gilt   xvii oz.
the vth parcel-gilt   xi oz.
Two Candlesticks of silver   lii oz.
One Ship of silver[1]   x oz.
i pair of Censers of silver xxviii½ oz.

ORNAMENTS.—Item, one whole Suit[2] of red branched Damask with a Cope of the same.

ii whole suits of Silk, partly green and partly yaller.

i Suit of blue Silk, with Birds and Trees on it, with one Cope of the same. And Albes to them.[3]

i Cope of Silk with Images wrought in Golde:

ii old Copes of red Silk with Branches of Gold inne them:

i Cope of greene Silk:

i Cope of black Sage:

vi Vestyments, namley ii of Red Damask, ii of red silk, i of Camlet, ii of white Fustian. Whereof v hath Albes.

Item, iv paynted Clothes pertayninge to Altars:

i Cloth for the sup. Altar[4] of branched Damask:

ii Curtaines of Silk.

iv Altar-clothys of douez [?]:

iii Altar-Clothes of Linen:

iii Surplices:

[1] A boat-shaped vessel containing incense.
[2] *I.e.*, Chasuble, stole, maniple, and amice.
[3] *I.e.*, Albs with apparels to match the chasubles, etc.
[4] The super-altar was the slab of stone forming the table.

iv diaper Towels:
v Corporal cloths, whereof iv with cases.
i Cross of Copper:
i Pyx of Copper.
Item. An olde cloth for Lent.

BELLS.—There is in the Steepul iv great Bells and one Sanctis [sic] Bell.[1]

All which Parcells above-writen be delyvered by us the sayde Commissioners unto the safe-kepyng of William Prior, John Eyworth, William Tottenham and Ric. Bourne, Parishioners there, to be at all times forthcoming and to be answeryd.

Except and reservyng one of the said Chalyces double gilt weighing xiii oz.: one other parcel-gilt weightyng xi oz: i Cope branched with damask: one other Cope of Red Sylke with branches of Gold: and i Vestment: delivered to the safe custodie of William Collin and Will. Brown Chyrchewardens there for the maintenaunce of Divine Service within the Paryshe Church.

  HENRY GOODRICK RICHARD WYLKES
  THOMAS HUDDLYSTONE THOMAS DRAPER
              Vicar there.

The delivery of the "Parcells above-writen" to the safe-keeping of the parishioners was a mere form to cover their confiscation, as they were immediately demanded (and "forthcoming") for the benefit of the Crown. The articles reserved "for the maintenaunce of Divine Service" seem also speedily to have disappeared in like manner.

§ 26. And, along with this material spoliation of their religion, the villagers suffered further grievous spiritual and intellectual damage by the accompanying suppression of the Chantries. From an early period it had been the

[1] The Sanctus bell was rung at the consecration and other parts of the Mass.

practice of pious benefactors to erect beside the churches these small memorial chapels, endowing them with provision for an incumbent, who should say Mass for the Founder's soul, and should also act as assistant curate to the parish priest. Not seldom he seems to have also filled the post of elementary teacher, instructing the children in the chantry building itself. Reading, at least, was thus a far more common accomplishment amongst the labourers of our [County during mediæval times than it afterwards became; and the fourteenth and fifteenth century seats still to be seen in so many of our churches are almost invariably constructed with book-boards. For scarcely a church but had at least one chantry attached to it. All was now swept away; the endowments (as being tainted with "superstition," through their connection with prayers for the departed) confiscated, and the fabrics sold for the value of their materials to the first bidder, by whom they were usually demolished.

§ 27. The general disturbance of rural life caused by these pseudo-Protestant excesses (carried out by men who—so far as they had any religious convictions at all—were mostly Catholics at heart, and energetically protested against by the truest Protestants, such as Latimer) was even greater than that following on the suppression of the abbeys. It was as if in every parish the local benefit societies, schools, and almshouses, were to be swept away together, and this in connection with sweeping religious changes, which (however desirable, or even inevitable, for the triumph of the Reformation) involved, as their first result, a chaotic overthrow of the simple reverence and religion of our rustics. "It was no light thing," writes Mr. Froude, "to the English peasant, to see the Royal Arms staring at him from the empty socket of the crucifix to which he had prayed," to find every touch of colour in his church obliterated beneath a uniform sheet of whitewash, and the altar-stones, which he had been taught to regard with supernatural awe, pulled down, put to every sort of vile use, and "made into bridges for cattle and sheep to go upon."

§ 28. "The effect upon the multitude of the sudden and violent change in religion had been to remove the restraints of a regular and recognised belief, to give them an excuse for laughing to scorn all holy things, for neglecting their ordinary duties, and for treating the Divine government of the world as a bugbear, once terrible, which every fool might now safely ridicule."[1]

§ 29. "Hospitals were gone, schools broken up, almshouses swept away; every institution which Catholic piety had bequeathed for the support of the poor was either abolished or suspended till it could be organized anew; and the poor themselves, smarting with rage and suffering, and seeing piety, honesty, duty, trampled under foot by their superiors, were fast sinking into savages."[2]

§ 30. "Between the popular preachers and the upper classes who were indulging in these oppressions there may have been, for the most part, a tolerable understanding. The Catholic priests, in the better days that were past, had said alike to rich and poor, 'By your actions ye shall be judged. Keep the Commandments; do justice and love mercy, or God will damn you.' The unfortunate persons who, for the sins of England, were its present teachers said, 'You cannot keep the Commandments; that has been done for you. Believe a certain speculative theory, and avoid the errors of Popery.' It was a view of things convenient to men who were indulging in avarice and tyranny.

* * * * *

"While the country was in the darkness of superstition, landowners and merchants were generous, the people prosperous, the necessaries of life cheap and abundant.

[1] Froude, "History of England," vol. v., p. 269
[2] *Ibid.*, vol. v., p. 273.

The light of the Gospel had come in, and with it selfishness, oppression, and misery. That was the appearance which England presented to the eyes of Latimer, and it was not for him to sit still and bear it."[1]

§ 31. "The once open hand was closed, the once open heart was hardened; the ancient loyalty of man to man was exchanged for the scuffling of selfishness; the change of faith had brought with it no increase of freedom, and less of charity. The prisons were crowded, as before, with sufferers for opinion, and the creed of a thousand years was made a crime by a doctrine of yesterday. Monks and nuns wandered by hedge and highway as missionaries of discontent, and pointed with bitter effect to the fruits of the new belief, which had been crimsoned in the blood of thousands of English peasants."[2]

§ 32. For in county after county, from one end of England to the other, these hideous grievances drove the peasantry to arms; and their revolts were suppressed (by the aid of German mercenaries) with a cruelty as remorseless as that which had goaded them into rebellion. Homesteads burnt, their inhabitants slaughtered, the parish priests hung from every church steeple: such were the scenes throughout many a lately happy and contented district of our land. But while this was the case all round our County—in Lincolnshire, in Buckinghamshire, in Norfolk, Suffolk, and Essex—no similar uprising seems to have taken place in Cambridgeshire, where the Protestant leaven was, as we have seen, already working effectually, and where, moreover, there were comparatively few of those "gentlemen" who, in most parts of England, perverted the doctrine of Justification by Faith only into a license for the entire disregard of good works—robbing churches, enclosing commons, rack-renting tenants, and, on the pretext of turning arable into

---

[1] Froude, "History of England," vol. v., p. 113.
[2] *Ibid.*, vol. vi., p 28.

pasture land, carrying out wholesale ejections of the peasantry, who were thus literally reduced to starvation.

§ 33. Thus it came about that when, on the death of Edward VI., Mary Tudor made her bid for the throne, and a general Catholic reaction set in throughout England, she found Cambridgeshire far from being wholly in sympathy with her. She was nearing London, on her way to her brother's sick-bed, when met by tidings of his death, together with a warning that the Council were preparing to entrap her, with a view to proclaiming Lady Jane Grey Queen. Cautiously retiring towards the East Anglian districts (where the horrible cruelty with which Northumberland had suppressed the peasant rising disposed the people to her side), she sought concealment and hospitality, by the way, at Sawston Hall, then, as now, the seat of the Huddleston family, who had recently migrated thither from their ancient home in Cumberland. Here her enemies all but surprised her. The Hall was attacked and burnt, seemingly by a local mob, so suddenly that she had barely time to escape, on a pillion behind one of Mr. Huddleston's servants, her course lighted by the flames. She shortly rewarded her host by knighthood and a post in her Court, giving him, moreover, materials (from the ruins of Cambridge Castle) for the rebuilding of his house, which still stands as thus re-erected, with its Catholic chapel in the roof, the family having ever remained constant to that faith. One of them was the priest who received Charles II., on his death-bed, into the Roman Catholic Church.

§ 34. Meanwhile Northumberland had marched out from London (" no man saying, 'God speed you' ") to apprehend her, having proclaimed his daughter-in-law Queen, and had reached Cambridge, where he was now Chancellor. Finding, however, how strongly the popular tide throughout England was setting in the contrary direction, he endeavoured to save himself by swimming with it. Accordingly, a few days later, on July 20, 1553, he proceeded to Market Hill (as the market-place of Cambridge is locally called), and "throwing up his cap for joy, yet with the tears running down his cheeks," himself led the cry, "God save Queen Mary!" It was too late; he was arrested almost immediately in his lodgings at King's College, and within a few days executed.

§ 35. Of the Marian reaction Cambridge felt the fuller effect, from its previous advanced Protestantism. Nearly every existing Head was dispossessed—amongst them Parker, now Master of Corpus. But Dr. Perne, Master of Peterhouse, retained his Lodge, atoning for his Edwardian Protestantism (which had made him the leader in the destruction of the University library) by decreeing, as Vice-Chancellor, that the bodies of the two celebrated Protestant teachers, Bucer and Fagius, who had lectured and died at Cambridge, should be exhumed and burnt. This ghastly ceremony was accordingly performed with full University pomp on Market Hill, the pile being chiefly composed of the printed works of the deceased and other Protestant publications. Otherwise the Marian persecution was little felt in our County. One man (John Hullier, Fellow of King's and Vicar of Babraham) was burnt as a heretic at Cambridge, on Jesus Green, and two others at Ely—William Wolsey and Robert Pigot, both of Wisbeach. Their offence was, calling the Sacrament of the Altar 'an idol.' Another Cambridgeshire man (William Flower, of Snailwell) was so zealous for Protestantism that he stabbed a priest while saying Mass at the altar of St. Margaret's, Westminster, so that his blood mingled with the chalice. For this outbreak Flower was burnt, after the hand with which the deed was done had first been cut off. The three most distinguished of the sufferers in this reign were, moreover, one and all Cambridge men; although it was at Oxford, not at Cambridge, that Cranmer, Latimer, and Ridley met their fate.

§ 36. The touching farewell to his old University left us by the last-named martyr, shows how close was the connection between Cambridge and those Protestant principles for which he laid down his life: "To whom, after my kinsfolk, should I offer farewell, before the University of Cambridge; where I have dwelt longer, found more faithful and hearty friends, received more benefits (the benefits of my natural parents only excepted), than ever I did in mine own native country wherein I was born?

§ 37. "Farewell, therefore, Cambridge, my loving mother and tender nurse! If I should not acknowledge thy manifold benefits, yea, if I should not for thy benefits at least love thee again, truly I were to be counted too ungrateful and unkind. What benefits hadst thou ever that thou usest to give and bestow upon thy best beloved children, that thou thoughtest too good for me? First to be Scholar, then to be Fellow; and, after my departure from thee, thou calledst me again to a Mastership of a right worshipful College. I thank thee, my loving mother, for all this thy kindness; and I pray God that His laws, and the sincere Gospel of Christ, may ever be truly taught and faithfully learned in thee.

§ 38. "Farewell, Pembroke Hall, of late mine own College, my care and my charge! What case thou art now in, God knoweth; I know not well. Thou wast ever named since I knew thee, which is now thirty years ago, to be studious, well learned, and a great setter forth of Christ's Gospel and of God's true Word. So I found thee, and, blessed be God, so I left thee indeed. Woe is me for thee, mine own dear College, if ever thou suffer thyself by any means to be brought from that trade. In thy orchard (the walls, butts, and trees, if they could speak, would bear me witness) I learned without book almost all Paul's Epistles; yea, and, I ween, all the Canonical

Epistles, save only the Apocalypse. Of which study, although in time a great part did depart from me, yet the sweet smell thereof I trust I shall carry with me into Heaven; for the profit thereof I think I have felt in all my lifetime ever after. And I ween of late (whether they abide now or no I cannot tell) there was that did the like. The Lord grant that this zeal and love toward that part of God's Word, which is a key and true commentary to all the Holy Scripture, may ever abide in that College so long as the world shall endure!"

§ 39. With the accession of Elizabeth came yet another counter-gale of reaction, which the inevitable Dr. Perne (from whose name the University wits now coined the word *pernare*, "to be a turn-coat") again succeeded, almost alone, in weathering.[1] By this time continuous instability, alike in its curriculum and in the personnel of its staff, had brought the University very low indeed. Already, under Cromwell's chancellorship, its numbers had so declined that it became practically bankrupt, and could barely pay its way by selling the books of the library and suspending the salaries of the Professors; while during the reign of Edward the number of B.A. degrees given annually averaged scarcely thirty. Macaulay also tells us that "in the reign of Edward the Sixth the state of the students at Cambridge is described to us, on the very best authority, as most wretched. Many of them dined on pottage made of a farthing's worth of beef with a little salt and oatmeal, and literally nothing else. This account we have from a contemporary Master of St. John's."[2]

[1] If Perne clung to his position, he did not make a bad use of it. He improved the Cambridge water-supply, and helped to re-establish the University Library, as he had helped to destroy it. To his college he was also a benefactor, and the weathercock there, which bore on either side his initials, A. P., was said to describe him as A Papist and A Protestant alternately.

[2] "Essays," vol. i., p. 258.

§ 40. "To the Universities," says Froude,[1] in his story of this reign, "the Reformation had brought with it desolation." "They were called stables of asses, stews, schools of the devil." "The Government cancelled the exhibitions which had been granted for the support of poor scholars. They suppressed the professorships and lectureships which had been founded by Henry VIII. Degrees were held anti-Christian. Learning was no necessary adjunct to a creed which 'lay in a nutshell.'" "College libraries were plundered and burnt. The Divinity Schools at Oxford were planted with cabbages, and the laundresses dried clothes in the School of Art."

§ 41. Things at Cambridge never became quite so bad as at Oxford, and during Mary's reign the chancellorship of Cardinal Pole doubled the number of resident students. But with the Elizabethan changes it fell lower than ever, only showing any permanent tendency to rise when the comparative security of the reign became evident, and put an end to the horrible see-saw of change and counterchange which had so long been distracting the nation.

§ 42. The utter unsettlement of the times in our County is strikingly set forth in such local church accounts as have survived. Those of the parish of March cover the whole of this period, and supply us with the following items:

1542	Payd to ye gold-smyth in pt of payment for a pyx and a crysmatary of sylver	-	- iijli.	
	Payd for makyn lx li wax at candyllmas	-		vij$d$.
	For a caes to cary ye pyxes -	-	-	ij$d$.
1543	For xvii elns of cloth for ye rochyt -	-	xs.	vj$d$.
	Payd for waxx at Stryrigg fayer	-	-	xxii$s$.
	Payd for makyn ye sepuker[2] lyght	-	-	ij$d$.
	Recayryd for godds lytt[3] -	-	-	vij$s$.

[1] "History of England," vol. v., pp. 269, 270.
[2] The sepulchre was a recess in which the Host was reserved from Good Friday to Easter.'
[3] *I.e.*, the lamp kept burning before the Sacrament.

1544	Payd in hernest of a santus bell		xx*d.*
	Payd for mendyng of ye coppys and sylk lases and thryd		x*d.*
	For a slevyd surplys	x*s.*	
1547	For baryn of ye banyars on Assessyon day		viij*d.*
	Payd for ye bybull	x*s.*	viij*d.*
	Payd for gyrdylls & tapys for vestments		ij*d.*
1547	Reign of Edward VI.		
	To Kyrspe for pluckynge doun emags[1] in the Chyrch		iij*d.*
	To Sams wyfe for drynkynge the fyrst tyme the emags war pluckyd doune		xii*d.*
	To Thomas Payne and Ihon Andrew for berying gers[2] furth of Church		x*d.*
	For whyghttynge of the Church	xxviiis.	iiij*d.*
1550	*Pd for breckyng down the alter and carrying forth ye stonns*		xii*d.*
1553	*Pd for ye new comunion boke*	v*s.*	
	Going to Wysbech for the same boke		iii*d.*
	For a tabull cloth		xxii*d.*
	For a boke to synge our salms on		xii*d.*
	Payd to Sams wyfe for a dener when we drew ye obstrayt[3] out of ye Church bok	ij*s.*	i*d.*
	It for goinge to Ely when we carryd ye plait[4]	xii*s.*	ij*d.*
1553	Reign of Queen Mary.		
	For to yards & a half of hayer cloth for ye hy alter		xvi*d.*
	For ye crismatory	iij*s.*	
	For a grayill &c.	xxii*s.*	
	For ye pyx	ij*s.*	
	For ye hy alter makynge	vi*s.*	viii*d.*
	For an alter cloth	ij*s.*	iiij*d.*
	For a gyrdyll		i*d.*
1554	For hangynge up ye sance bell		ij*d.*
	For books for ye Church & ye cariege of ye sam	iij*li.* vi*s.*	

[1] *I.e.,* images.

[2] *I.e.,* gear; probably the ornaments, banners, etc.

[3] *I.e.,* "obit straight." An obit was a service performed on the anniversary of the death of a benefactor, and contained prayers for his soul. It was, therefore, now erased as superstitious.

[4] See above, § 25.

For a fram to set on candells for lent and for workmanshyp about ye sepulker - -		xiv*d*.
Pd for a chein for ye sencer - -		iij*d*.
For ye rode Mary and Ihon and for costs¹ -	xxiij*s*.	iiij*d*.
1555 Pd to ye clark for makyng of small candell agaynst candelmas - - - -		iij*d*.
1557 Pd for thre pound wax and a quarter -	ij*s*.	viij*d*.
1558 Reign of Queen Elizabeth.		
Pd for ye comunion book - - -		v*s*.
Pd for paper to pricke forth stayne sams² for ye Quier - - - - -		iij*d*.
Pd for ye omiles³ - - - -		xx*d*.
Pd for pulling doun ye hy alter - -		vj*d*.
Pd for ye comunion tabull - - -		xxx*d*.
1560 Pd for one part of the phraphasis⁴ - -		v*s*.
Pd for pullyng doune ye roodloft - -		xij*d*.
Pd for removinge of ye organs - -		vj*d*.
1566 Pd for a comunion cup for ye church -		x*d*.

§ 43. Nor was it only in numbers that this long and general unsettlement had perniciously affected the University. Its *morale* had also grievously suffered. Dr. Caius, the Court Physician, on returning to Cambridge after many years' absence, in 1559, complains bitterly of the decline in academic decencies, the neglect of reverence to authority, the idleness in study, the extravagance, and the disuse of cap and gown amongst the undergraduates. The hostels which he had seen in old days swarming with students were now deserted to the townsfolk (freshmen were now indeed expected to inscribe not only their name, but their College, in the books of the Registrary at entrance); while the colleges themselves were not untainted by the all-pervading corruption, but gave Fellow-

[1] The roods were this year ordered to be set up again where "missing."

[2] *I.e.*, "certain psalms." The first metrical version of the Psalms was issued at this time, and became very popular.

[3] *I.e.*, homilies, of which every church had to keep a copy, very few of the clergy being licensed to preach during this reign.

[4] *I.e.*, the paraphrases of Erasmus, which were chained to the reading-desk beside the Bible.

ships and Scholarships rather by favour than by merit. To remedy these evils in some measure, his munificence transformed the decaying Gonville Hall into the College which still bears his name, and which he dedicated to his own chosen study, that of Medicine. He himself became the first Master; but the growing Protestantism of the age detected in his rooms a store of Popish vestments and service-books, burnt them in the College court, and drove him from his own foundation to end his days in London.

§ 44. This was in 1573, and not long afterwards this same growth of Protestant sentiment found further expression, in the foundation, on the site of the Dominican Convent, of the first college definitely intended to develop that sentiment. In 1584 Sir Walter Mildmay obtained a royal license " to erect and endow a certain college . . . for the propagation of the *pure* Gospel of Christ; to be called Emmanuel College "—a name which, like the Scriptural arms and motto of the Society, shows that we are now entering the Puritan era. In his Statutes the Founder exhorts to special watchfulness towards " extirpating Papistical heresies"; and in his architectural arrangements he was careful to build the College chapel north and south, instead of east and west, while he used the site of the old convent church for the College hall. Shortly afterwards yet another conventual site was utilized for Protestant purposes, by the foundation, in 1595, of Sidney Sussex College, on the grounds where the great Franciscan church and cloisters stood of old. Like Pembroke and Clare, this College was due to the generosity of a widow, Frances Sidney, relict of the third Earl of Sussex, and its armorial bearings still show her lozenge, charged with the broad arrow[1] which is the cognizance of the House of Sidney.

[1] The adoption of this device as the official stamp for Government property is said to have arisen from Sir R. Sidney having been Controller of the Ordnance under James I.

CHAPTER IX.

REFORMATION PERIOD—II.

§ 1—5. Oliver Cromwell at Sidney—The prisoners of Wisbeach—Protestantism loses favour—Elizabeth at Cambridge—Lancelot Andrews—Reactionary movement—James I. and Charles I. at Royston.

§ 6—23. Civil War—Associated counties—Royalist march on Cambridge—Ecclesiastical disturbances—Dowsing—Profanation of churches—Ejection of incumbents—Ship-money—Cromwell at Cambridge.

§ 24—27. Lack of funds—Discontent of the army—Triplow Heath—Cornet Joyce—Charles at Newmarket—March on London—King detained at Royston.

§ 28—34. Changes at Cambridge—Prayer-Book torn up—Oliva Pacis —Puritan license—Mr. Tripos—University humour—Thomas Fuller—Ode to Monmouth.

§ 1. ONE of the earliest students who learnt, at Sidney Sussex College, as the Founder's Statutes direct, "to detest and abhor Popery," was Oliver Cromwell, whose name introduces us to the second act of the Reformation drama.

§ 2. Already the performers in its early scenes were almost all in the tomb ere the College was founded. Amongst those who found graves in Cambridgeshire, we must not pass over "the prisoners of Wisbeach," the last survivors of the old Catholic hierarchy. Such of that hierarchy as were alive at Elizabeth's succession were, with one exception, deposed for refusing the Oath of Supremacy, to the number of fifteen. Shortly afterwards they were imprisoned, not by any process of law, but by the royal *fiat*, and continued under more or less severe restraint for the rest of their lives. This was wholly on account of their religion. Lord Burghley, a hostile witness (in his "Execution of Justice in England "[1]), testifies to their blameless characters, describing them as "faithful and quiet subjects," "persons of courteous natures," "of great modesty, learning and knowledge," secluded only "for their contrary opinions in religion, that savour not [like those of the seminary priests] of treason."

§ 3. Yet, though thus inoffensive, their doom was grievously heavy. Committed, to begin with, to solitary confinement in what Froude calls "the living death of the Tower," and other London prisons, for three or four years, they were afterwards quartered (singly) on the Protestant prelates, who were stringently ordered by the Council to prevent them from communication, either by word or letter, with anyone, and to see that they had neither paper to write withal, nor books to read (except Protestant ones). Thus, deprived of every intellectual, social, and religious solace, "pining away in miserable desolation, tossing and shifting from one keeper to another," they one by one drooped and died. But all remained steadfast to their faith; and finally the "obstinate" survivors were, in 1580, closely imprisoned, along with others in like case, in Wisbeach Castle, under the charge of the Bishop of Ely. Here they remained, "enclosed within a brick wall," and pestered by Protestant preachers (amongst them "Lancelot Andrewes of Pembroke Hall"), till death set them free. The latest to linger were Thomas Watson, Bishop of Lincoln, who died 1584, and Feckenham, the last Abbot of Westminster,

[1] This work was published in 1583, to justify the execution of the seminary priests in England. Burghley's point is that quiet Papists were not put to death.

who died 1585. Both are buried (as the parish registers testify) in Wisbeach Churchyard.[1]

§ 4. And now the current of Protestant feeling, which had long run so fiercely, was checked in its course by the action of the authorities. Even in the early days of her reign, Elizabeth, on her visit to Cambridgeshire, when a play was performed before her in King's College Chapel, was shocked and disgusted by the appearance on the stage of a dog trained to walk on its hind-legs with the consecrated Host in its mouth.[2] Afterwards, as years went by, her political instinct told her that Puritanism was likely to prove yet more antagonistic to the royal prerogative than Catholicism had, in her case, shown itself; thus leading her to favour such "reactionary" divines as Lancelot Andrewes, Master of Pembroke College and afterwards Bishop of Ely. And when her successor came to the throne, such divines were still more the objects of royal patronage, till, under Laud, their repudiation of Reformation doctrines and practices, and their persecution of the Nonconformists, who clung to Reformation principles, led to that renewed outburst of Protestantism which found expression in the Civil War.

§ 5. The monarchs whose pertinacious adherence to the reactionary cause brought about this outbreak were not infrequently in Cambridgeshire. James I. had at Royston one of his favourite hunting-boxes, and once passed there almost twelve months of seclusion. The house in which he resided is still called the "Palace," and the

[1] See Bridgett and Knox, "Queen Elizabeth and the Catholic Hierarchy," p. 197 *et seq.*

[2] This performance (got up by the undergraduates) had been intended as an afterpiece to the play at King's. The Queen, however, was not able to remain for it, but consented that the actors should follow her to her first stage on her journey from Cambridge, and there exhibit their composition. On seeing what it was, she rose, and with an indignant rebuke swept out of the room.—Froude, "Hist. England," vol. vii., p. 205.

three-cornered, richly-carved oaken chest in which his ruffs were kept is still preserved there. It was in this house that his unworthy favourite, the Earl of Somerset, was arrested in his very presence for the murder of Sir Thomas Overbury, and from this house that his son Charles, Prince of Wales, started, incognito, as John Smith, on his romantic wooing of the Spanish Infanta. In this house, moreover, at a later day, Charles I. took up his abode for a while, on his way from London to set up his standard at Nottingham at the first beginning of the Civil War; and in this house, at its close, he was lodged, on June 24, 1647, as a prisoner, by the Army, whose headquarters were for a while at Royston.

§ 6. Between these two last events Cambridgeshire had undergone its share of the stirring transactions of the civil strife. It was not the scene of any great battle, or, indeed, of any fighting at all ; for the Protestant County contained almost no Royalists, and (along with Norfolk, Suffolk, Lincoln, Bedfordshire, Huntingdonshire, and Essex) was one of the seven "Associated Counties," which combined for mutual defence, and "felt little of the war, save the cost."

§ 7. Once only, during the whole course of hostilities, did an action within our borders seem imminent. In August, 1645, the King made his last despairing effort to retrieve the ruin of his cause at Naseby by "undertaking, with a mere handful of men, a desperate march of over two hundred miles, traversing the heart of the enemies' country, entering their Associated Counties, where no army had ever yet come, and (in spite of all their victorious troops facing and following him) alarming even London itself, and returning safe to Oxford."

§ 8. From Wales, whither he had retreated after his fatal defeat, he marched, with troops of pursuing Scottish and Roundhead cavalry "on every side, like hounds started at a fresh stag," through Staffordshire, Warwickshire, Leicestershire, and Nottinghamshire, raised the siege of Newark, and thence struck southwards, by the Ermine Street, and entered Huntingdonshire. Here he was fairly on enemies' ground, and his dragoons plundered the country right and left, so that once again (and for the last time in history) the Isle of Ely was crowded with fugitives from hostile invasion. At Huntingdon itself a small body of Puritans, " not above two hundred, under one Bennet, a resolute officer, who stood in front of his men on the bridge with a pike in his hand," bravely defended the passage of the Ouse. Charge after charge of the Royalists was repulsed, and the resistance could not be overcome till a venturous soldier swam the river, " in the midst of a shower of musket balls," and succeeded in cutting out " a great flat-bottomed boat " from the flotilla secured to the southern bank. A party of the King's men was thus enabled to take the defenders of the bridge in rear, and Huntingdon was captured.

§ 9. "The town suffered for it, for our men left them but little of anything they could carry," and requisitions were levied from all the country about, including the western districts of Cambridgeshire, under threat of like plunder. Twice the King marched on Cambridge itself, with the design of passing into East Anglia, "where he had a party forming." His force, however, being wholly cavalry, and only 5,000 strong, was not equal to the assault of the fortifications which had been thrown up round the " Borough"; and the strategic value of Cambridge was manifested for the last time, when the royal army, unable to pass the Cam, gave up their East Anglian design, and retreated from before our earthworks, by the Newnham Road, to Woburn, Buckingham, and Oxford, carrying with them, as the fruit of their raid, " six waggons loaded with money, two thousand horses, and three thousand head of cattle."[1]

[1] See Defoe's " Memoirs of a Cavalier," chap. xvi.

§ 10. But, though scarcely a blow seems to have been struck in our County, the social and ecclesiastical disturbances accompanying the Rebellion were widespread within its boundaries, and are recorded with unusual minuteness in many contemporary publications, such as the "Querela Cantabrigiensis," in which the Royalists lament over the havoc wrought by Puritan fanaticism, and the treatise on the "Reformation of Religion," wherein the Puritans triumphantly detail the self-same transactions as a glorious victory for the Protestant cause.

§ 11. The latter work chiefly concerns itself with the organized iconoclasm carried out by the Parliamentary agent, William Dowsing, who has left an abiding mark on almost every parish church in the County. The usual type of entry in his diary is as follows:

"*Abington Magna.* 1643, *March* 20.—We breake forty superstitious pictures, two crucifixes, order a cross to be taken from the steeple, and the steps[1] to be levelled."

At Babraham "a holy lamb" is amongst the defaced "superstitions"; at Bassingbourn, and other places, "a superstition in brass: *Quorum animabus propitietur Deus*"; at Bourne, "a superstitious image of the Virgin Mary, and divers Popish pictures"; at Brinkley, "Christopher carrying Christ"; at Burrow Green, "Joseph and Mary together in the glass, as they were espoused"; at Cheveley, "two staring crosses"; at Comberton, "thirty-six Cherubim"; at Fowlmere, "the Twelve Patriarchs."

At Hatley St. George "there was written over a coat of arms: *William St. George gave a hide of land with his daughter to be a nun in Clerkenwell, temp. Henry II.* Which we burnt."

At Horseheath, "four pictures of the Prophets, Ezekiel, Daniel, Zephaniah, and Malachi," are mentioned especially; at Madingley, "Christ on the Cross and two

---

[1] *I.e.*, the ancient altar steps, which had hitherto survived in most places, though the altars themselves had been destroyed.

thieves by Him, Christ and the Virgin Mary in another window, Christ in the steeple window, ... and fourteen Cherubims in wood"; at Papworth Everard, "the four Evangelists, painted on the walls of the chancel, and Abraham offering his son Isaac." At Shelford Magna there were no fewer than "one hundred and twelve superstitious pictures, three crucifixes, twelve Cherubim, and two superstitious inscriptions"; at Swaffham Bulbeck, "one hundred superstitious pictures, twenty Cherubim, four Crucifixes (and Christ nailed to them), and four Crosses."

At Croxton "we brake a crucifix, the railes, and twenty superstitious pictures. To be taken down, one crucifix and two crosses, the one on the steeple and another in the highway."

At Teversham "there was JESUS written in great capital letters on six arches in the church, and in twelve places in the chancel. The six in the Church I did out, and six in the chancel, and the other six I could not reach, but gave orders to do them out. Also on one side of the altar Phil. ii. 10, *At the Name of Jesus every knee should bow*, and on the other side Psalm xcv., *O come let us worship and fall down*, &c. And four suns were painted: in the first was writ *God the Father*, in the second, *God the Son*, in the third, *God the Holy Ghost*, and in the fourth, *Three Persons and One God*."

§ 12. This last entry is interesting, as showing that the Laudian reaction was beginning to affect the district; for the texts, etc., here described were assuredly not mediæval. They were very probably the work of Wren, uncle to the famous architect, and Bishop of Ely from 1638 to 1667, who, before his elevation to the episcopate, had been Vicar of Teversham. He was a noted leader amongst the rising High Church party, and as Master of Peterhouse had built the existing chapel, the first attempt seen in England at an imitation of pre-Reformation architecture.

In this edifice he had further made an attempt at reviving something of pre-Reformation ritual; so that the current saying in Cambridge was, "Here is a little chapel but much Popery."

As Bishop of Ely he issued "Articles" to his clergy for the due observance of the Rubrics, ordering the Communion-tables to be permanently set up "altar-wise" at the east end of the chancels (instead of being merely boards, which were habitually leant against the walls, and were just placed on trestles in the middle of the naves for each administration), bidding communicants to kneel at the rails, instead of remaining in their seats, and the like. This deeply offended the Protestant laity, and led to Wren's imprisonment in 1642 by the Parliament. He remained in the Tower for no less than eighteen years, till released by the Restoration. This Bishop was one of a series of High Church leaders, having been chaplain to Bishop Andrewes, and the trainer of Bishop Cosin, who was under him at Peterhouse.

§ 13. Under Wren's influence many of the Cambridgeshire clergy seem to have developed those High Church proclivities which were so specially hateful to the Puritan feeling dominant at this period in the County. Accordingly, while Dowsing was on his iconoclastic rounds (for which he was paid 13s. 4d. for each church purified, and sometimes, as at King's College Chapel, was bribed or persuaded into taking the pay without doing the work), the Duke of Manchester, as Parliamentary Commissioner, was considering at Cambridge the "Articles of Complaint" preferred against incumbents of the wrong colour, and ejecting such "malignants" wholesale. The Puritan recorder dwells on these transactions with great gusto, for example :

"*Bartlow.* 22 *March*, 1643.—Mr. Baker, Parson thereof, had these Articles exhibited against him, viz., 'That he hoped the Earl of Essex would come to the same end with his father, and to see King Pym hanged for taking of bribes: that they were all traitors that took up arms on the Parliament side. And for refusing to take the Covenant.' Whereupon he was ejected, and William Hinton put in his place."

§ 14. At Bottisham, the complaint against "Mr. Crossland, Vicar thereof, and Senior Fellow of Trinity College, Cambridge," was:

"That he is a time-server, and one that observeth bowing towards the East, standing up at *Gloria Patri*, reading the Second Service at the Communion Table, and such-like superstitious worship and popish innovations. . . . Neither did he ever preach to edifying, neither is he able, as the deponents do verily believe. That he did say in his pulpit that we do take up arms against the King."

At Burrow Green the parson, "though he hath taken the Covenant yet he prays for Bishops, and still observes ceremonies, bowing towards the altar and at the Name of Jesus. He sayeth that he ought to shorten his sermons rather than neglect reading the Common Prayer, and that the Collects are to be preferred before Preaching."

§ 15. At Castle Camps the minister is deposed "for bowing at the Name of Jesus, for forcing the complainant (for the peace of a good conscience) to remove out of the parish, for making a new Communion Table and placing it altar-wise, for not suffering godly men, such as Mr. Faircloth and others, to preach in his church, for reading the King's proclamations and not those from the Parliament."

At Caldecot, "Mr. Thomas Saunders, Minister thereof, hath been a constant practiser of ceremonies, and an observer of Wren's Articles, railing the Communion Table, bowing at the Name of Jesus towards the East; and refuseth obedience to the ordinances of the Parliament." Whereupon, by Manchester's warrant, George Biker, "recommended by the Assembly of Divines," was put in his room.

At Cheveley we are told that the minister "read the King's Commission of Array,[1] and refused to read the Parliament's against it, that he refused to take the Covenant, that he never sent a man-at-arms to the Muster," etc.

§ 16. At Chesterton the complaint is:
"That the Vicar teacheth to pray for and yield obedience to Bishops ... that he neglected the true solemnity of the Parliament Fast, ... in Christ-tide last, saying *They did not use to fast at Christmas, it was a festival time.* ... That when the Covenant was to be taken he preached from Romans xiv. 3, and said, *Let not him that taketh the Covenant despise him that taketh it not; for we must not judge one another in things indifferent.*"

And at Coveney:
"That Mr. Hill, Minister thereof, sued one Catharine Holmes for a tithe calf, and with four nobles (for which the suit was composed) buying a Communion Table, which he set up in the chancel, with these words graven upon it, *Sin no more lest a worse thing come unto thee.*"

§ 17. At Downham the minister "preached against the Parliament, terming them a company of wicked Nabals ... worse than devils (for there is government in hell), and saying that it is a dangerous thing to preach extempore, and that now the people run about after false teachers who preach in tubs and pray by the spirit."

At Eversden the minister is said to be "a man of a troublesome spirit, for that he had presented the deponents in the Ecclesiastical Court for going out of

---

[1] The Commission of Array was the King's proclamation to all loyal subjects to take arms in his behalf under the leaders appointed by him. The Parliament, on their side, called out the County Militia, and ordered every parish to send its quota to the ranks. Every incumbent was required to find one man, fully equipped, for the muster.

the Church when he went up to the Altar to read Second Service. And that he hath also been a strict observer of ceremonies, signing children with the Sign of the Cross," etc.

§ 18. At Fen Ditton, Dr. Collins, Provost of King's, was Rector, and is denounced "for setting up a costly altar, his superstition being so great, and his doctrine so impossible to edify; . . . for sending, in his absence, none but malignant preachers, who exclaimed against the Parliament; of whom one preached that he hoped to see the King triumphantly return, with a sceptre in one hand and a sword in the other, . . . to cut down those rebels who are now raising forces against His Majesty. . . . For making feastings on the Sabbath days."

§ 19. At Fowlmere, Mr. Morden " preacheth but once on a Lord's Day, so that he is very unable and unfit to have charge of souls; for that he never preacheth but only some few sermons that are writ down, which he hath preached over and over by the space of twelve years past. By which these deponents can gather no benefit."

At Girton, " Mr. Ling, Minister thereof, having a wife and four small children," is ejected "for being a great fomenter of innovations, preaching in his surplice and hood."

At Hardwick the same fate befalls the parson, " with a wife and seven children," because " He refused to read anything from the Parliament, but read many things from the King at Oxford with great boldness; . . . he commonly useth altar-worship, east-worship, and dropping-worship, with bidding canonical prayer. And after his sermon he came out of the pulpit into the chancel, and there made an end of his will-worship."

§ 20. At Orwell, Dr. Row is sequestrated "for refusing obedience to the ordinances of Parliament for the taking away of the [Communion] rails, . . . for sending the

King £100, and for being the chief man in procuring the [Trinity] College plate to be sent to the King."

At Stretham the grievances against the incumbent are "for having caused his parishioners to expend £12 to rail in the Communion-table, and make new steps to the altar, himself bowing three times as he went up, and as often while he came down, to the great offence of his parishioners."

§ 21. At Wimpole the Rector and his curate are alike removed, "for being much given to play cards at night; for neglecting the Fast day; for sending a horse to the King, and bidding Thomas Lancaster, that rode him, to ride the horse to death rather than the Parliament should light on him; for not taking the Covenant, and refusing to tender it."

At Wisbeach the Vicar was accused "for saying *the Parliament had wit enough, had they but grace to use it;* for calling a godly minister (Mr. Alliston), *Brother Redface;* for drinking Prince Rupert's health; for saying (upon the loss of Gainsborough) that *Cromwell, as valiant as he was, turned his back before his enemies;* for preaching against extempore prayer, saying it was vain babbling," etc.

At Wilbraham, Mr. John Munday, Minister, "did not, at the meeting at Bottisham, subscribe anything to the Parliament, but said it was treason for any man to give any money against the King, . . . and in his sermons discouraged his parish from doing anything for the Parliament; saying, that, if he suffer, it shall be as an innocent. He was forward to pay the ship-money, but never paid the Parliament taxes till distrained."

§ 22. The collection of the ship-money had already proved a sort of touchstone throughout the County for testing the dispositions of men's minds. At Melbourne the attempt to collect it (in 1640) had given rise to a serious riot. The villagers gathered at the Cross, "and fell upon the sheriff's men with stones and staves and hedgestakes and forks, and beat them and wounded divers of them, and did drive them out of the highway into a woman's yard for their safety. And were forced for saving of their lives to get out of the town a back way; which notwithstanding, some 30 or 40 able men and boys pursued them above a quarter of a mile, stoning them, and driving the bailiffs into a ditch, where some of their horses stuck fast. And the multitude got some of the bailiffs' horses and carried them away, and would not redeem them without money."

§ 23. Meanwhile a like state of confusion reigned at Cambridge. The University was, for the most part, loyal, and ready to contribute its plate to the King's war-chest. Little, however, reached him; for Manchester and the hitherto unknown Cromwell pounced upon the town, made it the headquarters of the Grand Committee for the Associated Counties, threw up fortifications (at a cost of £2,000), and diverted to the service of the Parliament such College property as they thought fit. Thus the materials with which Clare was just then rebuilding itself were requisitioned for the repairs of the Castle, and contributions were levied on the University; for refusal of which the Vice-Chancellor, and other Heads, were shut up in the Public Schools on Good Friday, 1643, and kept there "all the cold night without fire or food." The Committee at the same time sent out warrants "inviting" like contributions from the villages—an invitation but slackly responded to, for in two months the sum thus raised amounted to little over £3,000 from the whole seven counties, of which some £2,000 had been found by Cambridgeshire.

§ 24. Want of funds was indeed the standing trouble on both sides throughout this war. Men and arms were forthcoming in fair plenty, but not the cash for the pay and provisioning of the soldiery. It was their impatience at the long arrears of their service-money which, when the last Cavalier resistance was overcome, led the army on June 10, 1647, to their famous concentration on Triplow Heath, in our County. Commissioners from the Parliament were in presence, with offers of two months' pay in cash, and debentures for the remainder, would they only disband — offers received with shouts of "Justice! justice!" and preparations for an immediate march on London, nominally under the orders of the King in person.

§ 25. For it was from this camp on Triplow Heath— till within living memory the same wide open expanse of turf around the "Nine Wells"[1] that it was then—that Cornet Joyce set forth on that memorable ride to Holmby House which gave the King's person into the power of the Army. Already surrendered by the Scots into the hands of Parliamentary Commissioners, he was now taken into other keeping, by authority of that other Commission, "written in fine legible characters" — the Cornet's stalwart troopers. From Holmby he was conveyed to Cheveley, in our County, where Fairfax and Cromwell "waited on" him, and arranged for his removal to Newmarket, where, as well as at Royston, his father had set up a hunting-box. The natural road from Holmby would have been through Cambridge, where the streets were decked with green boughs and "whole rose-bushes" to receive him. But fear of popular demonstration, amid these May Term gaieties, caused his escort to carry him round by Trumpington, where we hear of "much preparation for his Majesty, by strewing the streetes, cutting doune boughes, and preparing of benefiers" [bonfires].[2] At Newmarket he was kept under

---

[1] "Nine Wells" is the local term for each of those stes of springs which are found along the base of the chalk in Cambridgeshire. The number is used quite indefinitely, as in the Athenian 'εννεάκρουνος (Herodotus, vi. 837).

[2] Sanderson, p. 986.

careful guard, but "very pleasant and cheerful, and takes his recreation daily at tennis, and delights much in the company of Cornet Joyce."[1] Nor was this wholly pretence; for at the moment there did seem to be a real prospect that his power might be set up once more by the very hands which had pulled it down, and that the soldiers might believe a restored King would show himself more grateful, in the way of money, for their services, than the niggardly Parliament was doing.

§ 26. Having this trump card, then, in their hands, the Army, 20,000 strong, broke up from Triplow Heath, and that night encamped at Royston, whence Fairfax and Cromwell sent an ultimatum to the Corporation of London, significantly hinting that "a rich City may seem an enticing bait to poor beggarly soldiers to venture far to gain the wealth thereof; yet, if not provoked by you," and so forth. The provocation, they gave it to be understood, would be found in any further delay as to the just demands of the Army, which next morning, June 11, 1647, took up its march, not straight on London (where the train-bands were being called out, "on pain of death," to resist it), but along the Icknield Street, so leaving Cambridgeshire on the way to St. Albans.

§ 27. A fortnight later, and Charles himself followed by the same route. Army and Parliament had meanwhile been intriguing against each other for his custody; and the King himself was getting tired of his restraint at Newmarket, finding himself "an absolute prisoner," and not being reconciled to the case even by the presence of Hugh Peters, the famous army preacher, who "moved His Majesty to hear him preach, which His Majesty did rather decline." Finally, on Midsummer Day, he set off under escort, along the Icknield Street to Royston, in response to a Parliamentary message intreating him to come to Richmond—a place far too near London to suit the

[1] Whitelocke, p. 257.

Army, who on their part had resolved "that, if the King would not be diverted by persuasion (to which His Majesty was very opposite), they would stop him by force at Royston ... keeping continual guard against any power that should be sent by Parliament to take him from us ... and out-guards also kept to prevent his escape from us with the Commissioners." Stopped at Royston he accordingly was, and, after two days' confinement in the royal palace there, was escorted, not towards Richmond, but, on the track of the Army, to St. Albans. And with his departure ended the last high political transactions of which our County has formed the theatre.

§ 28. Puritanism was now triumphant throughout Cambridgeshire, and the University procedure was remodelled accordingly. That same cold Good Friday which the Vice-Chancellor and Heads passed under lock and key in the Schools saw the Book of Common Prayer solemnly torn up in Great St. Mary's, Cromwell himself presiding at the function; the College chapels, like the parish churches, were purified in Dowsing fashion, King's, alone, through some unknown influence, retaining its windows; while students were "examined of the Grace of God in them," and had to write upon such theses as "An in renatis peccata puniantur?" "Carnal learning" became more and more despised, soldiers were quartered in the Colleges, libraries were ransacked, trees and bridges cut down, and every graduate and undergraduate alike was required to take the Covenant, all who refused being summarily expelled. Oliver Cromwell became an object of such adulation that, in 1654, the Vice-Chancellor and many other of the leading University officials combined to dedicate to him a work called (in his honour) "*Oliva* Pacis," in which he is accorded the peculiar royal salutation of our earliest English monarchs: χαῖρε βασιλεῦ—the words which, as late as the days of John, implied recognition of sovereign claims,[1] and which were now used for the last time in English history.

§ 29. In University circles, however, Puritanism was not the wholly laughterless influence it is sometimes painted. Though such vanities as stage-plays, songs, dances, games, and amusements in general, were branded as profane, there was still left one direction in which license was not merely allowed, but encouraged. Anything which tended to develop a healthy Protestant contempt for the superstitions of popery, by turning the old Catholic ceremonies into ridicule, was actually patronized by the authorities, and every opportunity of so doing was eagerly seized upon by the students as the only permissible outlet for their youthful gaiety. Parodies of Catholic worship, scurrilous doggerel travestying Catholic doctrine, were thus performed and recited with universal applause and content; and, most especially, the solemnities which anciently accompanied the conferring of Degrees were turned into an elaborate farce.

§ 30. Of old the candidates for the Baccalaureate had been admitted by the Vice-Chancellor as part of a solemn Lenten function, which began with High Mass in the University church. When presented to him, they had to pass a *vivâ-voce* examination, so that the phrases " stare in quadragesima " and " ad respondendam quæstionem " denoted a very serious ordeal, even though the "father" of each College was allowed more or less to prompt his "sons." But when Protestantism became dominant, the questioning was made over to an "old bachelor" (*i.e.*, a man of nearly M.A. standing), seated on a three-legged

---

[1] See Chapter IV., § 11. Richard of Devizes (§ 48) tells us that John, when Regent, was vexed at not being saluted with the words " Chere Basileus," which he explains as " Dear Lord" (misled by the similarity between *cher* in French and χαῖρε in modern Greek). From the latter our English *cheer* is derived.

stool, and hence denominated "Mr. Tripos." His business was to chaff both the "questionists" and the "fathers"—the more personally the better—in his examination, to "vary"[1] his questions into the most absurd forms possible, and generally to turn the whole affair into ridicule.

§ 31. A like state of things prevailed at Oxford, where "Mr. Tripos" was represented by "Terræ Filius"; and one great object at either University was to make jokes, for the most part of incredible poverty, at the expense of the other. Such jokes formed the main staple of the address which these humorists were wont to deliver on some given thesis. Sometimes this thesis was physical: "An mundus confletur ex atomis?" "An cerebrum sit pars corporis frigidissimum?" "An Naturæ errores faciant ad ornamentum universi?"; sometimes literary: "An poeta nascatur?" "An pravitas scribendi sit scabies sæculi?"; sometimes philosophical: "An aliquid sciatur?" "An mundus senescendo fiat deterior?"; sometimes political: "An feminæ admittendæ sint ad publica consilia?"

All these were theses actually discussed between 1652 and 1660, at the very height of the Puritan ascendancy, and they are invariably treated with the broadest license. The Latin sequence was occasionally broken by a "Music Speech" in English, addressed to the ladies, and dealing with such delicate questions as the sex of Satan.

§ 32. The standing dish of Oxonian satire at this time is the poverty and antiquity of Cambridge jokes. "Dreadful quibles on wordes" are declared by a "Music" speaker to be "the grand charter of Cambridge"; whilst a Terræ

---

[1] Ingenious "varying" of the questions for disputation had long been held a mark of skill amongst the sophisters in the schools (see Chapter VI., § 9). Hence the words "sophistry" and "prevaricate" have come into our language. A *prævaricator* had indeed become a recognised University official in the conduct of scholastic exercises.

Filius avers that these "quibbles" "jam servantur in Archivis, ubi inter antiquitatis insignia jocos suos tanquam res antiquissimas ostendunt." Their dulness is ascribed to that of the Cambridge atmosphere, owing to the close contiguity of the Fens, "ubi vapores continuo ascendentes provocant somnum ";—a somnolence which enables Cantabs to sleep even on their local beds, where an Oxonian finds it impossible to repose, "for reasons which have just twice as many feet as a tripos." Even in the Schools a like slumberous atmosphere prevails, each Doctor being provided with a pillow on which to sleep out his neighbours' disputations, and with a pair of spectacles to read (instead of rehearsing) his own.

§ 33. In 1657 a man specially famous for this style of humour was Prævaricator, in whose honour an elaborate inter-University joke was got up. At the Oxford Comitia two undergraduates presented themselves disguised as hobby-horses, "equi saltantes." After their admission to a degree had been twice non-placeted, "a quodam moroso Asino," they were finally made Bachelors, on stating, in answer to the question what authors they had read, "equos ffabri philosophiam callere ad ungulos." (This was a reference to Smith's "Treatise on Logic," then a standard school book.) A condition, however, was annexed, "ut Cantabrigiæ determinarent." To Cambridge, accordingly, they went, and appeared in full costume before the Vice-Chancellor and Mr. Tripos, who proved equal to the occasion, and "cum inter doctores graviter consultatum est an ad Gradum equos saltantes admitterent, respondet hanc esse rem *æquissimam*." And this master of low comedy was no less a Puritan than Thomas Fuller the historian.

§ 34. With the Restoration more obvious forms of undergraduate amusement revived, and this peculiar kind of humour decayed at Cambridge. A specimen of it, however, is still to be found in an ode addressed, in

1662, to the Duke of Monmouth, on his visit to the University:

> "Magne Dux, qui titulum
> Sumis tibi ex Wallia,
> En tibi Academiam,
> Id est pileos et pallia,[1]
>
> "Cum omni supellectile,
> Punnis, Jocis, Quibbilis,
> Quos Dunces Oxonienses
> Derident ita sibilis.
>
> "Videbis Academiam nostram
> Ita pace plenam,
> Nam adeo fimo oblita est
> Ut nemo potest provocare in animum.
>
> "Doctores tibi dabunt anseres,
> Et multos, Dux, anates.
> Gratia Vestra gratias agat,
> Nam habebis omnia gratis.
>
> "Damus tibi duas damas
> (Sylvæ carent cervis),
> Sed ut servi tui habeant madamas
> Conamur omnibus nervis.
>
> "Flocci æstimamus oves,
> Et loquimur Bulls[2] de vitalibus,[3]
> Et ita Celsitutidini Tuæ
> Provisum est de victualibus.
>
> "Hic possis videre literas,
> Sed nullas hic lituras.
> Auriga, hæ sunt Scholæ nostræ,
> Be pleased to hold still your horses."

---

[1] *I.e.*, caps and gowns, the use of which had just been brought back by the Restoration.

[2] The word "Bulls" at this time was used for English as well as Irish jokes.

[3] Probably a mistake for *vitellabus*.

"Sorores novem suos hic
Semper exercent lusus,
Sed ita stabulis sunt similes
Ut sint aptiores Pegaso quam Musis.[1]

"In Collegio hoc Emmanuel,
Sunt omnes sub securi.[2]
Ffor that your Grace may understand me well,
Sunt omnes ibi puri.

"Si licuit Prometheo artem
Hic exercere tutam
Nullibi gentium melius poterit
Invenire lutum.

"Non opus sit ut ignem peteret
A sole vel a stella,
Abunde hoc suppeditabit
Trinitatis nostræ capella.

"Tanto zelo ardebat domus
Ut negligerent omnes jocos,
Et pro duas horas pugnarent acriter
Pro aris contra focos."[3]

---

[1] It does not appear on what this felicitous conceit was founded. Logan's contemporary print does not justify the comparison.

[2] The Puritan College having a specially strict discipline at this time, as existing records testify.

[3] This last reference is to the fire on Advent Sunday, November 30, 1662, when the Trinity Chapel clerk put the extinguished candles, as usual, under the altar, while one wick was still smouldering. The altar was thus destroyed, which was the more regretted as it was the only one in Cambridge to survive the Puritan cataclysm, having been hidden for nearly twenty years by a devout lady.

CHAPTER X.

MODERN PERIOD.

§ 1—5. Modern England begun at Restoration—Political conditions—Ecclesiastical—Social—Coinage—First coppers—Earlier tokens.
§ 6—8. First public vehicles—First postal deliveries—First newspapers.
§ 9—24. Newmarket Races—Stourbridge Fair.
§ 25—28. University progress in eighteenth century—The Tripos—George I. enlarges the Library—Epigrams.
§ 29—43. Draining of Fens—Early objections—Attempt by Charles I.—Bedford Level—Cromwell—Conservators—Wicken Fen—Decoys.
§ 44—51. Enclosure of wastes—Effect on peasantry—Agrarian discontent—Rising at Ely—Rick-burning—Victorian prosperity.
§ 52—58. Church restoration—Earlier decay—Visitation of 1685—State of fabrics—Services—Education—Nonconformity—Briefs—The great storm.
§ 59—61. University changes in nineteenth century.
§ 62—65. Elementary education—First (Sunday) schools—Local Government—Water-supply—Hobson's conduit—Present agricultural depression.

§ 1. WITH the reign of Charles II., as Lord Macaulay has pointed out, we enter the region of modern English history. The series of transmutations through which the civil and ecclesiastical constitution of the realm had been so long passing then issued in that resultant equilibrium between the various conflicting influences which has ever since been practically maintained. With the statesmen of earlier ages the British politician of to-day would find himself at issue in regard to the most fundamental principles of government. But these principles so far developed themselves, after the Restoration, on still existing lines, that he would be able at least to discuss them with the diplomatists of that reign on a common platform. From this reign dates the conception of a Ministry as part of our Constitution, and those great party names of Whig and Tory, which have divided the Ministerial Government between them even to our own day.

§ 2. In Cambridgeshire, no less than elsewhere, social and political life now assume their existing complexion. In every village the Prayer-Book was restored, never to be again disused; the dispossessed Church of England minister, if he survived the hardships consequent on his ejection,[1] returned to his cure; while his Puritan supplanter was (on "Black Bartholomew," 1662) in turn ejected, and, very probably, found a new vocation in ministering to those Nonconformist congregations which now sprang up everywhere, and have continued to this day. The squires, the farmers, the labourers, all now found their respective levels, ever since maintained, and scarcely yet shifted, even by the rapid changes which have marked the last quarter of the nineteenth century.

§ 3. An outward and visible token of the introduction, at this period, of modern conditions is to be found in the fact that our coinage now took its permanent form, the only subsequent change worthy of notice being that from the guinea to the sovereign in the present century. While older English money is entirely different in appearance to any now in use, coins of Charles II. (the best in design ever issued from a British mint) are still not infrequently found in circulation. This is especially

[1] See above, p. 218.

the case with those of the lesser denominations, the fourpenny, threepenny, and twopenny bits, now first struck; and above all with the copper, never before used by the State for money. The great significance of this last fact is commonly forgotten by historians; but few political developments have ever had more practical effect on the popular life of our country.

§ 4. When the lowest coin issued by Government was the silver penny, the purchasing power of which varied, between the twelfth and seventeenth centuries, from that of a florin to that of a sixpence, it was obviously necessary that some less valuable medium of exchange should be provided for use amongst the masses. This medium was found in a system of "tokens," thin, broad coins of bronze, often stamped with designs of the highest artistic merit. These were partly issued by the abbeys, for the convenience of their dependents, and partly imported from the prolific mint of Nuremberg, where the manufacture of the like cheap mintage is a speciality even to this day. The earliest of these Nuremberg tokens (which are found by hundreds in Cambridgeshire) are imitations of the Venetian "bezant," and bear the lion of St. Mark; the latest are impressed with Renaissance designs. They are usually inscribed with some pious German sentiment, such as:

> GOTTES . SEGEN . MACHT . REICH .,
> DAS . WORT . GOTTS . BLEIBT . EWICK .,
> GOTTES . GABEN . SOLL . MAN . LOB .,

and the like. These tokens passed current, for small and uncertain values, as suited the convenience of buyer and seller, till towards the end of the sixteenth century, when their place was taken by others, of much poorer workmanship, issued by local tradesmen, and current within the area of their local credit for the amount (usually a halfpenny) which they claim to represent. Of these, too, Cambridgeshire furnishes abundant examples, bearing such inscriptions as

THOMAS . POWELL . OF . CAMBRIDGE
HIS . HALFPENNY . 1666.

These tokens in turn died out with the seventeenth century. Towards the end of the eighteenth they were revived, in superior form, chiefly issued by local bodies, and continued in use till the Peace of 1814. Those current in our County bear on one side a hooded head (probably representing " Camus, reverend sire "[1]), and on the other a beehive, with the inscription INDUSTRY HAS ITS SURE REWARD.

§ 5. It was no small advance in material convenience when the restored monarchy took this small change business into its own hands, and sent out the first copper pence, halfpence, and farthings, all beautifully minted, with the familiar figure of Britannia on the reverse (copied from a Romano-British design of the Emperor Hadrian), and bearing the motto CAROLVS . A . CAROLO, by which Charles II. declared his immediate inheritance of the throne from his ill-fated father.

§ 6. Three other great factors of modern social life also take their rise at this period, the first public vehicles for passenger traffic making their appearance in the County, along with the establishment of the first regular postal service, and the first organized attempt to provide periodical information as to current events—political, social and literary. These most potent developments were necessarily, each and all, rude and imperfect in their embryonic conception. But the first "flying" coach which, in this reign, succeeded in covering the fifty-five miles[2] between Cam-

[1] Milton, "Lycidas."
[2] The first milestones ever seen in England (since Roman days) were set up on the road between Cambridge and London, in 1729, in connection with a local trust fund administered by Trinity Hall, whose arms are still to be seen on them.

bridge and London, during the light of a summer day, is connected, by a line of unbroken progress, with the express trains of to-day; and the first "news-letter" which brought to the solitary coffee-house of Cambridge the weekly gossip of the Metropolis[1] (not the mere garbled scraps which alone could appear in the official Gazette) is in like manner the progenitor of the London papers by which Cambridgeshire is now kept in daily touch with the furthest corners of the earth.

§ 7. The progress, however, though continuous, was for many decades very far from rapid. So late as the middle of the eighteenth century the postal letter-bags were still conveyed on horseback, and left Cambridge for London every night but Saturday at 5 or 6 p.m., the delivery being every noon but Monday "at the Post-house." Nor was there any other postal service in connection with Cambridge except to Bury St. Edmunds (daily), and (twice a week) to Caxton, where the line of the Great North Road was tapped; but a "licensed letter-carrier" started for London at 3 p.m. on Monday, Tuesday, Wednesday, and Friday, getting back at 11 a.m. on Thursday, Friday, Saturday, and Tuesday.

§ 8. These interesting, if humble, items of historical information are given in Carter's "History of Cambridgeshire," now an exceedingly rare book. From it we also learn that, at the date of his writing (1753), the London and Cambridge coaches started at 4 a.m., and were not due till 7 p.m. There were only two such coaches, one of which left Cambridge each Monday and Thursday, the other Tuesday and Friday, returning on the following days. Each coach had accommodation for six passengers (all being seated inside). The ordinary fare of the earliest coaches was about 2½d. per mile in summer, and somewhat more in winter. The cost of the journey from Cambridge to London was thus about 12s.—as

---

[1] Macaulay, "History of England," vol. i., p. 392.

much as a first-class return ticket by railway at the present day.

Six "stage waggons" also ran to London weekly in 1753, all alike starting on Monday or Tuesday, and getting back Friday or Saturday. But Cambridge was not connected by regular passenger vehicles with any town except London, though there were weekly carriers to Bury St. Edmunds, Haverhill, Huntingdon, Ipswich, St. Ives, Kettering, Lynn, Mepal, Newmarket, Northampton, Norwich, Stamford, and Yarmouth. There was, however, an organized system of connection by which goods could be forwarded by road to almost any part of England. Carter gives a list of no fewer than sixty-eight destinations, including such remote spots as Bangor, Kendal, St. David's, and Launceston. With Ely, and with Downham in Norfolk, there was regular communication by water, and, till the construction of the railway, fuel was brought to Cambridge almost wholly by this water carriage. Carter writes that (in 1753) "for the convenience of passengers and heavy goods to and from Cambridge, a passage-boat goes every Tuesday and Friday morning from Ely, and sets out on its return on Wednesday and Saturday noon from Cambridge. The distance by water is about twenty miles, and is generally done in about six hours." Cambridge is now (1897) the centre on which eight lines of railway converge,[1] while fifteen express trains either way daily cover the distance to London in less than an hour and a half. Letters, moreover, are delivered eight times a day in Cambridge, and at least twice in almost every village throughout the County.

§ 9. Nor must a Cambridgeshire historian pass over the establishment under Charles II. of one of the most distinctive features of our County, the Newmarket Races. Horse-racing had not been unknown in Cambridgeshire

[1] See Appendix D.

at an earlier date. Stow mentions a race-meeting held at Linton under the auspices of James I. That monarch had a hunting-box at Newmarket, which, after serving as a place of detention for his ill-starred son, was rebuilt by his grandson, whose keen eye for his own amusements saw how admirably adapted was the expanse of turf beside the Devil's Dyke for the new sport which he was so successful in making a part of English life.

§ 10. It is possible, however, that he was merely reviving an older local custom; for Newmarket had been from its first foundation the great centre of the Eastern Counties horse-trade. That centre had in ancient times been at the neighbouring village of Exning, the capital seat of Anna, the hero-King of East Anglia.[1] But an outbreak of the plague in 1227 had caused the old mart in the natural amphitheatre beside its springs to be deserted, and a New Market to be established on the Icknield Way, at the borders of Cambridgeshire and Suffolk. The exhibition of paces is an essential feature of any horse-fair, and the step from this to trials of speed and matches between the animals for sale is a very small one.

§ 11. But it was the Merry Monarch who first founded at Newmarket a regular race-meeting, and under his patronage the Heath became annually one of the gayest spots in England. "It was not uncommon," says Macaulay,[2] "for the whole Court and Cabinet to go down there," Charles himself, to the admiration of his subjects, posting down from London in a single day, with only two relays of fresh horses. "Jewellers and milliners, players and fiddlers, venal wits and venal beauties, followed in crowds. The streets were made impassable by coaches and six. In the places of public resort peers flirted with maids of honour, and officers of the Life Guards, all plumes and gold lace, jostled professors in trencher caps

[1] See above, p. 47.
[2] "History of England," vol. iv., p. 611.

and black gowns. For on such occasions the neighbouring University of Cambridge always sent her highest functionaries with loyal addresses, and selected her ablest theologians to preach before the Sovereign and his splendid retinue. In the wild days before the Revolution, indeed, the most learned and eloquent divine might fail to draw a fashionable audience, particularly if Buckingham announced his intention of holding forth; for sometimes his Grace would enliven the dulness of a Sunday morning by addressing to the bevy of fine gentlemen and fine ladies a ribald exhortation which he called a sermon. With lords and ladies from St. James's and Soho, and with doctors from Trinity College and King's College, were mingled the provincial aristocracy, fox-hunting squires and their rosy-cheeked daughters, who had come in queer-looking family coaches, drawn by cart-horses, from the remotest parishes of three or four counties to see their Sovereign.

* * * * *

"Racing was only one of the many amusements of that festive season. On fine mornings there was hunting. For those who preferred hawking, choice falcons were brought from Holland. On rainy days the cock-pit was encircled by stars and blue ribbons.

* * * * *

"The Heath was fringed by a wild, gipsy-like camp of vast extent. For the hope of being able to feed on the leavings of many sumptuous tables, and to pick up some of the guineas and crowns which the spendthrifts of London were throwing about, attracted thousands of peasants from a circle of many miles."[1]

Yet the place itself was of so little importance that even in 1753, as Carter's "History" tells us, it had no

[1] A specially brilliant race-meeting was held in 1698, when Tallard, the French Ambassador, opened the first negotiations with William III. on the Spanish Succession (Macaulay, "Hist.," v. 115).

resident butcher, all meat being brought in from adjoining villages. He adds that "during the races such is the resort that a bed is let for a guinea a night, and a hackney horse in Cambridge is not to be got for money."

§ 12. Newmarket thus became the first of these great horse-racing gatherings, which have thence spread with the spread of the Anglo-Saxon race and influence throughout the world. Its new race-meetings rivalled in the crowds they drew together the older County institution of Stourbridge Fair, which in the seventeenth and eighteenth centuries boasted itself the largest in Europe.

As such, Bunyan made it the prototype of his "Vanity Fair." During his Bedfordshire youth he must often have been drawn to its attractions, and we may easily recognise, in the description given by the Cambridgeshire historian, Carter, the features which we know so well in "Pilgrim's Progress." The many kinds of merchandise sold, "As Houses, Lands, Trades, Places, Honours, Preferments, Titles, Countreys, Kingdoms, Lusts, Pleasures and Delights of all sorts, as Whores, Bauds, Wives, Husbands, Children, Masters, Servants, Lives, Blood, Bodies, Souls, Silver, Gold, Pearls, precious Stones, and what not"; the varied frivolities, "Juglings, Cheats, Games, Plays, Fools, Apes, Knaves, and Rogues, and that of all sorts"; the darker side of the festivities, which gave "to be seen, and that for nothing, Thefts, Murders, Adulteries, False-swearings, and that of a blood-red colour"; the disposition of the Fair into "the proper Places, Rows, Streets, where the Wares of this Fair are soonest to be found"; the peremptory Court of Justice under "the Great One of the Fair," ever ready to take immediate cognizance of any "hubbub in the Fair"—all these are touches drawn from the life.

§ 13. Carter's description is as follows:

"Near half a mile east of this village [Barnwell] Sturbridge Fair is kept, which is set out annually on St. Bartholomew by the Mayor, Aldermen, and the rest of the Corporation of Cambridge; who all ride thither in a grand procession, with music playing before them, and most of the boys in the town on horseback after them, who, as soon as the ceremony is read over, ride races about the place; when returning to Cambridge each boy has a cake and some ale at the Town Hall. On the 7th of September they ride in the same manner to proclaim it; which being done, the Fair begins, and continues three weeks; though the greatest part is over in a fortnight.

§ 14. "This Fair, which was thought some years ago to be the greatest in Europe, is kept in a cornfield, about half a mile square, having the River Cam running on the north side thereof, and the rivulet called the Stour (from which and the bridge over it the Fair received its name) on the east side, and it is about two miles east of Cambridge market-place; where, during the Fair, coaches, chaises, and chariots attend to carry persons to the Fair. The chief diversions at Sturbridge are drolls, rope-dancing, and sometimes a music-booth; but there is an Act of Parliament which prohibits the acting of plays within fifteen miles of Cambridge.[1]

§ 15. "If the field (on which the Fair is kept) is not cleared of the corn by the 24th of August, the builders may trample it underfoot to build their booths; and, on the other hand, if the same be not cleared of the booths and materials belonging thereto by Michaelmas Day at noon, the plough-men may enter the same with their horses, ploughs, and carts, and destroy whatever they find on the premises. The filth, dung, straw, etc., left behind by the fair-keepers, make amends for their trampling and hardening of the ground.

§ 16. "The shops or booths are built in rows like streets, having each their name; as Garlick Row, Booksellers'-

---

[1] This Act continued to be enforced till the middle of the nineteenth century.

row, Cook-row, etc. And every commodity has its proper place, as the Cheese Fair, Hop Fair, Wool Fair, etc.; and here, as in several other streets or rows, are all sorts of traders, who sell by wholesale or retail, as goldsmiths, toy-men, brasiers, turners, milliners, haberdashers, hatters, mercers, drapers, pewterers, china warehouses, and, in a word, most trades that can be found in London, from whence many of them come. Here are also taverns, coffee-houses, and eating-houses in great plenty, and all kept in booths, in any of which (except the coffee-booth) you may at any time be accommodated with hot or cold roast goose, roast or boiled pork, etc.

§ 17. "Crossing the main road at the south end of Garlick Row, and a little to the left hand, is a great Square, formed of the largest booths, called the Duddery, the area of which Square is from 240 to 300 feet, chiefly taken up with woollen drapers, wholesale tailors, and sellers of second-hand clothes;[1] where the dealers have a room before their booths, to take down and open their packs, and bring in waggons to load and unload the same. In the centre of this Square was (till within these three years) erected a tall May-pole, with a vane at the top; and in this Square, on the two chief Sundays during the fair, both forenoon and afternoon, Divine Service is read, and a sermon preached from a pulpit placed in the open air, by the Minister of Barnwell; who is very well paid for the same by the contribution of the fair-keepers.

§ 18. "In this Duddery only, it is said, there have been sold £100,000 worth of woollen manufactures in less than a week's time; besides the prodigious trade carried on

---

[1] The special development of the woollen trade in this fair is said (by Fuller) to have been due to certain traders from Kendal in Westmorland (famed through many centuries for its manufacture of cloth), who were here weather-bound on their way to the great entrepot at Norwich, and found a ready sale for the goods which they spread out to dry.

here, by the wholesale tailors from London, and most other parts of England, who transact their business wholly in their pocket-books, and meeting here their chapmen from all parts, make up their accounts, receive money chiefly in bills, and take further orders. These, they say, exceed by far the sale of goods actually brought to the Fair, and delivered in kind; it being frequent for the London wholesale men to carry back orders from their dealers for £10,000 worth of goods a man, and some much more. And once in this Duddery, it is said, there was a booth consisting of six apartments, all belonging to a dealer in Norwich stuffs only, who had there above £20,000 worth of those goods.

§ 19. "The trade for wool, hops, and leather here is prodigious; the quantity of wool only sold at one fair is said to have amounted to £50,000 or £60,000, and of hops very little less.

"September 14, being the Horse Fair day, is the day of the greatest hurry, when it is almost incredible to conceive what number of people there are, and the quantity of victuals that day consumed by them.

"During the Fair, Colchester oysters and white herrings, just coming into season, are in great request, at least by such as live in the inland parts of the kingdom, where they are seldom to be had fresh, especially the latter.[1]

§ 20. "The Fair is like a well-governed city; and less disorder and confusion to be seen there than in any other place where there is so great a concourse of people: here is a Court of Justice always open from morning till night, where the Mayor of Cambridge, or his Deputy, sits as Judge, determining all controversies in matters arising from the business of the Fair, and seeing the Peace thereof kept; for which purpose he hath eight servants, called

[1] A dish of fresh herrings was invariably set before the Vice-Chancellor at the official banquet when the fair was declared open.

Red-coats, attending him during the time of the Fair and other public occasions, one or other of which are constantly at hand in most parts of the Fair: and if any dispute arise between buyer and seller, on calling out 'Red-coat,' you have instantly one or more come running to you; and if the dispute is not quickly decided, the offender is carried to the said Court, where the case is decided in a summary way, from which sentence there lies no appeal.

§ 21. "About two or three days after the Horse Fair day, when the hurry of the wholesale business is over, the country gentry for about ten or twelve miles round begin to come in with their sons and daughters; and though diversion is what chiefly brings them, yet it is not a little money they lay out among the tradesmen, toy-shops, etc., besides what is flung away to see the puppet shows, drolls, rope-dancing, live creatures, etc., of which there is commonly plenty.

§ 22. "The last observation I shall make concerning this Fair is, how inconveniently a multitude of people are lodged there who keep it; their bed (if I may so call it) is laid on two or three boards, nailed to four pieces that bear it about a foot from the ground, and four boards round it, to keep the persons and their clothes from falling off, and is about five feet long, standing abroad all day if it rains not. At night it is taken into their booths, and put in to the best manner they can; at bed-time they get into it, and lie neck and heels together until the morning, if the wind and rain do not force them out sooner; for a high wind often blows down their booths, as it did A.D. 1741, and a heavy rain forces through the hair-cloth that covers it.

§ 23. "Though the Corporation of Cambridge has the tolls of this Fair,[1] and the government as aforesaid, yet

---

[1] The tolls were originally granted (by King John) to the Lepers' Hospital at Stourbridge. See p. 141.

the body of the University has the oversight of the weights and measures thereof (as well as at Midsummer[1] and Reach Fairs[2]) and the licensing of all show-booths, live creatures, etc.; and the Proctors of the University keep a Court there also to hear complaints about weights and measures,[3] seek out and punish lewd women,[4] and see that their Gownsmen commit no disorders."

§ 24. These rights of the University in the Fair were a fertile theme for the satire of the Oxford "Terræ Filius" mentioned in our last chapter.[5] In one speech this functionary describes the Cambridge Proctors as having there a booth of their own for the sale of beer, the Pro-proctors acting as potmen. No wonder, he continues, that they are so strict in forbidding undergraduates to enter public-houses. It would spoil their own trade.

[1] Midsummer Fair is held on Midsummer Common, between Cambridge and Barnwell, and was of old connected with Barnwell Priory. The Common derives its name from the fair.

[2] Reach is situated at the Fenward extremity of the Devil's Dyke (see above, p. 14), and is about seven miles from Cambridge. It is now quite a small village, but its position made it a place of great importance in early times. A Roman villa has been unearthed there, and local tradition declares that the place once possessed seven churches. Its situation at the River Gate of the Icenian and East Anglian realms must have made it from the first a place of traffic, and its Fair remained famous for many centuries.

[3] See above, p. 125.

[4] An ordinance of Edward I. (Patent Rolls, 1327, March 13) provides that no *publica mulier* shall stay within the town or suburbs of Cambridge, and that proclamation be made of this four times a year by the Mayor and Bailiffs on information of the Vice-Chancellor or Chancellor, and that any such woman found three days after such proclamation be imprisoned. By the charter of Elizabeth the University authorities have power to arrest and imprison such in a special place of confinement known as the Spinning House, where further chastisement used to be inflicted. "Thither," says Carter, "doth the Toun Cryer oft-times resort, to discipline the Ladies of Pleasure with his whip."

[5] See above, p. 228.

§ 25. But before the eighteenth century was far advanced, the license introduced in the sixteenth had practically died out, and the admission to degrees once more became a serious proceeding. In 1740 " Mr. Tripos " was formally abolished, and his satirical outpourings confined to the Latin or Greek " Tripos Verses"; which to this day are usually the production of some "old Bachelor,"[1] and are supposed to deal, in a spirit of modified license, with the current topics of interest in the University. The printing on the back of the " Tripos Verse" sheet of the "Honour" lists led to the Honour Examination itself becoming known as the Tripos.

§ 26. And about the same period the series of public disputations, which had hitherto been the sole gauge of a student's proficiency, became first supplemented and then supplanted by the more accurate test of a single written examination. The still surviving nomenclature of the Mathematical Tripos (within living memory the only Honour Examination for Cambridge Degrees) bears witness to the gradual nature and recent development of the new system. Originally the " Wranglers " were those abler and more ambitious students who *habitually* took part in the disputations (instead of confining themselves to the minimum required by statute), and whose comparative powers thus became well known to the "Moderators" presiding over these exercises. These authorities, together with the Proctors, arranged the Honour list at their discretion; adding to the Wranglers those students who had won the approving formula, "Optime quidem disputasti," and thus became known as "Senior (or Junior) Optimes." But not till the beginning of the nineteenth century did the old system entirely make way for that which still exists.

§ 27. In the latter part of the seventeenth century the studies of the University assumed that specially

[1] See above, p. 227.

mathematical colouring which was for a long time their exclusive, and is still their chief, characteristic. Originally mathematical theses seem to have been favoured by disputants in the Schools on account of the difficulty of confuting them; but the glory of such men as Sir Isaac Newton led to a less sordid conception of their value, and during the eighteenth century they formed the main part of the training of every candidate for Honours.

§ 28. From 1730 the Tripos was held in the newly-built Senate House, adjoining the University Library, which, by a grant from George I., was able to enlarge itself by thirty thousand volumes. This grant was made in recognition of the Hanoverian principles current at Cambridge, the Jacobitism of Oxford being at the same time punished by the quartering of cavalry upon that city; a difference in treatment which called forth from an Oxford wit the following quatrain:

> "King George, observing with judicious eyes
> The state of both his Universities,
> To Oxford sent a troop of horse: and why?
> That Learned Body wanted Loyalty.
> To Cambridge books he sent,—as well discerning
> How much that Loyal Body wanted Learning."

The Cantab reply, composed by Sir Thomas Browne, the founder of the University prize for Greek and Latin Epigrams, ran thus:

> "The King to Oxford sent his troops of horse,
> For Tories own no argument but force.
> With equal wit to Cambridge books he sent,
> For Whigs admit no force but argument."

In 1769, at their own petition, the soft round hats with a brim of black velvet which had hitherto been the head-gear of the undergraduates gave place to the square trencher cap, which has ever since been associated with University costume.

§ 29. And while the University was thus modernizing its curriculum, the physical aspect of the County was being modified towards its present condition by two mighty changes, the Draining of the Fens in its northern regions, and the Enclosure of the Wastes in the southern districts. The former operation was by far the greater, and began far earlier. Certain limited tracts had been reclaimed by the monks of the great abbeys, and in the fifteenth century Bishop Morton, of Ely, and others undertook the work on a much larger scale. "Vast sums," says Carter, "were expended in making ditches and banks, impregnable, as they thought, against all assaults of inundation.

§ 30. "But the next winter being wet and windy, down comes the bailiff of Bedford (for so the country people call the overflowing of the river Ouse), attended, like a person of quality, with many servants (the accession of tributary brooks), and breaks down all their paper banks as not waterproof, reducing all to their former condition.

§ 31. "This accident put the wits of that and succeeding ages upon the dispute of the feasibility of the design; and let us sum up the arguments for and against this great undertaking.

"*Argument* 1.—Some objected that God said to the water, ' Hitherto shalt thou come, and no further.' It is therefore a trespass on the Divine prerogative, for man to presume to give other bounds to the water than what God hath appointed.

"*Answer* 1.—The argument holdeth in application to the Ocean, which is a wild horse, only to be broke, backed, and bridled by Him who is the Maker thereof; but it is a false and lazy principle if applied to fresh waters, from which human industry may and hath rescued many considerable parcels of ground.

§ 32. "*Argument* 2.—Many have attempted, but not effected it. None ever wrestled with it, but it gave them a foil, if not a fall, to the bruising, if not breaking, of their backs. Many have burnt their fingers in these waters, and instead of draining the Fens have emptied their pockets.

"*Answer* 2.—Many men's undertaking thereof implies the possibility of the project; for it is not likely so many wise men should seek for what is not to be found; the failing is not in the improbability of the design, but in the undertakers either wanting heads, or hearts, to pursue, or pay the people employed therein.

* * * * *

§ 33. "*Argument* 4.—An alderman of Cambridge affirmed the Fens to be like a crust of bread swimming in a dish of water. So that under eight or ten feet earth it is nothing but mere water. Impossible therefore the draining thereof, if surrounded by that liquid element both above and below.

"*Answer* 4.—Interest betrayed his judgment to an evident error; and his brains seemed rather to swim than the floating earth; for such as have sounded the depth of that ground, find it to be Terra Firma, and no doubt as solid to the centre as any other earth in England.

§ 34. "*Argument* 5.—The river Grant or Cam (call it what you will), running by Cambridge, will have its stream dried up by the draining of the Fens. Now, as Cambridge is concerned in its river, so that whole county, yea, this whole kindgom, is concerned in Cambridge. No reason, therefore, that private men's particular profit should be preferred before an universal good, or good of an University.

"*Answer* 5.—It is granted the water by Cambridge kindles and keeps in the fire therein:[1] no hope of sufficient fuel on reasonable rates, except care be taken for preserving the river navigable, which may be done, and the

---

[1] See above, § 8. In 1753, Carter tells us, "Newcastle coals are sold at fifteen shillings per sack (which contains two bushels), and good turf about five shillings per thousand, from the riverside." Coal now costs in Cambridge from fifteen to twenty shillings per ton.

Fens drained nevertheless. To take away the thief is no wasting or weakening of the wick of the candle. Assurances may be given that no damage shall rebound to the stream of Grant by stopping other superfluous waters.

§ 35. "*Argument* 6.—The Fens preserved in their present property afford great plenty and variety of fish and fowl, which have their seminaries and nurseries, which will be destroyed on the draining thereof, so that none will be had but at excessive prices.

"*Answer* 6.—A large first makes recompense for the shorter second course at any man's table. And who will not prefer a tame sheep before a wild duck? a good fat ox before a well-grown eel?

"*Argument* 7.—The Fens afford plenty of sedge, turf, and reed; the want whereof will be found if their nature be altered.

"*Answer* 7.—These commodities are inconsiderable to balance the profit of good grass and grain, which those grounds, if drained, will produce. He cannot complain of wrong, who hath a suit of buckram taken from him, and one of velvet given instead thereof. Besides, provision may be made that a sufficiency of such ware-trash may still be preserved.

"*Argument* 8.—Many thousands of poor people are maintained by fishing and fowling in the Fens, which will all be at a loss for a livelihood if their farms be burnt; that is, if the Fens be drained.

"*Answer* 8.—It is confessed that many who love idleness live (and only live) by that employment. But such, if the Fens were drained, would quit their idleness, and betake themselves to more lucrative manufactures.

§ 36. "*Argument* 9.—Grant that the Fens be drained with great difficulty, they will quickly revert to their old condition like to the Pontine Marshes in Italy.

"*Answer* 9.—If a patient, perfectly cured, will be careless of his health, none will pity his relapse. Moderate cost with constant care will easily preserve what is drained, the Low Countries affording many proofs thereof.

"*Argument* 10.—Grant them drained and so continuing; as now the great fishes prey upon the less, so then wealthy men would devour the poorer sort of people; injurious partage would follow upon the inclosures, and rich men (to make room for themselves) would jostle the poor people out of their commons.

"*Answer* 10.—Oppression is not essential either to draining or enclosing, though too often a concomitant of both. Order may be taken by Commissioners of quality impowered for that purpose, that such a proportion of commons may be allotted to the poor that all private persons may be pleased and advance accrue hereby to the Commonwealth."

§ 37. These polemics date from the early years of the seventeenth century, when, in 1630, the second great attempt to drain the Fens was being undertaken by Francis, Earl of Bedford, to whose family Thorney Abbey with its estates (including only 300 acres of arable land) had been granted in 1539. The work was begun under the auspices of Charles I., who brought skilled labourers over from Holland to superintend it. The complaints of the Fenmen at these innovations met accordingly with strong support from the Parliamentary party, and very particularly from Oliver Cromwell. The new-made dykes were cut, and the reclaimed lands once more drowned. But when Cromwell was established as Protector, he himself caused the work to be resumed, the Earl of Bedford again undertaking the responsibility[1] in consideration of a grant of 95,000 acres. "And after the further expenditure of £300,000 (in addition to £100,000 spent by his father), it was finished and completed nearly as we now see it (in 1753),

[1] Hence the new channels cut for the Ouse are called the Bedford Rivers, and the reclaimed area the Bedford Level.

to the undoing of many who were admitted sharers and adventurers with him therein, the sum being much more than the 95,000 acres were worth."

§ 38. And to this day the "adventure" retains the same luckless reputation as a commercial speculation. The lion's share has always been held by the Earls (now Dukes) of Bedford, who during the nineteenth century alone have expended on their Thorney estates nearly £2,000,000. Yet the Thorney property does not even pay its way. The noble owners have, however, their reward in the genuine success which has crowned the experiment from a philanthropic point of view. Thanks to their efforts, Thorney is again, as in the old days of the Benedictines, a smiling, well-wooded oasis amid the dreary Fenland[1]; where the welfare of the tenantry is, as of old, the chief object of the landlord, and where, in consequence, pauperism, drunkenness, and crime are alike practically unknown.[2]

§ 39. Finally, in 1664, King Charles II. constituted a Corporation for governing the Level, "by the name of the Governors, Bailiffs, and Commonalty of the Company of the Conservators of the Great Level of the Fens. This Corporation consists of a Governor, six Bailiffs, twenty Conservators, and Commonalty, who are vested with power to do whatever in their judgments they shall think best, in order to the support and preservation of the Great Level." Under this authority the work of drainage has been steadily continued; but not till the nineteenth century was far advanced can it be said to have been completed, leaving only the few acres of "Wicken Fen" to show what, within living memory, was the characteristic of the whole "boundless plain"[3] of the Fenland.

[1] See Chapter VI., § 37.
[2] See "A Great Agricultural Estate," by the Duke of Bedford (1897).
[3] Macaulay, "Armada."

§ 40. And even in Wicken Fen, though the sedge and the rushes and the reeds still rise, as of old, from the water-logged soil, the swarming animal life which was once so conspicuous a feature of the district can be seen no longer. Now and then a Swallow-tail butterfly is still to be beheld flitting over the water-courses and reed-beds; but its companion, the Great Copper, is utterly extinct, along with the whole population of ruffs and reeves and water-fowl of every tribe, whose cries and motions made a never-ceasing stir throughout what is now the most silent expanse in England.

"In these fens," writes Carter in 1753, "are several of those admirable contrivances called decoys, in which it is incredible what quantities of duck, teal, widgeon, and all kind of wild fowl, are taken every week during the season. There is one near Ely which lets for £500 a year, and from that alone they generally send up to London 3,000 couple a week."

§ 41. These "decoys," the use of which is now wholly obsolete, consisted of a curved ditch called the "pipe," leading from the open water of the mere for some fifty yards into the reed-bed.[1] As it curved, this ditch also narrowed, from about twelve feet at its mouth to only two feet at its shoreward extremity. Along its course poles were driven into the ground, close to its edge, on each side, and the tops were bent over across the ditch and tied together. These poles, thus bent, formed at the entrance of the ditch or pipe an arch, the top of which was ten feet distant from the surface of the water. This arch was made to decrease in height as the pipe decreased in width, so that the remote end was not more than eighteen inches in height. The poles were placed about six feet from each other, and connected by poles laid lengthwise across the arch and tied together. Over the whole was thrown a net, which was made fast to a

[1] This description is from Knight's "Animated Nature."

reed fence at the entrance, and nine or ten yards up the ditch, and afterwards strongly pegged to the ground. At the end of the pipe farthest from the entrance was fixed a "tunnel-net," as it was called, about four yards in length, of a round form, and kept open by a number of hoops, about eighteen inches in diameter, placed at a small distance from each other to keep it distended. Supposing the circular bend of the pipe to be to the right of its issue from the mere, then on the left-hand side a number of reed fences were constructed, called " shootings," for the purpose of screening the " decoy-man " from observation, and in such a manner that the fowl in the mere might not be alarmed while he was driving those that were in the pipe. These shootings, which were ten in number, were about four yards in length, and about six feet high. From the end of the last shooting a person could not be seen from the mere, owing to the bend of the pipes, and there was then no further occasion for shelter. Had it not been for these shootings, the fowl that remained about the mouth of the pipe would have been alarmed if the person driving the fowl already under the net should have been exposed, and would have become so shy as entirely to forsake the place.

§ 42. The first thing that the decoy-man did when he approached the pipe was to take a piece of lighted turf or peat, and hold it near his mouth to prevent the birds from smelling him. He was attended by a dog, trained for the purpose of rendering him assistance. He would then walk very silently about half-way up the shootings, where a small piece of wood was thrust through the reed fence, which made an aperture just large enough to enable him to see if any fowl were in; if not, he walked forward to see if any were about the entrance of the pipe. If there were, he stopped and made a motion to his dog, and gave him a piece of cheese, or something else, to eat; and, having received this, the animal went directly to a hole through the reed fence, and the birds immediately flew off the bank into the water. The dog returned along the bank between the reed fences, and came out to his master at another hole. The man then gave him something to reward and encourage him, and the animal repeated his round until the birds were attracted by his motions, and followed him to the mouth of the pipe. This operation was called "working" them. The man then retreated farther back, working the dog at different holes until the ducks were sufficiently under the net. He then commanded his dog to lie down behind the fence, and going himself forward to the end of the pipe next the mere, he took off his hat and gave it a wave between the shootings. All the birds that were under the net could then see him, but none that were in the mere could do so. The former flew forward, and the man then ran to the next shooting, and waved his hat, and so on, driving them along until they came to the tunnel net, into which they crept. When they were all in, the man gave the net a twist, so as to prevent them from getting back. He then took the net off from the end of the pipe, and, taking out one by one the ducks that were in it, dislocated their necks.

§ 43. The net was afterwards hung on again for the repetition of the process, and in this manner five or six dozen were sometimes taken at one drift. When the wind blew directly in or out of the pipes, the fowl seldom worked well, especially when it blew into the pipe. The reason of this was that the ducks always preferred swimming against the wind, otherwise the wind, blowing from behind, caught and ruffled their feathers. If many pipes were made in the same mere, they were so constructed as to suit different winds, and were worked accordingly. The better to entice the fowl into the pipe, hemp-seed was occasionally strewn on the water. The season allowed by Act of Parliament for taking ducks in this way was from the latter end of October until February. Instead of the dog, a tame duck—the "decoy duck"—was sometimes employed. The bird was trained to mingle with the other water-fowl, and gradually to entice them into the pipe. This method was more effective than the other, but was less often used, as the duck was much less readily trained than the dog, and had to be much more frequently replaced.

§ 44. The enclosure of the County was for the most part the work of the early years of the nineteenth century. Even at the accession of Queen Victoria, the general aspect of the southern district, as seen from any hill-top, was that of a gently undulating prairie, out of which the villages, with their trees and hedges, rose like islands. Bustards were still occasionally to be met with, roaming this open expanse of down, and the sheep and cattle of the villagers found ample grazing space on its wide expanse of sparse herbage.

§ 45. The transformation scene from this primitive wilderness to the present condition of the County, of which almost every acre has been brought under husbandry, was not effected without considerable suffering to the peasantry, who everywhere lost, by the Enclosure Acts, the advantages which the waste lands had afforded them, receiving in exchange a scanty portion of "town land" in each parish, the rent of which is applied to local charities. And in every instance the policy of the Government placed these "town lands" in the least accessible corner of the parish, for the express purpose of preventing labourers from acquiring allotments in them and thus becoming less dependent on their wages.

§ 46. Widespread agricultural discontent marked, accordingly, the early years of this century, and the period of special exhaustion which followed Waterloo brought with it pressure so extreme that, in the Isle of Ely, the peasantry actually took arms. Assembling, by sound of horn, at Littleport, they sacked some of the houses of the more prosperous, levied contributions on others, and then marched on Ely in formidable force, armed with guns, pistols, scythes, etc., and under cover of a waggon, on which they had mounted four punt guns. These formidable weapons, used for wild-fowl shooting, with barrels eight feet long, whose charge was no less than a pound of gunpowder, projected over the front of the vehicle to clear the way, if needful. But though the leading inhabitants of Ely had hastily armed themselves, and been sworn in as special constables, they were not prepared to face this artillery, and the town passed without resistance into the power of the mob, who repeated their Littleport doings on a larger scale, though with little bodily hurt to anyone.

§ 47. The rioters had, indeed, no clear idea what they wanted. It was a mere blind outbreak of starvation. Wages were nine shillings per week, and wheat at one hundred and three shillings per quarter. Their one demand was that their pay should be raised to the price of "a stone of flour a day," which would be equivalent, at *present* prices, to the not exorbitant sum of eleven shillings per week. Much sympathy was felt for their case by those better off than themselves, some of whom actually appeared at their head; but the movement speedily degenerated into a mere drunken riot, the chief sufferers in which were, as usual, those who had done most for the relief of the poor—the local shopkeepers, who had aided them by credit, and the local clergy, who had organized soup-kitchens for them.

§ 48. At the first approach of the military force sent for to suppress them, the rioters retreated in good order, still under cover of their armed waggon, to Littleport, where, however, only a handful made any sort of stand when the soldiers actually arrived. The rest were hunted through the Fens by squads of the Hanoverian regiment charged with the suppression of the revolt, who treated the district with true German thoroughness. Local tradition still hands down the tale of the poor thatcher who was engaged on the roof of the great tithe barn at Ely (the largest in the kingdom) at the moment when a detachment of these foreigners was marching past. The usual thatcher's cry to his assistant, "Bunch! bunch!" was interpreted by the German officer in command as an insult to his troops. On the instant he halted them beside the barn, and gave the order to fire. Pierced by a dozen musket-balls, the unhappy thatcher rolled from the roof, his body falling upon the great folding door of the barn, which happened to be half open. There it hung, dripping with blood, for over three days, the officer swearing that anyone who dared to remove it should share the same fate, as an example to all to behave with due respect to their oppressors.

§ 49. Finally, a Special Commission was held for the trial of the unhappy men, over eighty in number, who had been arrested. In spite of strong testimony to character, five were hanged, and five more transported for life, the rest undergoing various terms of imprisonment, all to the accompaniment of ecclesiastical rejoicings; the Bishop (the last to exercise his old palatine jurisdiction in the Isle)[1] entering the Cathedral in solemn procession, to the strains of the triumphal anthem, "Why do the heathen rage?" with his Sword of State borne before him (by his butler!) and escorted by fifty of the principal inhabitants, carrying white wands. No fewer than three hundred of these wand-bearers guarded the execution of the five rioters; yet the sympathy for them was so strong that the Bishop could not get a cart to carry them to the gallows under five guineas for the trip.

§ 50. Eighteen years after the riots at Ely, agrarian discontent once more found expression in the outbreak

[1] See above, p. 73.

of rick-burning which, in Cambridgeshire as throughout England, marked the reign of William IV. The fires, however, were not seldom the work of the very men paid to extinguish them; and the last execution for arson in the County was that of the captain of the Sawston fire-brigade, who had invented so ingenious a device that he caused no fewer than twenty-three fires before being detected. He had discovered that a ball of kindled turf, wrapped in greased rag, would smoulder for hours before bursting into flame, and he used to stroll out at dusk with this infernal device in his pocket till he found an opportunity of sticking it into some rick. Then he quietly went home, to be praised a few hours later for the zeal with which he turned out to cope with the flames which had mysteriously burst forth, often beneath the very eyes of the watchmen. His only motive was the pay—five shillings—which each fire brought him.

§ 51. With the accession of Queen Victoria things improved; the County shared in the general prosperity of English agriculture, and from 1850 onwards had a special " boom " of its own through the setting up of the coprolite[1] industry. The sale of these minerals not only raised the value of land by some £150 per acre, but created such a demand for labour that ordinary wages went up to twenty-four shillings per week, whilst a good " fossil-digger," working by the piece, could earn almost double that sum. Population increased accordingly, and for nearly a generation our County was about the most prosperous in England, the rent running from £2 to £3 per acre.

§ 52. This golden period has left an abiding mark upon the district in the restoration of almost every one of the ancient parish churches. But many men still living can recall a state of things, in matters ecclesiastical, not materially different from that set forth in the records of

[1] See above, p. 5.

the Archidiaconal Visitation in 1685.[1] These documents show that, notwithstanding the High Church reaction which followed the Restoration, the results of the Puritan iconoclasm were still to be seen, after a lapse of forty years, in shattered windows, still unglazed, uprooted pavements, broken doors, and heaps of ruins yet lying unremoved where Dowsing had left them.[2]

§ 53. Thus, at Stapleford: "The Chancell windows are broaken," and "the Church very foul, full of heaps of tile and dust."

At Longstowe: "The Chancell in a wofull Case; the Windows and Dore broaken. . . . The Surplice, Communion Plate, Clerks Bible and Prayer-booke, stolen, and . . . the Pulpit broak."

At Toft: "The Chancell all fould wth Pidgeons; the Church a dove-house. Mortar is made in the Church. Heaps of brick, stones, and dust all over it."

At Rampton: "The Church dilapidated and very nasty. The windows all over broaken. The Pidgeons horribly as well as Owls bedaub ye Church."

At Barton, again: "The Church is made a dovehouse . . . the windows at both ends much broaken. The Font foul . . . they use a Bason, or rather a black nasty dish. Noe Patin.' [These last entries as to the font and paten are almost universal. For the latter we sometimes find used "a trencher," as at Burwell; sometimes "a Napkin," as at Little Gransden.]

At Meldreth: "The Church a dovehouse, the Windows unglazed. . . . Seats broaken miserably. The Chancell in a sad pickle. . . . Gravestones lie about the Church, and great heaps of other stones and dust . . . the Font foul. . . . The pavement very faulty." [This, again, is an almost constant entry.]

[1] Their full text is to be found in "The Collected Works of Henry Bradshaw," University Librarian.
[2] See above, p. 216.

At Sawston: "The Chancell a dungeon, the Windows stopt up with pease-straw ... the Dore so broaken y^t Hoggs may creep under it. The Churchyard weedy and full of elders. [This, too, is all but always noted.] The Hoggs have rooted up the graves. The Vicaridge-house turned to an Ale-house and a sign on the Dore. It rents for £5 per Ann."

§ 54. The fact that "the Minister is non-resident" is here recorded. But this is far from a general complaint. Miserably small as was the value of the livings (averaging scarcely over £50 per annum, and almost never exceeding £100), the great majority of the incumbents resided in the parsonages; a state of things contrasting favourably with later periods, when the parishes were frequently served in batches by peregrinating ministers. Thus, in 1685, Sunday services (morning and afternoon) were universal, while the better worked parishes had also prayers on Wednesdays and Fridays, as well as on Holy-days. The Sacrament was administered quarterly, and the number of communicants (where recorded) is often astonishingly large. Harlton, with only 30 families, had from 70 to 80 communicants; Witcham, 192; Balsham, no fewer than 250.

§ 55. Catechizing in church was a very general practice; and we also find instruction given by secular school-masters and "Dames," supposed to be licensed by the Bishop. Thus, at Mepal "the Schoolmaster is licensed and teaches our Catechism"; at Orwell and at Sutton "the School is taught in the Church"; at Balsham "there is one good School Dame, constant at Church, but another never comes"; at Cottenham and at Rampton we find "a Whigg unlicensed School Dame." At Bassingbourn and Willingham the teachers are also unlicensed; while at Gamlingay, not only does the schoolmaster teach without a license, but is also excommunicate. At Oakington, " the most scandalous parish and worst in the Diocese, the people being most vile," the local education is in the hands of "A Fanatick Schoolmaster"; and at Witchford there is an entry: "*Quære*. Is not the Schoolmaster a Fanatick? I was told that hee is one. Then lett him be prohibited."

§ 56. Open Dissent was, however, far from general, James II. not having yet introduced into English ecclesiasticism that principle of religious toleration which was to cost him so dear. Such Nonconformity as existed seems chiefly to have been amongst the Quakers, while there are occasional returns of Papists, Anabaptists and Independents, or Congregationalists. Of these last, some are described as "Mr. Holdsworth's disciples." This Holdsworth was a Cambridge student who devoted himself to preaching in the villages around, the churches of which were often served by Fellows of Colleges, who rode out from Cambridge for that purpose. The story runs that young Holdsworth, finding one of the ministers indisposed, on a certain Sabbath, to start on his errand, himself mounted the horse, and held an open-air service in the first village to which it took him; afterwards frequently returning thither, and likewise resorting for the same purpose to others in the neighbourhood. In one case (that of Holy Trinity, Cambridge) we meet with an aggressive Dissenter, by trade a tanner, who "hangs his skins on the church walls," and keeps his dunghill in the churchyard. But in a large number of parishes "Noe Dissenter," "Never a Dissenter," is the entry. This absence of competition does not always seem to have been wholly beneficial to the Church. There is a latent significance in the Bassingbourn return: "Noe Dissenters, but Many Sluggards"; and in that from St. Benet's, Cambridge: "No Dissenter. Many idle." Nonconformist places of worship, chiefly Independent, Baptist, and Wesleyan, are at the present day to be found in almost every village throughout the County. But the Quakers, once so conspicuous, are now strong only in the neighbourhood of Wisbeach.

§ 57. At the period of this Visitation a notable ecclesiastical feature of life was the system of frequent appeals by Episcopal Brief to the congregations of the diocese, for this or that charitable object. These Briefs were read during service, at the time appointed by the rubric, and the resultant offertory handed over. A record preserved in the Great Gransden register, extending over twenty-two years, from 1686 to 1707, contains no fewer than 110 such Briefs.

Those on whose behalf they were issued are usually sufferers from local fires, the loss in each case being stated. Thus, a conflagration at Grantchester, in 1695, is said to have caused damage to the extent of £1,250; another at Soham (1698), £759; another at Chatteris (1706), £1,787; another at Littleport (1707), £3,931 18s. 5d.; while, from outside the County, come plaints that St. Ives (Huntingdonshire) is thus the poorer by £12,000, and Bungay (Suffolk) by no less than £30,000.

Church restoration is sometimes an object; Ely Cathedral, in 1701, thus attempting to raise £2,800, and Orford Church (Suffolk), £1,450.

Other appeals are made, for "the French Protestants or Vaudois"[1] (who get four Briefs); for "the Irish Protestants"[2] (two Briefs); for "loss by French Privateers," at Teignmouth in Devon and Widdrington in Northumberland;[3] for "redemption of captives" amongst the

---

[1] This is a misnomer. The Huguenots of France were distinct both in origin and tenets from the earlier Vaudois. Those here referred to are the sufferers by the Revocation of the Edict of Nantes (1685).

[2] The Protestants of Ireland had sustained heavy loss during the disturbances accompanying the Revolution of 1688.

[3] This collection was made throughout the kingdom (Macaulay, "Hist. England," vol. iii., p. 654). Teignmouth was sacked in 1690, not, however, by privateers, but by the French fleet under Tourville.

Moors; for "French Refugees in the Principality of Orange";[1] and for "Seamen's Widows, &c., whose husbands perished in ye late great storm."

§ 58. This last reference is to the fearful hurricane which, on November 26, 1704, desolated the southern half of England, and was thought to have caused the death of at least thirty thousand sailors around our coasts. A contemporary letter from Ely tells us that "the Cathedral Church of Ely, by the Providence of God, did, contrary to all men's expectations, stand out the shock, but suffered very much in every part of it, especially that which is called the body of it, the lead being torn and rent up a considerable way together, about 40 lights of glass blown down and shattered to pieces, one ornamental pinnacle belonging to the north isle demolished, and the lead in divers other parts of it blown up into great heaps; ... the loss which the church and college of Ely sustained being, by computation, near £2,000 ... and the general loss [in the town] about £20,000."[2] But our County was near the northern limit of the storm area, and thus escaped with little injury, comparatively.

§ 59. In the University the nineteenth century has made a greater change than any since its foundation. The traditional barriers have been broken down on all hands, ancient privileges everywhere abolished, the curriculum expanded to include every branch of human knowledge, and the doors thrown open to men of every creed and nationality. So sweeping and rapid has been this change that it now seems hardly credible that, only a few decades back, all students were required to be members, and all tutors clergy, of the Established Church, that in

---

[1] This little district (from which William III. took his title) lies on the Rhone, near Avignon, and served as an asylum for the dragonaded Huguenots of the neighbourhood. It was, in consequence, seized and annexed by Louis XIV. in 1687.

[2] De Foe, "The Storm."

mathematics alone could an Honour Degree be taken, and that celibacy, as well as ordination, was essential for retaining a Fellowship. Few Fellows now fulfil either of these conditions. Non-collegiate students, such as originally made up the University, are once more to be found within its bounds; and a crowd of quasi-collegiate edifices, more or less connected with the University, enable multitudes of both sexes to share in its advantages. All these have been founded within the last three decades of the nineteenth century; the list comprising Denominational Colleges (recognised by the University only as Public Hostels), for Anglicans, Roman Catholics and Presbyterians, and Colleges for Women (at Newnham and Girton), whose inmates are accorded a place in the University lecture-rooms and class lists, without as yet (1897) being granted any University, or even honorary, degree.

§ 60. Besides these more modern institutions, this century has also witnessed the creation of the latest College founded on the old system and recognised as a College by the University. So far back as 1717, Sir George Downing, of Gamlingay in Cambridgeshire, provided in his will for the building and endowment of a College at Cambridge, to be called by his family name. Legal difficulties, however, prevented his purpose from being carried into effect till 1800, when, at length, his design took visible form in what was then considered the acme of classical elegance. Maria Edgeworth, however, in a letter written shortly afterwards, confesses that so poor is her taste, she fears she shall never think it equal to King's College Chapel (!).

§ 61. And, meanwhile, what is perhaps the very greatest change of all has been brought about in the development of the physical side of education, by the successive introduction of rowing, cricket, football, and other sports into University life. In the seventeenth century her statutes stringently forbade any such vanities, even bathing being prohibited, under penalty of flogging for an undergraduate and confinement in the College stocks for a Bachelor; while now almost the best-known application of her name is that which connects it with the University boat-race, the University cricket match, and the University sports.[1]

§ 62. But great as has been the widening of University education during the nineteenth century, that of elementary education has been yet more marked. At the present day the parish school is a marked feature in every village in the County, and fills so important a place in our rural life that it is hard to realize how short a while back that place was vacant. Yet it is certain that at the beginning of the century only a few favoured parishes contained a school of any kind whatever. The Visitation questions of the Bishop of Ely in 1791 clearly bring out this fact. And what schools there were were the "Dames'" schools, painted by Miss Edgeworth and by Kingsley in the "Water Babies," where children paid twopence per week to learn their "Chris-cros row," with perhaps a little writing. But few labourers could afford the money, and still fewer the time of their children, for such learning; while many employers made ability to read and write a positive disqualification in engaging servants.

§ 63. Under these discouraging auspices began the first revival of that peasant education provided of old by the Chantries.[2] Private benevolence set on foot a scheme for utilizing as the time of education those Sunday hours on which alone the children were not occupied in labour. And thus came in with the century the earliest Sunday-schools—institutions originally not for religious instruction (for which the almost universal "catechizing" in church was supposed to provide sufficiently), but to teach the elements of reading. These schools were free, and

---

[1] The Oxford and Cambridge boat-race began in 1829, the cricket match in 1827.
[2] See Chapter VIII., § 26.

the attendance of the children, of course, purely voluntary. They were held in any available building, sometimes in a cottage, sometimes in a barn, sometimes (as at Melbourne) in the parvis-chamber over the church porch, and occasionally in the church itself. For the movement was a purely Church movement, though the idea of Sunday gatherings for religious teaching only, such as we now associate with the word 'Sunday-school,' originated with the Nonconformists of the next generation. In every case attendance at church formed part of the school course, and made the school hours very long; from half-past eight to half-past twelve in the morning, and from two to six in the afternoon, being the usual arrangement. The children were required to appear "with clean face and hands, hair combed, and decently clothed according to the ability of the parents," and were arranged according to proficiency, the lowest class learning the alphabet, the next spelling, and the highest reading. Monitors from each class instructed the class below, under the supervision of the head-teacher, who was almost always a salaried official, the salary for the master at Royston amounting (in 1808) to six guineas a year. Children coming late, or otherwise misbehaving, had often to wear a placard bearing the word NAUGHTY, "in large letters," during church. Boys were expected to attend from the ages of six to twelve, girls from six to fourteen.

Such was the system which the Victorian era has superseded by the State-aided National Schools (erected and maintained by the Church) which still retain almost the whole of the elementary education throughout Cambridgeshire. The more recent development of undenominational Board Schools has made little way in this County; March alone of the towns having adopted it, and only thirteen out of the one hundred and twenty-three villages.

§ 64. Local Government has also signally changed

during this century, especially in the rural districts of our County. The Parish Constable, so great an official when it commenced, has become a mere survival at its close, and the rural policeman reigns in his stead. And along with the constables have disappeared the Lock-ups, the Stocks, and the Pounds, over which they presided, and which were once to be found in every parish.[1] The ancient Hundreds have been superseded by the Unions, while Quarter Sessions, Boards of Guardians, and Parish Vestries, once so potent, have given place to County, District, and Parish Councils. Sanitary Authorities, Relieving Officers, and Inspectors of Nuisances have all come into being; their work being in no small degree aided by the abundant supply of pure water (from the Greensand) which has resulted from the many artesian wells bored for the use of the coprolite diggers during the prosperous days of that industry.[2] Previously the inhabitants had taken their water from ponds, surface wells, or streams, all usually polluted. At Ely, till recently, the supply was drawn from the river, and carried up the hill for sale in leathern bags slung across horses. Cambridge, however, has for over two hundred and fifty years enjoyed an excellent water-supply from the neighbouring chalk, brought into the town partly by Dr. Perne, the time-serving reformer,[3] partly by Hobson, the Puritan Mayor and carrier sung by Milton,[4] whose uncompromising system of horse-letting originated the well-known phrase, "Hobson's choice."

§ 65. The period of inflation due to the coprolite industry[5] lasted about thirty years, from 1850 till near 1880. Unhappily, that period of inflation has been followed by twenty years of continuous and increasing depression

[1] The parish stocks are still to be seen in a few places—*e.g.*, Meldreth; and the lock-ups at others—*e.g.*, Littlington.
[2] See above, p. 5.
[3] See above, viii., 39.
[4] "Occasional Poems," xi. and xii.
[5] See above, p. 259.

throughout the whole County. The coprolites have become exhausted, agriculture has failed, wages have sunk to ten shillings per week, rents have gone down from pounds to shillings (thus bringing many of the Colleges into most severe pecuniary difficulties), and nearly a third of the acreage once under the plough has already gone out of cultivation. Many labourers are unemployed, and many more have left the County, the population of which (in the rural districts) is rapidly sinking.[1] Nor does there seem any probability that the near future will bring alleviation; though the tentative introduction of cement manufacturing, for which the local deposits appear adapted, may ultimately do something (along the upper reaches of the Cam) to render the distress less acute; while the introduction of fruit culture promises relief in the more northerly districts around Histon and Wisbeach.

§ 66. Meanwhile, Cambridgeshire has become for the time one of the poorest counties in England, a poverty emphasized and enhanced by the secession of the border towns of Royston and Newmarket, which have recently voted themselves into the richer shires of Hertford and Suffolk respectively. But its inhabitants and authorities are making as brave a stand against their troubles as their forefathers made at Ringmere[2]; and, whatever may be the immediate future, nothing can take away from our County the history of its past, to which we may fairly apply Henry of Huntingdon's encomium, "Laus Grantabrigiensis Provinciæ splendide floruit.'

[1] See Appendix C.   [2] See above, p. 76.

APPENDIX A.

THE HUNDREDS OF CAMBRIDGESHIRE.

THE Isle of Ely contains five Hundreds, namely:

1. The Hundred of Ely, including the Parishes of—
    1. Ely.
    2. Chettisham.
    3. Downham.
    4. Littleport.
    5. Prickwillow.
    6. Stuntney.

2. The Hundred of Thorney, including the Parishes of—
    1. Thorney.
    2. Whittlesea.

3. The Hundred of Witchford (North), including the Parishes of—
    1. Benwick.
    2. Chatteris.
    3. Doddington.
    4. March.
    5. Wimblington.

4. The Hundred of Witchford (South), including the Parishes of—
    1. Coveney.
    2. Haddenham.
    3. Manea.
    4. Mepal.
    5. Stretham.
    6. Sutton.
    7. Wentworth.
    8. Wilburton.
    9. Witcham.
    10. Witchford.

5. The Hundred of Wisbeach, including the Parishes of—
    1. Elm.
    2. Guyhirn.
    3. Leverington.
    4. Newton-in-the-Isle.
    5. Tydd St. Giles.
    6. Wisbeach.

Appendix A.

In the remainder of the County there are fourteen Hundreds (besides the "Liberty" of Cambridge), namely :

1. The Hundred of Armingford, including the Parishes of—
    1. Abington.
    2. Bassingbourn.
    3. Croydon.
    4. East Hatley.
    5. Melbourne.
    6. Meldreth.
    7. Guilden Morden.
    8. Steeple Morden.
    9. Shingay.
    10. Wendy.
    11. Whaddon.
2. The Hundred of Chesterton, including the Parishes of—
    1. Chesterton.
    2. Cottenham.
    3. Dry Drayton.
    4. Histon.
3. The Hundred of Cheveley, including the Parishes of—
    1. Ashley.
    2. Borough Green.
    3. Cheveley.
    4. Wood Ditton.
    5. Kirtling.
    6. Silverley.
4. The Hundred of Chilford, including the Parishes of—
    1. Great Abington.
    2. Little Abington.
    3. Babraham.
    4. Bartlow.
    5. Castle Camps.
    6. Chudy Camps.
    7. Hildersham.
    8. Horseheath.
    9. Linton.
    10. Pampisford.
    11. West Wickham.
5. The Hundred of Flendish, including the Parishes of—
    1. Cherry Hinton.
    2. Fen Ditton.
    3. Horningsea.
    4. Teversham.
6. The Hundred of Long Stow, including the Parishes of—
    1. Bourne.
    2. Caldecote.
    3. Caxton.
    4. Comberton.
    5. Croxton.
    6. Eltisley.
    7. Great Eversden.
    8. Little Eversden.
    9. Gamlingay.
    10. Little Gransden.
    11. Hardwicke.
    12. Hatley St. George.
    13. Kingston.
    14. Long Stow.
    15. Toft.
7. The Hundred of North Stow, including the Parishes of—
    1. Childerley.
    2. Girton.
    3. Impington.
    4. Landbeach.
    5. Lolworth.
    6. Long Stanton.
    7. Oakington.
    8. Rampton.
    9. Waterbeach.

8. The Hundred of Papworth, including the Parishes of—

1. Boxworth.
2. Conington.
3. Elsworth.
4. Fen Drayton.
5. Graveley.
6. Knapwell.
7. Over.
8. Papworth Agnes.
9. Papworth Everard.
10. Swavesey.
11. Willingham.

9. The Hundred of Radfield, including the Parishes of—

1. Balsham.
2. Brinkley.
3. Carlton.
4. Dullingham.
5. Stetchworth.
6. Weston Colville.
7. Westley Waterless.
8. West Wratting.

10. The Hundred of Stane, including the Parishes of—

1. Bottisham.
2. Quy-cum-Stow.
3. Swaffham Bulbeck.
4. Swaffham Prior.
5. Great Wilbraham.
6. Little Wilbraham.

11. The Hundred of Staploe, including the Parishes of—

1. Burwell.
2. Chippenham.
3. Fordham.
4. Isleham.
5. Landwade.
6. Snailwell.
7. Soham.
8. Upware.
9. Wicken.

12. The Hundred of Triplow, including the Parishes of—

1. Fowlmere.
2. Foxton.
3. Harston.
4. Hauxton.
5. Newton.
6. Great Shelford.
7. Little Shelford.
8. Shepreth.
9. Stapleford.
10. Triplow.
11. Trumpington.

13. The Hundred of Wetherley, including the Parishes of—

1. Arrington.
2. Barrington.
3. Barton.
4. Comberton.
5. Coton.
6. Grantchester.
7. Harlton.
8. Haslingfield.
9. Orwell.
10. Wimpole.

14. The Hundred of Whittlesford, including the Parishes of—

1. Duxford.
2. Hinxton.
3. Ickleton.
4. Sawston.
5. Whittlesford.

APPENDIX B.

ECCLESIASTICAL DIVISIONS OF CAMBRIDGESHIRE.

The ecclesiastical divisions of Cambridgeshire are as follows:

THE ISLE OF ELY,

under the immediate jurisdiction of the Bishop of Ely. It contains 3 Rural Deaneries and 46 Benefices.

Deanery of Ely.

Coveney.	Ely, Stuntney.	Stretham, with Thetford.
Downham.	Haddenham.	Sutton.
Ely, St. Mary.	Littleport.	Wentworth.
„ Holy Trinity.	Littleport St. Matthew.	Wilburton.
„ Chettisham.	Mepal.	Witcham.
„ Prickwillow St. Peter.	Little Ouse, St. John.	Witchford.

Deanery of March.

Benwick.	March.	Whittlesey St. Andrew.
Chatteris.	March St. John.	„ St. Mary.
Doddington.	March St. Mary.	„ Coates.
Manea.	March St. Peter.	Wimblington.

Deanery of Wisbeach.

Coldham.	Leverington.	Wisbeach, St. Peter and St. Paul.
Elm.	Newton, with St. Mary in the Marsh.	
Emneth.	Parson Drove.	„ St. Augustine.
Friday Bridge.	Southsea, with Murrow.	„ Chapel of Ease.
Gorefield.	Thorney Abbey.	
Guyhirn, with Ring's End.	Tydd St. Giles.	„ St. Mary.

THE ARCHDEACONRY OF ELY

is within the County of Cambridge. It contains 7 Rural Deaneries and 118 Benefices.

Deanery of Barton.

Arrington.	Grantchester.	Shelford, Great.
Barrington.	Harlton.	„ Little.
Barton.	Harston.	Shepreth.
Comberton.	Haslingfield	Stapleford.
Coton.	Hauxton, with Newton.	Triplow or Thriplow.
Fowlmere.		Trumpington.
Foxton.	Orwell	Wimpole.

Deanery of Bourn.

Bourn.	Eversden, Great.	Kingston.
Boxworth.	Eversden, Little.	Knapwell.
Caxton.	Fen Drayton.	Lolworth.
Childerley.	Gamlingay.	Longstowe.
Conington.	Gransden, Little.	Papworth St. Agnes.
Croxton.	Graveley.	,, Everard.
Elsworth.	Hardwicke.	Swavesey.
Eltisley.	Hatley St. George.	Toft, with Caldecote.

Deanery of Cambridge.

Cambridge, All Saints.	Cambridge, St. Edward.	Cambridge, St. Michael.
,, St. Andrew the Great.	,, St. Giles, with St. Peter.	,, St. Paul.
,, St. Andrew the Less, and Christ Church.	,, Holy Trinity.	,, St. Sepulchre.
	,, St. Mary the Great.	Cherry Hinton.
		Fen Ditton.
,, St. Barnabas.	,, St. Mary the Less.	Fulburn All Saints, with St. Vigors.
,, St. Benedict.		Horningsey.
,, St. Botolph.	,, St. Matthew.	Teversham.
,, St. Clement.		

Deanery of Camps.

FIRST DIVISION.

Balsham.	Stow cum Quy.	Wilbraham, Great.
Bottisham.	Swaffham Bulbeck.	Wilbraham, Little.
Bottisham Lode and Long Meadow.	Swaffham Prior, with St. Cyriac.	Wratting, West.

SECOND DIVISION.

Abington, Great.	Duxford St. John, with St. Peter.	Ickleton.
Abington, Little.		Linton.
Babraham.	Hildersham.	Pampisford.
Bartlow.	Hinxton.	Sawston.
Castle Camps.	Horseheath.	Shudy Camps.
Whittlesford.		Wickham, West.

Deanery of Chesterton.

Chesterton.	Impington.	Over.
,, St. Luke.	Landbeach.	Rampton.
Cottenham.	Madingley.	Stanton, Long.
Dry Drayton.	Milton.	Stanton, St. Michael.
Girton.	Oakington (Hockington).	Waterbeach.
Histon St. Andrew, with St. Etheldred.		Willingham.

Appendix C.

Deanery of Shingay.

Abington Pigotts.	Hatley East, with Tadlow.	Meldreth.
Bassingbourne.		Steeple Morden.
Croydon, with Clapton.	Litlington.	Wendy, with Shingay.
Guilden Morden.	Melbourn.	Whaddon.

Deanery of Fordham (to Archdeaconry of Sudbury).

Brinkley.	Exning, with Landwade.	Soham, with Barway.
Burrough Green.		Stetchworth.
Burwell.	Exning, St. Agnes.	Wicken.
Carlton, with Willingham.	Fordham.	Westley Waterless.
	Newmarket, All Saints.	Weston Colville.
Dullingham.	Newmarket, St. Mary.	Wood Ditton.

APPENDIX C.

The rise and fall of the rural population of Cambridgeshire during the present century is exhibited in the following comparative tables. Since 1891 the depletion of the rural villages has been proceeding at a greatly accelerated rate, and it is probable that few of them in the census of 1901 will show higher figures than in 1801.

Parish.	1801.	1841.	1871.	1891.	Hundred.
Abington, Great	272	358	300	314	Chilford.
„ Little	185	232	339	262	„
„ Pigotts	177	277	197	228	Armingford.
Arrington	190	317	305	209	Wetherley.
Ashley	272	417	562	485	Cheveley.
Babraham	196	404	298	280	Chilford.
Balsham	542	1,271	1,102	890	Radfield.
Barrington	348	533	727	582	Wetherley.
Bartlow	83	89	93	90	Chilford.
Barton	218	319	419	281	Wetherley.
Bassingbourn	948	1,774	2,730	1,374	Armingford.
Benwick	346	...	857	794	Witchford, N.
Bottisham	864	1,497	1,653	695	Stane.
Bourne	554	909	973	785	Long Stow.
Boxworth	220	326	331	273	Papworth.
Brinkley	275	366	298	289	Radfield.
Burrough Green	276	452	429	178	Cheveley.
Burwell	1,250	1,820	2,106	1,998	Staploe.
Cambridge	10,087	...	...	36,983	

276   *History of Cambridgeshire.*

Parish.	1801.	1841.	1871.	1891.	Hundred.
Camps, Castle	546	854	632	839	Chilford.
,, Shudy	349	...	322	369	,,
Carlton	229	424	447	213	Radfield.
Caxton	336	554	631	420	Long Stow.
Chatteris	2,393	4,813	4,765	4,587	Witchford, N.
Chesterton	741	1,617	4,102	7,650	Chesterton.
Cheveley	398	645	639	608	Cheveley.
Chippenham	524	666	722	620	Staploe.
Comberton	295	520	619	453	Wetherley.
Conington	182	196	202	111	Papworth.
Coton	126	307	340	263	Wetherley.
Cottenham	1,088	1,833	2,496	2,458	Chesterton.
Coveney (with Manea)	712	1,532	1,857	1,837	Witchford, S.
Croydon	208	441	545	426	Armingford.
Croxton	171	264	308	293	Long Stow.
Ditton, Fen	337	537	649	675	Flendish.
,, Wood	648	1,016	1,472	895	Cheveley.
Doddington	374	...	1,440	1,366	Witchford, N.
Downham	844	2,140	2,156	1,873	Ely.
Drayton, Dry	376	478	477	330	Chesterton.
,, Fen	256	381	458	297	Papworth.
Dullingham	468	758	818	823	Radfield.
Duxford	464	763	881	777	Whittlesford.
Elm	951	...	865	789	Wisbeach.
Elsworth	585	915	802	673	Papworth.
Eltisley	250	372	504	465	Long Stow.
Ely (with Chettisham, Prickwillow, and Stuntney)	3,948	7,071	9,805	8,689	Ely.
Eversden, Great	212	300	380	269	Long Stow.
,, Little	150	225	261	212	,,
Fordham	700	1,416	1,266	1,284	Radfield.
Fowlmere	420	610	603	542	Triplow.
Foxton	322	452	513	435	,,
Fulbourn	702	1,405	1,390	1,295	Flendish.
Gamlingay	847	1,434	2,063	1,734	Long Stow.
Girton	232	351	465	480	North Stow.
Grantchester	294	606	844	1,199	Wetherley.
Gransden, Little	232	273	305	227	Long Stow.
Gravely	156	294	294	175	Papworth.
Haddenham	1,090	2,103	2,055	1,719	Witchford, S.
Hardwicke	152	202	248	150	Long Stow.
Harlton	156	259	335	265	Wetherley.
Harston	412	662	917	767	Triplow.
Haslingfield	387	689	871	550	Wetherley.
Hatley St. George	101	136	97	90	? Long Stow.
,, East	94	98	155	127	,,

Appendix C. 277

Parish.	1801.	1841.	1871.	1891.	Hundred.
Hauxton	144	313	289	286	Triplow.
Hildersham	170	238	241	190	Chilford.
Hinxton	270	382	400	336	Whittlesford.
Histon	523	859	1,017	969	Chesterton.
Horningsea	293	298	438	436	Flendish.
Horseheath	343	523	578	507	Chilford.
Ickleton	493	700	677	604	Whittlesford.
Impington	92	248	387	399	North Stow.
Isleham	1,212	2,127	1,819	1,698	Staploe.
Kennet	111	228	159	164	Staploe.
Kingston	225	307	322	278	Long Stow.
Kirtling	458	803	877	821	Cheveley.
Knapwell	97	155	154	188	Papworth.
Landbeach	235	468	480	476	North Stow.
Leverington	1,047	2,782	2,549	2,088	Wisbeach.
Linton	1,157	1,838	1,838	1,726	Chilford.
Litlington	350	722	768	580	Armingford.
Littleport	1,602	3,365	3,500	3,008	Ely.
Lolworth	98	122	171	139	North Stow.
Madingley	190	282	267	215	,,
March	2,514	...	5,854	6,988	Witchford, N.
Melbourn	819	1,724	1,759	1,613	Armingford.
Meldreth	444	730	757	713	,,
Milton	273	452	576	518	North Stow.
Morden, Guilden	428	808	1,059	820	Armingford.
,, Steeple	430	797	1,018	810	,,
Newton	114	183	218	196	Triplow.
Newton in the Isle	283	400	562	322	Wisbeach.
Oakington	317	619	605	450	North Stow.
Orwell	375	583	801	689	Wetherley.
Over	689	1,119	1,155	1,004	Papworth.
Pampisford	202	333	355	329	Chilford.
Papworth-Agnes	80	148	155	120	Papworth.
Papworth-Everard	111	117	137	126	,,
Rampton	162	194	256	220	North Stow.
Sawston	465	992	1,729	1,882	Whittlesford.
Shelford Magna	570	803	1,005	1,020	Triplow.
,, Parva	220	527	510	494	,,
Shepreth	202	353	376	375	,,
Snailwell	200	273	226	181	Staploe.
Soham	2,000	4,162	4,283	4,138	,,
Stanton, Long	400	548	534	454	North Stow.
Stapleford	235	447	594	519	Triplow.
Stetchworth	342	673	662	714	Radfield.
Stow, Long	176	276	277	131	Long Stow.
Stow cum Quy	235	445	373	378	Stane.
Stretham	753	1,357	1,462	1,273	Witchford, S.
Sutton	944	1,519	1,717	1,432	,,
Swaffham Bulbeck	540	806	912	800	Stane.

278   *History of Cambridgeshire.*

Parish.	1801.	1841.	1871.	1891.	Hundred.
Swaffham Prior	791	1,226	1,396	1,000	Stane.
Swavesey	831	1,273	1,335	1,070	Papworth.
Tadlow	101	173	232	193	Armingford.
Teversham	154	220	286	285	Flendish.
Thorney	1,598	2,159	2,099	1,860	Thorney.
Toft	282	453	478	217	Long Stow.
Triplow	334	477	522	442	Triplow.
Trumpington	494	759	841	975	"
Tydd St. Giles	535	863	944	835	Wisbeach.
Waterbeach	553	1,270	1,619	1,340	North Stow.
Wendy	151	288	354	201	Armingford.
Wentworth	115	155	180	143	Witchford, N.
Westley	126	194	212	198	Radfield.
Weston-Colville	318	530	538	320	"
Whaddon	221	345	...	216	Armingford.
Whittlesea	3,841	6,874	6,594	6,107	Thorney.
Whittlesford	416	579	821	875	Whittlesford.
Wicken	614	945	1,133	716	Staploe.
Wickham, West	332	572	522	415	Chilford.
Wilbraham, Great	354	564	...	542	Stane.
" Little	183	345	371	396	"
Wilburton	301	500	546	452	Witchford, S.
Willingham	795	1,424	1,619	1,630	Papworth.
Wimblington	844	...	1,209	1,140	Witchford, N.
Wimpole	324	464	419	287	Wetherley.
Wisbeach	5,541	10,461	11,161	11,112	Wisbeach.
Witcham	323	502	478	321	Witchford, S.
Witchford	294	561	534	428	"
Wratting, West	541	912	705	535	Radfield.

Besides the above-mentioned localities, the towns of Royston and Newmarket also were, until lately, partly in Cambridgeshire (the Icknield Street, running through either town, forming the County boundary). The former town, however, transferred itself to Hertfordshire in 1896, the latter to Suffolk.

APPENDIX D.

CAMBRIDGESHIRE RAILWAYS.

The lines throughout the County mostly form part of the Great Eastern system. But three other railway companies also run to Cambridge: the Great Northern from Hitchin, the Midland from

Huntingdon and Kettering, and the London and North-Western from Bedford and Bletchley.

The various lines were opened at the following dates :
1. The G.E.R. Main Line from London to Norwich, entering the County at Chesterford and leaving it at Mildenhall, after passing through Cambridge and Ely - 30 July, 1845.
2. Ely to March and Peterborough (G.E.R.) - 9 December, 1846.
3. March to Wisbeach (G.E.R.) - - 3 May, 1847.
4. Cambridge to St. Ives and Huntingdon (G.E.R.) - - - - - 17 August, 1847.
5. Ely to Lynn (G.E.R.) - - - 26 October, 1847.
6. March to St. Ives (G.E.R.) - - - 1 February, 1848.
7. Chesterford to Newmarket[1] (G.E.R.) - 4 April, 1848.
8. Hitchin to Shepreth (G.N.R.), entering the County at Royston[2] - - - 1 April, 1851.
9. Shepreth to Shelford (G.E.R.)[2] - - 25 April, 1852.
10. Cambridge to Six Mile Bottom and Newmarket (G.E.R.) - - - - 9 October, 1852.
11. Bedford to Cambridge (L.N.W.R.), entering the County at Potton - - - 1 August, 1862.
12. Shelford to Sudbury (G.E.R.), leaving the County at Haverhill - - - 1 June, 1865.
13. Kettering to Cambridge (Midland)[3] - 1 March, 1866.
14. March to Spalding (G.E.R.) - - 1866.
15. Cambridge to Mildenhall (G.E.R.) - - 1 April, 1885.

[1] The section of this line from Chesterford to Six Mile Bottom (about 12 miles in length) was abandoned in 1852, on the opening of the line from Six Mile Bottom to Cambridge. The deserted cuttings and embankments are still striking features of the landscape.

[2] The G.N.R. were compelled by their Act to permit the G.E.R. to meet them at Shepreth, and did not get running powers over the line to Cambridge till 1866. Before the Shelford and Shepreth line was made, the G.N.R. used to run coaches from Shepreth to Cambridge by road, in connection with their trains, timed to do the distance (9 miles) in 40 minutes.

[3] The Midland trains run over the G.E.R. line from Huntingdon to Cambridge.

APPENDIX E.

ABBESSES, ABBOTS, AND BISHOPS OF ELY.

ABBESSES.

A.D.
I. 673—679. Etheldred, Queen of Northumbria (p. 48).
II. 679—699. Sexburga, Queen of Kent, sister to Etheldred (pp. 48, 51).
III. 699— ? Ermenilda, Queen of Mercia, daughter of Sexburga (p. 48).

The arms of the See of Ely (gules, three crowns or) commemorated these three Royal Superiors. IV. ?—? Werburga, daughter of Ermenilda (p. 74). After Werburga the succession of Abbesses is not accurately known. It continued until the destruction of the Abbey by the Danes in 870, after which there are no further records till its restoration, a century later (see Chapter VI., § 23).

ABBOTS.

A.D.
I. 970— 981. Brithnoth, Prior of Winchester (p. 73).
II. 981—1016. Ælfsige (p. 71), or Elsin (p. 100).
III. 1016—1022. Leofwin.
IV. 1022—1029. Leofric.
V. 1029—1045. Leofsin.
VI. 1045—1066. Wilfric.
VII. 1066—1072. Thurstan. Last Saxon Abbot.
VIII. 1072—1075. Theodwine of Jumièges. Never fully appointed. After him an administrator was put in by the Conqueror (p. 104.).
IX. 1081—1093. Simeon, Prior of Winchester. Under him the existing Minster was begun (p. 110).
1093—1100. The abbacy remained vacant for seven years (p. 112).
X. 1100—1107. Richard of Bec. Under him the Minster was reopened (p. 112).

BISHOPS.

A.D.
I. 1109—1131. Hervey, Bishop of Bangor (p. 111).
II. 1133—1169. Nigel, Prebendary of St. Paul's (p. 114); Founder of St. John's Hospital, Cambridge (p. 116).

A.D.	
1169—1174.	The See remained vacant.
III. 1174—1189.	Geoffrey Ridel, Archdeacon of Canterbury. Under him the Minster was completed (p. 110).
IV. 1189—1197.	William Longchamps, Chancellor of England (p. 127).
V. 1198—1215.	Eustace, Chancellor of England. Under him was built the Galilee (p. 130).
1215—1220.	The See remained vacant (p. 135).
VI. 1220—1225.	John, Abbot of Fountains.
VII. 1225—1229.	Geoffrey de Burgh, Archdeacon of Norwich.
VIII. 1229—1254.	Hugh de Northwold, Abbot of Bury. Under him the E. end of the Minster was built (p. 119).
IX. 1254—1257.	William de Kilkenny, Archdeacon of Coventry.
X. 1257—1286.	Hugh de Balsham, Sub-Prior of Ely. He founded Peterhouse (p. 127).[1]
XI. 1286—1290.	John de Kirkby, Archdeacon of Coventry.
XII. 1290—1298.	William de Louth, Archdeacon of Durham.
XIII. 1299—1302.	Ralph de Walpole, Bishop of Norwich.
XIV. 1302—1310.	Robert de Orford, Prior of Ely.
XV. 1310—1316.	John de Ketton, Almoner of Ely.
XVI. 1316—1337.	John Hotham, Chancellor of England. Under him the Octagon and Lady Chapel were begun (p. 158).
XVII. 1337—1345.	Simon de Montacute, Bishop of Worcester.
XVIII. 1345—1361.	Thomas de L'Isle, Prior of Winchester.[2]
XIX. 1362—1366.	Simon Langham, Abbot of Westminster. He was afterwards Archbishop of Canterbury and Cardinal.
XX. 1366—1373.	John Barnet, Bishop of Wells.
XXI. 1374—1388.	Thomas Arundel, Archdeacon of Taunton; afterwards Archbishop of Canterbury and Cardinal.
XXII. 1388—1425.	John Fordham, Dean of Wells.

[1] He was the only Cambridgeshire man to occupy the See, except Bishop Cox (p. 195). Under him the monks obtained a Papal dispensation to wear caps "on account of the exposed situation of the church."

[2] The monks had chosen Alan de Walsingham (p. 158), but their choice at this period was constantly set aside by Papal authority.

	A.D.	
XXIII.	1426—1435.	Philip Morgan, Bishop of Worcester. Under him the See lost its visitatorial powers over the University of Cambridge (p. 167).
	1435—1438.	The See remained vacant.
XXIV.	1438—1443.	Lewis de Luxemburg, Archbishop of Rouen and Cardinal. He defended Paris for the English, 1435.
XXV.	1443—1454.	Thomas Bourchier, Bishop of Worcester; afterwards Archbishop of Canterbury and Cardinal.
XXVI.	1454—1478.	William Gray, Archdeacon of Richmond.
XXVII.	1478—1486.	John Morton, Archdeacon of Leicester;[1] afterwards Archbishop of Canterbury and Cardinal. He attempted the draining of the Fens (p. 248).
XXVIII.	1486—1500.	John Alcock, Bishop of Worcester. He founded Jesus College, Cambridge (p. 176).
XXIX.	1501—1505.	Richard Redman, Bishop of Exeter.
XXX.	1506—1515.	James Stanley, Archdeacon of Richmond.
XXXI.	1515—1533.	Nicholas West, Archdeacon of Derby (p. 185).
XXXII.	1533—1554.	Thomas Goodrych, Chaplain to Henry VIII. (p. 188). Under him the Abbey was suppressed (p. 191). He wrote the Duty to God and the Duty to our Neighbour in the Church Catechism.
XXXIII.	1554—1559.	Thomas Thirlby, Bishop of Norwich. Last of the old Roman Catholic Hierarchy. Deposed by Elizabeth (p. 211). Died in imprisonment, 1570.
XXXIV.	1559—1581.	Richard Cox, Dean of Christ Church, Oxford. First of the Protestant Hierarchy, appointed without Papal sanction (p. 195). Spoliation of See by Elizabeth.
	1581—1600.	The See remained vacant (p. 168).
XXXV.	1600—1609.	Martin Heton, Dean of Winchester.
XXXVI.	1609—1619.	Lancelot Andrewes, Bishop of Chichester (p. 218); afterwards Bishop of Winchester.

---

[1] This is the Bishop who figures in Shakespeare's "Richard III." He took a prominent part against that monarch.

Appendix E. 283

	A.D.	
XXXVII.	1619—1626.	Nicholas Felton, Bishop of Bristol. One of the Translators of the Authorized Version.
	1626—1628.	The See remained vacant.
XXXVIII.	1628—1631.	John Buckeridge, Bishop of Rochester.
XXXIX.	1631—1637.	Francis White, Bishop of Norwich.
XL.	1638—1667.	Matthew Wren, Bishop of Norwich. Imprisoned for eighteen years under the Commonwealth (p. 217).
XLI.	1667—1674.	Benjamin Laney, Bishop of Lincoln.
XLII.	1675—1683.	Peter Gunning, Bishop of Chichester. He composed the Prayer For all Sorts and Conditions of Men.
XLIII.	1684—1691.	Francis Turner, Bishop of Rochester. He was one of the seven Bishops prosecuted by James II., and was afterwards deprived as a Nonjuror by William III. Died, 1700.
XLIV.	1691—1707.	Simon Patrick, Bishop of Chichester.
XLV.	1707—1714.	John Moore, Bishop of Norwich.
XLVI.	1714—1723.	William Fleetwood, Bishop of St. Asaph.
XLVII.	1723—1738.	Thomas Greene, Bishop of Norwich.
XLVIII.	1738—1748.	Robert Butts, Bishop of Norwich.
XLIX.	1748—1754.	Sir Thomas Gooch, Bishop of Norwich.
L.	1754—1771.	Matthias Mawson, Bishop of Chichester. He made the first carriage-road from Ely to Cambridge.
LI.	1771—1781.	Edmund Keene, Bishop of Chester.
LII.	1781—1808.	James Yorke, Bishop of Gloucester.
LIII.	1808—1812.	Thomas Dampien, Bishop of Rochester.
LIV.	1812—1836.	Bowyer Edward Sparke, Bishop of Chester. He was the last Bishop possessed of palatine jurisdiction over the Isle of Ely (p. 258).
LV.	1836—1845.	Joseph Allen, Bishop of Bristol. Under him the diocese was extended beyond Cambridgeshire (p. 111).
LVI.	1845—1864.	Thomas Turton, Dean of Westminster.
LVII.	1864—1873.	Edward Harold Browne, Canon of Exeter; afterwards Bishop of Winchester.
LVIII.	1873—1885.	James Russell Woodford, Vicar of Leeds. Under him was founded the Ely Theological College.
LIX.	1885.	Lord Alwyne Compton, Dean of Worcester.

APPENDIX F.

ADDENDA.

CHAPTER V., § 37, PAGE 112.

That monks (like Fellows) were supposed to dress and live like gentlemen appears from the Chamberlain's accounts, given by Dean Stubbs in his "Historic Memorials of the Church of Ely." These show us that in 1334 the clothing for the 45 monks then forming the convent cost £87 18s. 11¾d., or nearly £2 a piece, equivalent to at least £30 to-day. Clothing, however, was much dearer than now. The items for *each* monk comprised:

	s.	d.	Approximate modern equivalent. £ s. d.
1 cowl (*capucium*)	at 1	0	1 0 0
1 pellice (*i.e.*, cassock lined with lambskin)[1]	,, 3	3	3 0 0
1 winter tunic	,, 4	9	4 10 0
1 summer ,,	,, 4	4	4 5 0
1 flannel shirt [?] (*Straminea*)	,, 2	5	2 5 0
1 Wilkok[2]	,,	6	10 0
1 Frock	,, 5	11	5 10 0
1 pr linen drawers	,, 3	4	3 0 0
1 pr winter Boots[3]	,, 1	3	1 0 0
1 pr summer ,,	,, 1	4	1 0 0
1 pr "Caligæ et Pedulæ yemales"[4]	,, 1	5	1 0 0

Besides these, each monk was supplied with a coopertarium (counterpane?), at 4s. 6d., a stragula (coverlet?), at 2s., and a blanket, 3½ yards (the present regulation size) in length, at 7d. Their beds were stuffed with hay, which the Chamberlain was required to change once a year, at the annual cleaning of the dormitory.

Dean Stubbs also gives us the refectory account for the week ending Saturday, August 11, 1336, from which it appears that the weekly cost for each monk was about 1s. 4d., or some £3 10s. per annum.

---

[1] The surplice (super-pelliceum) is so called because worn over this garment.

[2] This may perhaps be the head-covering mentioned p. 281. It is not impossible that the name still survives in the modern "billycock."

[3] The boots were of soft leather, rising to the knee.

[4] The exact nature of these articles is a matter of dispute amongst antiquaries. They probably correspond to gaiters and slippers.

This, however, is only the kitchen bill, as it would be termed in a college, and does not include the buttery account for bread and beer, nor the cellarer's provision of wine. The allowance for a monk's food, therefore, notably exceeded the four marks (£2 13s. 4d.) considered by Archbishop Islip sufficient for an Assistant Curate.[1]

The fare provided by the Chamberlain for the week included 2,450 eggs, at 1d. per dozen; 8 fowls, at 1d. each; 6 pigeons, at ½d. each; mutton (*mult'*), to the value of 10¼d.; other meat, 5s. 2½d.; salt cod, 3s. 3d.; white herrings, 1s. 3d.; fresh fish (*pisc' rect'*), 6s. 6d.; and milk, 1s. 7½d. We learn also from a Manual "De Signis," containing a list of the signs used by the monks in the Refectory (where strict silence was enforced), that there were five different kinds of bread, which might thus be beckoned for, the best being "panis monachorum," and beer of four several strengths—"bona," "mediocris," "debilis," and "skegman." There are also signs given for wine, wineglass, and tumbler. The regulations of the Augustinians at Barnwell tell us that each Brother of that House was entitled to a daily allowance of a loaf of bread, a gallon of beer, and a dish from the kitchen.[2]

The monastic life, it must be remembered, implies a very severe call upon the physical powers. To have every night broken by a long service at midnight, to rise again by 6 a.m. for a day of study and manual labour, including at least six hours more of exhausting services, with no food till noon, and almost no recreation, is far from being the lazy existence popularly credited to conventual régime, and would not be possible, for a continuance, without a fair allowance of good food.

The clothing of the Barnwell Canons was on a somewhat superior scale to that of the Ely monks, new articles being served out twice a year, at Easter and Michaelmas, viz.:

    1 surplice.
    1 sheet [?] (*lintheamen*).
    3 pair linen drawers.
    1 ,, summer boots (of soft leather).
    1 ,, winter ,, lined with felt.
    1 ,, summer *Caligæ* (of serge or canvas).
    1 ,, winter ,, (*de blanketo*).
    1 ,, summer *Pedulæ* (of leather).
    1 ,, winter ,, (*de blanketo*).
    1 cope of frieze, for outdoor wear.
    1 pellice of lambskin.

---

[1] See p. 288.
[2] Clark, "Customs of Augustinian Canons," p. 217.

Towels were also supplied in the lavatory, and tablecloths in the refectory, the Brethren being strictly warned to use neither for the purpose of a pocket-handkerchief. The linen was under the charge of the Chamberlain (*camerarius*), who had to provide a laundress "of good character and reputation" to mend and wash every article fortnightly in summer and once in three weeks during winter. He also had to provide warm water for shaving, and soap for the baths "if asked for." At Ely we read of the laundry-man (*allutor*), the bath-attendant (*balneator*), and the barber (*barbitonsor*), whose pay was 6s. 8d. per annum.

CHAPTER VI., § 35, PAGE 141.

The dedication of the "Abbey Church" to St. Andrew is a recollection of the first place of worship set up at Barnwell. The "Liber Memorandorum Ecclesiæ de Barnwell" (1296) tells us that before the Priory of St. Giles was removed thither (by Pain Peverel, who had been standard-bearer to Robert Curthose in the First Crusade, and had been granted the forfeited Picot estates in 1112), there had lived on the spot a hermit named Godesone, a man of special sanctity, who had built there a small wooden oratory in honour of St. Andrew. He died but a short while before the removal, "leaving the place without habitation and his oratory without a keeper."[1]

§ 43, PAGE 146.

A single example of the ancient confessionals is still to be seen in the church of Guilden Morden, at the extreme south-west of our county. The fourteenth-century Rood Screen (one of the very few surviving in Cambridgeshire, where their almost universal disappearance bears witness to the pronounced Protestantism of the district) is so constructed as to be available for the hearing of confessions, and bears the inscription, in Old English letters :

> Fac . me . confessum . rogo . te . Deus . ante . recessum .
> Et . post . decessum . cœlo . mihi . dirige . gressum .
> Ad . mortem . duram . Jhesu . de . me . cape . curam .
> Vitam . venturam . post . mortem . redde . securam .

§ 60, PAGE 158 (NOTE).

The eight great angle-posts of the lantern are each 63 feet long, giving a sapless scantling of 3 feet 4 inches by 2 feet 8 inches. The trees must have been far larger than any oak now growing in England, and even then were only procured with the utmost difficulty, after a

---

[1] Clark, "Customs of Augustinian Canons," p. xii.

long search extending over the whole kingdom, and at a very large price. The whole structure of the lantern shows a truly marvellous skill in timber work. Fuller[1] tells us that when the bells were rung "the woodwork thereof shaketh and gapeth (no defect, but perfection of structure) and exactly chocketh into the joints again." Alan de Walsingham truly deserved the title given him by his contemporaries, "Flos operatorum."[2]

CHAPTER VII., § 12, PAGE 167.

Another source of revenue to the See was found in the "oblations payable at the Whitsun visit, which all devout Churchmen were expected to make to the Cathedral. Thus, on April 30, 1377, the Bishop sends the following warning "to all Rectors, Vicars and Parish Chaplains" of the Deanery of Ely : "Although, by ancient custom of the Church of England [Ecclesia Anglicana], all sons of the same Church, viz., Rectors, Vicars, Parish Priests, and Parishioners, have been wont devoutly, with Oblations, to visit their Cathedral Churches in procession at Whitsuntide, and our church of Ely has been from time immemorial in peaceful possession of such visitations : Nevertheless, many Clerics and Laics of your Deanery, from carelessness or pressure of business, have neglected the Visitation and Oblations, to the considerable hurt of ourselves and our church : We therefore command you piously to observe these Oblations, that for your good labour in this matter you may have merit from God : But know that whomsoever we shall find remiss herein, we shall punish him sharply for his demerits."

The above-mentioned "Oblations" seem to have been known as "Ely Pence." In 1379, a dispute having arisen between the Vicar of Whittlesea St. Mary and the Abbey of Thorney, impropriators of the church, the following composition was effected : "The Abbot and Convent of Thorney to have all the Tithes, great and small, with all Oblations, Mortuaries and other emoluments belonging to the church. The Vicar to receive £20 per ann. from the Abbey, with use of the Vicarage House, which is to be kept in repair by him. Also he is to hold the acre of [arable] land and 2½ acres of meadow anciently belonging to the Vicarage. Also he is to be answerable for all ordinary charges upon the church, viz., Synodals, Procurations, Peter Pence, Ely Pence. Also to find bread, wine, and candles for priests saying Mass in the church."

The scale of remuneration here set forth appears very liberal in the light of a Mandate issued that same year by the Archbishop of

---

[1] "Worthies of England" (Cambridgeshire).
[2] Stubbs, "Historical Memorials," pp. 148-153.

Canterbury to the Bishops of his Province. "It is well known," runs this document, "that the Priests of to-day, not content with reasonable remuneration, demand and receive excessive salaries for their labour, and have become so greedy and delicate in their manner of life and so sunken in gluttony that they be a pernicious scandal and a detestable example to the laity. Our predecessor, Simon Islip, had ordered that Chaplains celebrating Annuals [*i.e.*, commemorative Masses] should receive five marks by the year, or, if officiating in Parish Churches or Chapels, six marks. We, however, considering the state (*qualitatem*) of the times, decree that the Priests celebrating Annuals shall receive seven marks a year, or food and three marks; those who serve Cure of Souls, eight marks, or food and four marks."

Four marks are £2 13s. 4d., which gives about a shilling per week as the allowance for food—equivalent to at least 15s. at the modern value of money. The Archbishop expected the priests to live like gentlemen, but not extravagantly. In his increase of their pay we may see the rise in wages consequent on the Black Death, the ravages of which amongst the clergy led to the exorbitant salaries demanded by the survivors, and thus to the issue of this Mandate.

CHAPTER VIII., § 17, PAGE 193.

The word "divorce" was commonly applied to Henry's repudiation of his marriage with Catherine of Aragon. But what he actually aimed at (and procured from his own courts, in defiance of the Pope) was a decree of Nullity of Marriage. The issue of such decrees by the Ecclesiastical Courts is illustrated by a Papal Bull sent, in 1380, to the Bishop of Ely, on the petition of Lady Mary Percy. The petitioner complains that, being of tender years, she was induced by her tutor [*i.e.*, guardian], John de Suthray, a man of illegitimate birth, to contract matrimony with him by form of words. After having lived for some time, against her will, with his mother, she fled to her own relations, and publicly denounced the marriage. She accordingly supplicates the Holy See that, being now come to age, her marriage may be declared null and void; leaving her at liberty to marry "some worthy person." "You are to cite all concerned," decrees the Bull, "and make enquiry into the matter."

The Bishop accordingly cites both parties to appear before his Commission "in the Church of St. Mary outside Trumpington Gate."

§ 42, PAGE 209.

The very mean "Communion Cups," of which the last entry in the March accounts gives us a specimen, were generally superseded, in

1562, throughout the county by chalices of silver, with covers capable of being used as patens. These chalices (of which examples still survive at Barrington, Shepreth, and many other churches), are all of the same very incorrect pattern, and all inscribed FOR . THE . TOWNE . OF . such and such a place. They vary in size, according to the size of the parish. All bear one silversmith's mark, a nondescript stamp, which some antiquarians hold to be a fish, others a dove "displayed."

CHAPTER IX., § 13, PAGE 219.

In 1643 the Parliament ordered that in every parish church on a given Sunday the "Covenant" should be read, and taken by all present, every adult parishioner being compelled under severe penalties to be in attendance. "The Minister to read the whole Covenant distinctly and audibly in the Pulpit: And, during the time of reading thereof the whole Congregation to be uncovered: And at the end of the reading thereof, all to take it, standing, lifting up their Right Hands bare : And then afterward to subscribe it severally, by writing their Names or their Marks in a parchment Roll or Book, whereunto the Covenant is to be inserted, purposely provided for that end, and kept as a Record in the parish."

The full title of the document was "The Solemn League and Covenant for the Reformation and Defence of Religion, the Honour and Happiness of the King, and the Peace and Safety of the Three Kingdoms of Scotland, England and Ireland." It was founded upon the earlier agreements of like nature entered into by the Scottish Protestants. It is a very long and wordy composition, the essential phrases of which are as follows :

"We Noblemen . . . and Commons of all sorts, in the Kingdoms of Scotland, England, and Ireland, by the Providence of God living under one King, and being of one Reformed Religion, having before our eyes the Glory of God . . . the Honour and Happiness of the King's Majesty . . . and the true Public Liberty, Safety and Peace of the Kingdoms . . .: And calling to mind the . . . practices of the enemies of God against the True Religion . . . : We have now, at last, (after other means of Supplication, Remonstrance, Protestation and Sufferings) for the preservation of our Religion from utter ruin and destruction . . . determined to enter into a mutual and solemn League and Covenant, wherein we all subscribe, and each one of us for himself, with our hands lifted up to the Most High God, do swear

"That we shall sincerely, really, and constantly, through the Grace of God, endeavour, in our several places and callings, the preservation of the Reformed Religion in the Church of Scotland, in Doctrine, Worship, Discipline, and Government, against our common enemies; the Reformation of Religion in the Kingdoms of England and Ireland . . . according to the Word of God and the example of the best Reformed Churches: And shall endeavour to bring the Churches in the three Kingdoms to . . . Uniformity in Religion, Confession of Faith, Church Government, Worship and Catechising . . .

"That we shall in like manner, without respect of persons, endeavour the extirpation of Popery, Prelacy (that is Church Government by Archbishops, Bishops, . . . Deans, Chapters, Archdeacons, and all other Ecclesiastical Officers depending on that Hierarchy), Superstition . . . and whatsoever is contrary to Sound Doctrine . . .

"We shall . . . endeavour, with our Estates and Lives, mutually to preserve the Rights and Privileges of the Parliaments and the Liberties of the Kingdoms: And to defend . . . the King's Majesty's Person and Authority in the preservation of the True Religion . . .; that the world may bear witness with our conscience of our Loyalty, and that we have no thoughts nor intentions to diminish His Majesty's just Power and Greatness.

"We shall also . . . endeavour the discovery of all such as have been or shall be incendiaries or malignants . . . by hindering the Reformation of Religion, dividing the King from his People, . . . or making any faction . . . contrary to this League and Covenant; that they may . . . receive condign punishment. . . .

"We shall also . . . assist and defend all that enter into this Covenant . . .; and shall not suffer ourselves . . . by whatsoever persuasion or terror, to be divided from this Blessed Union . . . or to give ourselves to a detestable indifference and neutrality in that which so much concerneth the Glory of God . . .; but shall, all the days of our lives, zealously and constantly continue therein . . . against all lets and impediments whatsoever: And what we are not able ourselves to suppress, we shall reveal and make known that it may be timely prevented. All which we shall do as in the sight of God. . . .

"And this Covenant we make in the presence of Almighty God, the Searcher of all hearts, with a true intention to perform the same, as we shall answer at that Great Day when the secrets of all hearts shall be disclosed: Most humbly beseeching the Lord . . . to bless our proceedings with such success as may be encouragement to other Christian Churches, groaning under . . . Antichristian Tyranny, to join in the same . . . Covenant, to the Glory of God. . . ."

Any person refusing to "take the Covenant" was liable to be imprisoned till he did.

§ 25, PAGE 224.

In his escape to the Scottish Army (then besieging Newark) in 1646 Charles had passed through this same district of Cambridgeshire. Finding the position of Oxford hopeless, with his own forces shattered and the Parliamentary armies closing in upon the town from all sides, the King cut off his hair and beard, and in the disguise of a servant, carrying the cloak-bag of the two faithful chaplains who accompanied him, stole away at three in the morning, on Monday, April 27, 1646, from the beleaguered city, which had been his headquarters for so long. A long day's ride brought the party that night to Wheat-hamstead, near St. Albans, where a faithful adherent was found to give him shelter, though the Parliament were proclaiming, with drum and trumpet, that " what person soever shall harbour and conceal, or know of the harbouring and concealing of the King's Person, and shall not immediately reveal it to both Houses, shall be proceeded against as a traitor, forfeit his whole estate, and die without mercy." The next day, Tuesday, in clerical attire this time, and with only one companion, Mr. Ashburnham, the hunted Monarch entered Cambridgeshire (avoiding the towns), and that night slept "at a small village, seven miles from Newmarket." This village, Mr. Kingston (to whose " Hertfordshire during the Civil War " I am indebted for this portion of my history) thinks may have been Bottisham, whence Charles could have reached Downham, his next stage, by water.

CHAPTER X., § 6, PAGE 236.

John Gibson's MS. tells us that in 1668, the Prevaricator, in his usual derision of Oxford humour (see p. 228), declared it to be as inferior to Cambridge wit as the Gazette is to a Newsletter.

CHAPTER X., § 23, PAGE 244.

Midsummer Fair derives its name from an immemorial custom, referred to in the "Liber Memorandorum Ecclesiæ de Barnwell." Speaking of the foundation of Barnwell Priory, the author says:

"From the midst of the site there bubble up springs of fresh clear water, called by the English Barnewelle, the children's springs, because that once a year, on the Eve of St. John Baptist, boys and lads met there, and amused themselves in the English fashion by wrestling matches and other games, and applauded each other in singing and playing on instruments of music. Hence, by reason of the crowd of boys and girls who met and played there, a custom grew up that on the same day a crowd of buyers and sellers should meet in the same place to do business."

INDEX.

ABBEY CHURCH, origin of, 141, 286
Abbeys, introduction of, 49
   list of, 143
   abolition, 189
Abelard lectures on logic, 121
Abington, on Brent Ditch, 14
   non-resident vicar, 150
   church desecrated, 216
Accounts, Shingay, 128
   Bassingbourn, 178
   March, 207
Acre, first measure of, 37
Adwulf, King of East Anglia, helps to build Ely, 51
Ælfrinus, Abbot of Ely, 100
Ælfsige, Abbot of Ely, 71
Aetius appealed to by Britons, 32
Agrarian Riots, 256
Aidan converts Northumbria, 46
Akeman Street, 23
Alan, Count, 90
Alan of Walsingham builds Lantern of Ely, 158, 287
Albans, St., home of Matthew Paris, 134
   Charles I. conveyed there, 226
Alcock, Bishop of Ely, founds Jesus College, 176
Alderman, original position of, 66
Aldreth, 99
"Ales," 178
Alfred the Great, 3
   edits Anglo-Saxon Chronicle, 45

Alfred the Great, cedes Cambridgeshire to Danes, 59
   local government, 61
   founds College at Ely, 72
Alfred Etheling slain at Ely, 86
Alien Priories, 143
Allectus, Emperor in Britain, 29
All Saints Church, Cambridge, 150
Altars done away, 201, 209
Alwyn, Lady, founds Chatteris Abbey, 143
Ancarig, site of Thorney Abbey, 49
Anderida, utter destruction of, 36
Andrew the Less, St., Cambridge, 141, 286
Andrewes, Master of Pembroke College, 212
   Bishop of Ely, 218
Angle-kin, first name of England, 56
Anglesey Abbey, 143
Anglo-Saxons, authority for name, 83
Anglo-Saxon Chronicle edited by Alfred, 45
Anna, King of East Anglia, 47
Annuals, 285
Anselm, Archbishop of Canterbury, 121
Antoninus, Itineraries of, 24
Archdeaconries, 273
Architectural styles, 119

Index. 293

Aristotle, 164
Arithmetic, place in earliest University course, 124
"Army of the Church," 132
Artesian wells, 5, 268
Arthur, King, source of some legends, 17, 32
"Arts," original meaning of, 164
Aryan immigration, 11
Ashdon, site of Assandun, 79
Ashwell, source of Cam, 4
   inscription about Black Death, 157
Assandun, battle of, 79
Assize of Barnwell, 167
"Associated Counties," 214
Astronomy, place in earliest University course, 124
Audley, Sir Thomas, founds Magdalene College, 194
Audrey, origin of name, 50
Augusti (Diocletian), 30
Augustinian Canons, 143. See Barnwell
Augustinian Friars, 120, 141

Babraham, Vicar burnt for heresy, 204
   desecration of church, 216
Badew founds University Hall, 166
"Bachelors," original meaning of word, 124
Bailiffs of Cambridge incorporated by John, 137
Bailiwick of Shingay, 124
Balsham, on Fleam Dyke, 14
   Danish massacre at, 77
   belonging to Ely, 85
   episcopal residence, 167
   communicants (1685), 261
Balsham, Hugh de, Bishop of Ely, founds Peterhouse, 127
Bangor "Use" current at Royston, 182
Baptists, 262
Bardney Moor, freebooters in, 149
Barking Abbey founded by daughter of Anna, 48
Barnwell Priory founded, 110, 286
   road to, 114
   school at, 117
   fair granted, 138

Barnwell Priory sacked by patriots, 140
   position of, 141
   sacked by rioters, 155
   Assize of, 167
   customs of, 285
Barons' War, 130
Barrington, features of Church, 5, 119
   British village at, 15
   destroyed by Romans, 22
   Anglo-Saxon cemetery, 38
   Danish attack upon, 78
   faction fights (1327), 139
   White Hill Chapel, 144
   inventory of Church goods (1559), 197
Bartlow church built by Canute (?), 82
   parson ejected by Puritans, 218
Barton, rights of Templars in, 139
   state of church (1685), 260
Basileus, title of Anglo-Saxon Kings, 63
Basket-making a British industry, 42
Bassingbourn, gallows at, 140
   parish accounts (1498), 178
   desecration of church (1643), 216
   state of church (1685), 261
Bateson, Bishop, founds Trinity Hall, 164
Battle Bridge, Boadicea's victory at, 22
Bayeux tapestry, 74
Becket, Archbishop, portrait at Hauxton, 113
Bede, his forecast, 54
Bedford, Dukes of, drain the Fens, 251
Beer, Monastic, 285
Belsar's Hill, 99
Benedict Biscop, 51
Benedictines, the first monks, 48
   houses in Cambridgeshire, 141
Benet's, St., Cambridge, Saxon architecture, 87
   used as College Chapel, 147
   state in 1685, 262
Beornwulf, King of Mercia, conquered by Egbert, 57

Bethlehem Friars, in charge of Lepers' Hospital, 141
Bill, Anglo-Saxon, 39
Bishopric of Ely founded, 110
Bishop's Delf, boundary of Isle of Ely, 73
"Black Bartholomew," 233
Black Death, 156, 288
Black Friars, 120, 141
Blankets, 284
Boadicea, 21
Bologna, the first University, 121
Boots, monastic, 284
"The Borough," 114
Bottisham, parson ejected, 1643, 219
    Charles I. there [?] 291
Boulder clay, 5
Bourne, desecration of church (1643), 216
Boxworth, rights of Templars in, 139
Brand Ditch, 14
Brandon, flint workings, 10
    waterway to Ely, 74
Brent Ditch, 14
Brentford, battle of, 78
"Brethren of Penance," 141
Bretwaldas, list of, 44
Bridge Street, Cambridge, built, 115
Brie, Abbey of, school for English girls, 48
Briefs, Episcopal, 263
Brinkley, desecration of church (1643), 216
Brithnoth, Alderman of East Anglia, 66
    buried at Ely, 71
    benefactions to the Abbey, 74
British clans, 12
    coins, 13
    Empire, 62
    fleet, 19
    names in Fenland, 42, 104
    sees, 21
    villages, 15
Brownies, 9
Bryce, St., massacre of, 75
Bucer, 204
Buckingham College, 194
Bulla, Papal, 145
Bull Inn, Cambridge, 193

Bulls, Irish, 230
Bungay, fire at, 263
Bunyan, Vanity Fair, 240
Burgesses of Cambridge, 137
Burgh, Elizabeth de, founds Clare College, 166
Burgraed, King of Mercia, annexes Isle of Ely, 73
Burrow Green, church desecrated (1643), 216
    parson ejected (1643), 219
Burwell, Stephen's Castle, 114
Bury St. Edmund's, Abbey founded by Canute, 84
    post to Cambridge, 1753, 236
Buss-carls, 98

Caer Grant, 25
Cæsar, Julius, 17
Cæsars in Diocletian system, 30
Caius College, first origin, 162
    refounded, 209
Caldecot, 219
Calixtus II., Pope, 176
Cam River, origin of name, 25
    course of, 4
    carriage by, 237, 249
Camboritum, 25
Cambridge (town), site, 25
    strategic point, 131, 215
    Roman town, 25
    destroyed by Saxons, 36
    rebuilt by Egbert, 57
    occupied by Danes, 59
    re-conquered by English, 61
    burnt by Sweyn, 77
    fortified by William the Conqueror, 91, 98
    extends across the Cam, 115
    sacked by Maundeville, 114
    seized by Barons, 131
    enclosed by King's Ditch, 140
    incorporated, 137
    dower of Queen Margaret, 138
    public buildings, 141
    held by Cromwell, 223
    state in 1753, 236
Cambridge (University), origin, 121
    early organization, 123, 125
    town and gown, 122, 123
    collegiate system, 126
    eight first Colleges, 162-166

Index. 295

Cambridge (University), early College life, 163
  King's and Queens', 168-175
  S. Catherine's and Jesus, 176
  the new learning, 184
  the new theology, 193
  libraries destroyed, 195, 196
  Marian reaction, 204
  Ridley's farewell, 205
  Puritan changes, 226
Camelodunum, 17
Camp of refuge, 97
Canute, 78-84
Cap and gown, 247
Caractacus, 19
Carausius, 29
Carmelites, 141
Carriers, 237
Cassivellaunus, 16
Castle Camps, 82, 219
Castle Hill, 25
Catechizing, 261
Catharine's, St., College, 167
Catharine of Aragon, 188
Catharine of Siena, 145
Catharine Parr aids to found Trinity College, 194
Catholic Hierarchy, fate of, 211
Caxton, 236
Cells, 143
Celts, 11
Cement works, 269
Cenimagni, 12
Chad, St., converts Mercia, 48
  his death, 54
Chain measure, its early origin, 37
  used by Danes, 59
Chalices, 288
Chantries, suppression of, 199
Chapel Bush, 145
Charlemagne, his imperial pretensions over Britain, 63
Charles I. attempts Cambridge, 215
  captive at Newmarket, 224
  flight through Cambridgeshire, 291
Charles II., first copper coinage, 233
  first postal deliveries, 235
  first Newmarket races, 237
Charters of Richard II., 154

Chatteris, foundation of Abbey, 143
  misdoings at (1378), 148
  fire (1695), 263
Chaucer, 166
Cheer, origin of word, 227
Cherry Hill, 101
Cherry Hinton, chancel built, 119
Chester, road to, 23
  lay waste, 36
Chesterford, doubtful fight at, 62
Chesterton, origin of name, 36
  parson deprived (1643), 220
Cheveley, church desecrated (1643), 216
  parson deprived (1643), 220
  Charles I. confined there, 224
Children of the Chapel Royal, 163
Chippenham, rights of Templars in, 139
  transferred to Hospitallers, 143
  sacked by rioters (1381), 156
Christian, Bishop, leads Danes to Ely, 95
Christ's College founded, 167, 186
Christmas fast (1643), 220
Chronicle, Anglo-Saxon, in Library of Corpus Christi College, 196
Church of England in Magna Charta, 132
Churls, original status, 38
  sink to villenage, 90
Cicero on British civilization, 12
Clare College, foundation, 166
  under Cromwell, 223
Clare, Gilbert de, 100
Clerical incomes (1338), 129; (1380), 151, 287
Clarkson, anti-slavery champion, 105
Close Rolls, extracts from, 135
Clothing, Monastic, 284
Clunch pits, 144
Coaches, Cambridge and London, 235
Coffee-house, 236
Coinage, British, 12
  Roman, 27
  Anglo-Saxon, 39, 57, 63, 73
  modern, 233
Colchester under Cunobelin, 17
  a Roman colony, 23

Coldingham, 51
Colours, English, 80
Comberton, church desecrated (1643), 216
Communion cups, 209, 288
Common fields, 37
Confessionals, 146, 286
Constance, Council of, 167
Constantine the Great, 30
Constantine the Briton, 31
Constantinople, effects of fall, 184
Constantius, Cæsar of the West, 29
Coprolites, composition of, 5
   results of digging, 268
Corpus Christi College, connected with S. Benet's, 147
   founders, 165
   library, 196
Cottars, 90
Cottenham, belonging to Ely, 85
   school dame (1685), 261
Count of Britain, 28
Count of Saxon Shore, 28
Covenant, 219, 289
Coveney, ejection of parson (1643), 220
Cox, Bishop of Ely, spoliation of see, 168
   extreme Protestantism, 195
Cranmer, student at Jesus College, 178
   plans divorce of Henry VIII., 193
   burnt at Oxford, 205
Cromwell, Oliver, student at Sidney College, 211
   fortifies Cambridge, 223
   confines King at Newmarket, 224
   ultimatum to London, 225
   draining of Fens, 251
Cromwell, Thomas, revolutionizes University, 188
Crowland, founded, 49
   sacked by Danes, 58
   plundered, 77
Croxton, given to Ely, 71
   Church desecrated (1643), 217
Crutched Friars, 143
Cunobelin, 13, 17
"Cursory," origin of word, 124
"Customary" tenants, 129, 153
Cyneard the Etheling, 66

Cynewulf, King of West Saxons, 66
Danegeld, 68, 75
Danelagh, 59
Decentius, Emperor in the West, 30
Decoys, 253
"Decorated" architecture, 161
Dedication festivals, 146
Deeds introduced at Conquest, 92
Denny Abbey, 142
   connection with Pembroke College, 165
Denominational Colleges, 265
Dereham Abbey, 48, 74
Deva, 23
De Vere, Alberie, 90
Devil's Dyke, 14
Dialect, local, 43
Diocese of Britain, 28
   of Ely, extent of, 111
Diocletian system, 27
Disputations, 123, 246
Dissenters, 262
Ditton, origin of name, 14
Divorce (Henry VIII.) proceedings in University Senate, 193, 288
Doddington, denunciation at, 149
   episcopal residence, 167
Dominicans established at Cambridge, 119
   allowed degrees, 126
   their house destroyed, 195
   Emmanuel College on site, [210
Doomsday Survey, 88
Dorchester, Bishopric of, 53
Downham, episcopal residence at, 167
   parson ejected (1643), 220
Downing College, 265
Dowsing desecrates churches, 216
Drainage of Fens, 247
Druids, 13
Ducking-stool, 140
Duddery at Stourbridge Fair, 242
Duke of the Britains, 28
Dullingham, gallows, etc., 139
Dunwich, Bishopric of, 53
Dykes, the five, 14
   stormed by Ostorius, 19
   forced by Penda, 47
   last defence of, 60
Eadred, King of England, 61

Index.   297

Earpwald, King of East Anglia, 45
East Anglia bounded by Cam, 43
  converted to Christianity, 45
  conquered by Mercia, 54
  annexed to Wessex, 56
  Danish stronghold, 57
  under an Alderman, 66
Ebba, foundress of Coldingham Abbey, 51
Ecclesiastical Courts, 148
Edgar the Peaceful, 64
Edric betrays England to Danes, 81
Edmund Ironside, 78-83
Edmund, last King of East Anglia, 58, 65
St. Edmund's Hall, Cambridge, 126
Education, elementary, given in chantries, 200
  revival of, 266
Edwin, King of Northumbria, 45
Edward the Confessor, 85
Edward I. captures Ely, 133
Edward II. supports students at Cambridge, 163
Edward III. founds King's Hall, 163
Edward IV. continues King's College Chapel, 174
Edward VI., Greek pronunciation, 188
  libraries destroyed, 195
  parochial spoliations, 197
  wretched state of University, 206
Egbert, first King of the English, 56
Egric, King of East Anglia, 47
Eleanor of Aquitaine, 127
Elizabeth Tudor confiscates property of See of Ely, 168
  visits Cambridge, 213
Elizabeth Woodville completes Queens' College, 174
Elm in thirteenth century, 150
Eltisley cyclone (1234), 133, 142
  Abbey, 142
Ely, Abbey of:
  founded by Etheldred, 48
  destroyed by Danes, 58
  refounded by Edgar, 73
  favoured by Canute, 83

Ely, Abbey of:
  conquered by William, 95-100
  made a Cathedral, 110
  patriot stronghold, 130-133
  dissolved, 192
  monks of, 84, 112, 284
  officers, 85
  income, 111
  manors, 71, 85
Ely, College of, 72
" Ely farthings," 167
" Ely pence," 287
Ely House, Holborn, 167
Ely, Isle of:
  extent, 52
  British principality, 42
  tributary to East Anglia, 47
  Dowry of Etheldred, 48
  ravaged by Danes, 58
  annexed by Mercians, 73
  regranted to Abbey, 73
Ely, See of:
  created, 110
  registers of, 146
  jurisdiction over Isle, 4, 73, 258, 283
  powers in University, 167
Emma, Queen of England, 84
Emmanuel College, foundation, 210
Puritanism, 231
Enclosure of wastes, 256
England, name first used by Canute, 83
English colours, 80
Eorls, 37
Epigrams, 247
Erasmus at Cambridge, 186
  paraphrases, 209
Eric, Danish King, 60, 61
Erkenwald, Bishop of London, 47
Ermenilda, Queen of Mercia, 48, 280
Ermine Street, 23
Etheldred, St., founds Ely, 48
  death and burial, 51
Ethelfied, Lady of the Mercians, 3, 60
Ethelred the Unready, 65, 69, 78
Ethelwald the Etheling, 59
Ethelwine, Bishop of Durham, 97
Ethelwold, Bishop of Winchester, 73

Eudo Dapifer, 113
Eugenius IV., Pope, 167
Eustace, Bishop of Ely, 119, 130
   of Boulogne, 90
Eversden, parson ejected (1643), 220
Evesham, battle of, 131
Excommunication, 149
Exning, capital of East Anglia, 47
   alms to, indulgenced, 147
   centre for horse-trade, 238
"Faculties" at University, 123
Fagius burnt after death, 204
"Fairy Cart," origin of tradition, 128
Fairfax, 224
"Family," a measure of land, 52
Fare of monks, 112
Feckenham, last Abbot of Westminster, 213
Felix, St., converter of East Anglia, 46
Fellows of Colleges at foundation, 162, 164, 166
Fenland, extent of, 3
   once forest, 6
   formation, 41
   held by Girvii, 42
   ravaged by Danes, 58
   brigand fortress, 72
   draining, 247
   present state, 4
   old fauna, 6, 253
Fen Ditton at end of Dyke, 14:
   bulla found, 145
   manse enlarged (1389), 151
   parson ejected (1643), 221
Fisher, Cardinal, influence on Cambridge, 185
Flag of England, 80
Flavia Cæsariensis, 28
Fleam Dyke, 14
Flint weapons, 8
Florence, Council of, 167
Food, Monastic, 284
Fossils, 5
Foss road, 23
Founder's Day (Eton), 169
Fowlmere, Round Moats, 14
   gallows (thirteenth century), 140
      church desecrated (1643), 216
      parson ejected (1643), 221

Foxe, 188
Foxton, belonging to Ely, 85
   chancel, 119
   faction fights (1327), 139
Franciscans settle at Cambridge, 119
   site of their house, 126
   connection with Pembroke College, 165
   fate of their church, 194
   their conduit, 195
   Sidney College on their site, 210
Frankish axe, 69
Friars settle at Cambridge, 120
   list of their convents, 141
Froude, effects of Reformation, 200-206, 207
Fruit-culture, 269
Fuel, prices at Cambridge, 249
Fuller, prevaricator and historian, 229
Furlong, origin of name, 37

Galilee, Ely, built, 119
Galfrid de Maundeville, 113
Gallows, 140
Gamlingay, 265
Garret Hostel, 126, 195
Gaul, connection with Britain, 12
   overrun by barbarians, 31
Gault, 5
Geology, 4
Geometry, 124
Geraint, 32
"Germans," early Protestants so called, 193
Gilbert of Ghent, 90
Gilbert, St., of Sempringham, 143
Gilbertine Canons at Cambridge, 141
   houses in County, 143
Giles, St., founded by Picot, 110
   trees in churchyard, 150
Girton parson ejected (1643), 221
   Ladies' College, 265
Girvii, a British tribe, 42
"Goddam," 161
Godmanchester, 23
Godwin, Earl, 86
"God's House," 186
Gog Magog Hills, 14
Gomer, 11

Index. 299

Gonville Hall, foundation of, 162
Goodrich, Bishop of Ely, destroys shrines, 188
Græco-British coinage, 13
Grammar, meaning of, 107, 123
Gransden, state in 1685, 260
    Register of briefs, 263
    Little, 150
Granta River, 4
Granchester, name of, 36
    Bede's mention of, 52
    rights of Templars in, 139
    "ordination" of vicarage, 151
    fire in 1695, 263
Gratian, Emperor, 31
Greek, revival of, 186
Greensand, 5
Gregory XI., 145
Grey Friars, 141
Grey, Lady Jane, 203
Guarin de Montaigu, seal of, 130
Guilden Morden, confessional, 286
Guilds, Cambridge, 165
    parochial, 196
Gunpowder Plot, 184
Gurney of Earlham, 72
Gyrth, Earl of East Anglia, 93

Haddenham, Cross of Ovinus at, 54
    dedication festival, 146
Hadham, episcopal residence, 167
"Hæretha-land," 56
Hanoverians suppress Ely riots, 258
Hardwick belongs to Ely, 71
    parson ejected (1643), 221
Harlton communicants (1685), 261
Harmony, part of first University course, 124
Harold, 93
Harold Harefoot, 86
Harthacnut, 86
Haslingfield, 144
Hastings, flint weapons used at, 10
    no English cavalry, 68
    "dies fatalis Angliæ," 90
    campaign of, 93
    night before battle, 107
Hatfield, residence of Bishop of Ely, 167
Hatley, Church desecrated (1643), 216

Hauxton belongs to Ely, 85
    picture of Thomas à Becket, 113
Helena, mother of Constantine, 30
Henry of Huntingdon, praise of Cambridgeshire, 76, 88, 269
Henry Beauclerk, 105
Henry III., visit to Cambridge, 137
    Charter to Templars, 139
    makes the King's Ditch, 140
Henry VI. founds King's College, 168
    his will, 170-172
Henry VII. finishes King's Chapel, 174
Henry VIII., divorce, 183, 288
Heptarchy, 54
Herduin de Scalers, 90
Hereward defends Ely against Normans, 95-99
Hermitages, 144
Hervey, first Bishop of Ely, 111
Hide, measure of land, 52
    acres in, 101
Hilda, St., foundress of Whitby, 48, 50
Hildersham, the birthplace of Matthew Paris, 134
Hills Road, Cambridge, 114
Histon, 150
Historians, twelfth-century, 120
Hobson, 268.
"Hocus pocus," 188
Holborn House, 167
Holdsworth, 262
Holmby House, 224
Homilies, 209
Honorius, Emperor of Rome, 31
    Archbishop of Canterbury, 46
"Honours," University, 246
Horningsea belongs to Ely, 85
Horseheath church decorated (1643), 216
Hospitallers, 128-130
Hospital of St. John founded by Bishop Nigel, 116
    attempt to make College of, 127
    granted "forfeited victual," 138
    made into College, 186
Hospitals, 143

Hostels, origin of, 125
  destruction of, 186
  existing, 265
House-carls, 93
Huddleston family, 203
Huddlestone, quarry for King's Chapel, 174
Huguenots relieved by brief, 263
Hundreds, old English, 61
Huntingdon taken by Charles I., 215

Iceni, greatest British tribe, 12
  subdued by Cunobelin, 17
  friendly to Romans, 18
  revolt, and are crushed, 19
  revolt under Boadicea, 21
Ickleton, 12
  nunnery at, 143
Icknield Way, 12
Imperial style of English monarchs, 63
Impington, given to Ely by Brithnoth, 71
  rights of Templars in, 139
Independents, 262
Indulgences, 148
Infallibility, Papal, 176
"Infang-thief," 140
Inventories, Bassingbourn Church, 182
  Barrington Church, 197
Iona, extent of, 52
Irish Protestants relieved by brief, 263
Islip, Archbishop, regulates clerical salaries, 287
Ives, St., colony from Cornwall, 60

Jadite axe, 10
James I. resides at Royston, 213
  holds race-meeting at Linton, 237
James II., 262
Jarrow, 51
Jesus College founded by Bishop Alcock, 176
Jewry at Cambridge, 115
Joan of Arc, 161
"John Bull," earliest use of name, 161
John, King, crosses Wash at Wisbeach, 131

John grants Charter to Cambridge, 137
John, St., Knights of, 128-130
John of Wisbeach builds Lady Chapel at Ely, 158
John's College, St., founded by Bishop Fisher, 186
  state under Edward VI., 206
John's Hospital, St., founded by Bishop Nigel, 116
  attempt to make College, 127
  granted "forfeited victual," 138
  made into College, 186
Joyce, Cornet, 224
"Judæa Capta," coin of Vespasian, 27
Judith, Countess, 90
Julius Cæsar, 16

Kenwalk, King of Wessex, 46
King of England, first, 83
King's College founded, 166-173
King's Cross, battle of, 22
King's Ditch, 140
King's Hall, 162, 163
Kingston, 150
Kingston-on-Thames, 65
Knapwell, rights of Templars in, 139
Knight-service required of Ely, 112

Labarum, 30
Lady Chapel, Ely, built, 158
  defaced, 191
Landbeach, rights of Templars in, 139
Lanfranc, Archbishop, 120
Lantern, Ely, built, 158, 286
Latimer, protests against wrongdoings of Reformers, 190
  martyred, 205
Laundry, Monastic, 286
Lawmen of Cambridge, 91
Leofric, Earl, 95
Leper Chapel at Stourbridge, 141
  granted toll of Stourbridge Fair, 244
Leverington Hospital, 144
  licensed oratories, 146
Libraries destroyed, 195
Licentiate, 124

Index. 301

Lichfield, 54
Lincoln, 23
Linton, alien Priory, 143
   races under James I., 237
Litanies, 147
Litlington, gallows at, 140
   lock-up, 268
Littleport agricultural riots, 257
   fire (1707), 263
Logic taught by Abelard, 121
   part of first University course, 123
Longchamps, Bishop of Ely, 127
Longstowe Hospital, 144
   state of church (1685), 260
Louis the Dauphin, 131

Maccus, 67
Madingley, rights of Templars in, 139
   church desecrated (1643), 216
Magdalen College, Oxford, 168
Magdalene College founded, 194
Magna Charta, 132
"Magna Societas," 156
Magnentius, Emperor in West, 30
Maldon, battle of, 66
Malmesbury, William of, on Conquest, 105
Manchester, Duke of, ejects ministers, 218
Mandeville, Galfrid de, 113
Manumission of serfs, 151
Map of Cambridge, first, 194
March parish accounts, 207
   School Board, 267
"Mareway," 144
Margaret of Anjou founds Queen's College, 173
Lady Margaret, 186
"Market Hill," Cambridge, 203
Marks, Anglo-Saxon, 38
Mark, value of, 101
Martin V., Pope, bulla, 145
   Assize of Barnwell, 167
Mary Tudor at Sawston Hall, 203
Mary's, Little St., dedication, 147
"Masuræ," 91
Matthew Paris, 122, 134
Maximus, Emperor, 31
Mayor of Cambridge first appointed, 137
   at Stourbridge Fair, 243

Maypole, Orwell, 144
Melbourne, Ship-money Riot, 222
   Sunday-school, 267
Meldreth, state of church (1685), 260
   stocks, 268
Mendicant Orders appear in Cambridge, 120
   allowed degrees, 126
   excused Poll-tax, 152
Mepal, carrier from Cambridge (1753), 237
   school in 1685, 261
Merchant Guild of Cambridge, 137
Mercia, last heathen district of England, 46
   converted, 48
   wide power, 54
   conquered by Wessex, 57
Meridian of Greenwich, 144
Merton College statutes, 127
Michael House founded, 162
   Fisher, Master of, 186
   absorbed in Trinity College, 194
Midsummer Fair, 244, 291
Mildmay, Sir W., founds Emmanuel College, 210
Milestones first in England, 235
Milton, 174
Minor Orders, 142
Mitred Abbot, 142
Money, value of, in 1070, 101
   in 1338, 129
   in 1500, 179
Monks of Ely, 84, 111, 284
Monmouth, Duke of, Cambridge ode to, 230
Moors in British army, 28
More, Sir Thomas, reference to spindle-whorls, 40
   defence of Erasmus, 187
Morcar, Earl, 97
Morden, Guilden, confessional at 286
Morden, Steeple, gallows and pillory at, 140
Moreton, Bishop of Ely, begins drainage of fens, 248
Mursa, battle of, 31
"Music Speeches," 228

Naseby, battle of, 214

National schools, 267
"Nations," University, 124
"Nativi," 151, 153
Neolithic period, 8, 16
New College, Oxford, 169
"New Learning," 193
Newmarket, Charles I. confined there, 224
race-meetings, 237
Newnham, Carmelites at, 120
rights of Templars in, 139
Ladies' College, 265
News-letters, 235, 291
Newton, belonging to Ely, 85
Newton-in-the-Isle, College at, 144
Newton, Sir Isaac, 247
Nigel, Bishop of Ely, fights against Stephen, 114
founds Hospital of St. John, 116
"Nine Wells," 224
Nomenclature, national, 104
Nonconformists steadfast to Reformation principles, 213
Ministers ejected (1662), 233
numbers in 1685, 262
Norman architecture, 109, 119
characteristics, 108
Normans, lands of, confiscated, 137
Norsemen first land in England, 56
North road, 23, 93, 144, 236
Northampton, abortive University set up, 122
Northumbria converted under Edwin, 45
conquered by heathen, 46
restored to Christianity, 48
annexed to Wessex, 57
overrun by Danes, 58
ravaged by Eadred, 61
submits to Charlemagne, 62
so-called "Duke" of, 71
harried by Conqueror, 95
Northwold, Bishop, builds east end of Ely Minster, 119
Notitia, 23
Nunneries, 143
Nuremberg tokens, 234

Oakington, state in 1685, 261
Obits, 208

Offa, King of Mercia,
Officers of Ely, 84
Ogres, 9
"Oliva Pacis," 226
"Optimes," 246
Orange, Principality of, 264
Orwell, Maypole, 144
parson ejected (1643), 221
church school (1685), 261
Osbiorn, Earl, 95
Oseney, 195
Ostorius, 18
Oswald, 46
Otford, battle of, 79
Otterburn, 148
Overbury, 214
Ovinus, Alderman of Girvii, 53
Oxford, origin of University, 121
sends colonists to Cambridge, 123
leads in collegiate movement, 127
eels sent from Cambridge, 136
suffers at Reformation, 207
headquarters of Charles I., 228, 291

"Paigles," 43
Palæolithic period, 7
Pandiona, St., 142
Panta River, 66
Papworth, given to Ely, 71
Parish accounts, Bassingbourn, March, 207 [179
Paris University, 121
Parisians settled on Humber, 12
Parker, Archbishop, makes first plan of Cambridge, 194
creates library at Corpus Christi College, 196
Master of Corpus Christi College, 204
Patens, 260, 289
Patent Rolls, references to, 135
Paulinus converts Northumbria, 46
Peakirk Drove, 43
Pecocke, Bishop, dies at Thorney, 176
Pega, 43
Pembroke College founded, 165
- Ridley, Master, 205
Andrewes, Master, 213

Index. 303

Pen, Battle of, 78
Penda, King of Mercia, 46
"Penitenciaries," Diocesan, 146
Pensioners, College, 186
Perne, Master of Peterhouse, 204, 206
   improves Cambridge water-supply, 268
Perpendicular architecture, 160
Peterborough founded, 49
   destroyed by Danes, 58, 77, 96
Peterhouse founded, 127, 162
   special connection with See of Ely, 47
   Perne, Master of, 206, 208
   Bishop Wren, Master, 217
Peters, Hugh, 225
Peverel, Pain, founds Barnwell Abbey, 286
Picot, Sheriff of County, 90
   founds church of St. Giles, 110
Picts, 32
Pilgrims' Way, 144
Pillories, 140
Pixies, 9
Plautius, Proprætor of Britain, 18
Pole, Cardinal, Chancellor of University, 207
Poll-tax, 152
Population, 275
Pottery, Roman, 26
Prævaricator, 228, 291
Prasutagus, King of the Iceni, 21
Prayer-book, first suggestion of, 182
   burnt by Puritans, 226
   restored, 233
Prefectures in Diocletian system, 27
Prices (1334), 284; (1338), 128; (1379), 167; (1500), 179; (1753), 249
Probus deports vandals to Britain, 29
Processions, 147
Proctors, first appointed, 124
   duties at Stourbrige Fair, 245
Professorships, Lady Margaret, 186
   Regius, 195
Pronunciation of Greek, 187

Protestantism of County, 192
Provinces in Diocletian system, 28
Puritans, 210, 227
Pym, 219

Quakers in County, 262
Quadrivium, 124
Queen's College founded, 173
   Fisher, President, 186
"Querela Cantabrigiensis," 216
Questionists, 228

Races, Newmarket, 237
   University, 266
Radagaisus, 31
Railways, 237
Ramsey Abbey founded, 49
   destroyed by Danes, 58
   Cartulary, 101, 110
   sends fish to Cambridge, 137
Rampton, Rights of Templars in, 139
   state of church (1685), 260
   parish school (1685), 261
Reach, 245
Redwald, King of East Anglia, 45
Refectory account, Ely, 284
Regents, 123
Registers, Episcopal, 146
Regius Professors, 195
Regrating, 138
Remigius, Bishop of Lincoln, 111
Renaissance, 185
Rents (1088), 101; (1338), 128; (1380), 151; (1383), 152; (1875), 259; (1897), 269
Residences of Bishop, 167
Reserved cases, 146
Rhadegunde's, St., Priory, 119 141, 147
   suppressed, 176
Rhee River, 4
Rhetoric, 123
Rhyme in Anglo-Saxon poetry, 68
Richard, Abbot of Ely, 111
Richard of Devizes, 115
Richard I., 127
Richard II., his share in Wat Tyler's rising, 154
Richard III., patron of Clare College, 166

Rick-burning, 258
Ridel, Bishop of Ely, completes nave of Minster, 110
Ridley, Bishop, his farewell to Cambridge, 205
Ringmere, battle of, 76
River-bed men, 7
Ripon burnt, 62
Robert Curthose, 109, 286
Roesia, foundress of Royston, 113
Roman ashpits, 26
   coins, 27, 30
   conquest, 17
   greed, 18
   influence, 22
   miles, 24
   peace, 22
   pottery, 26
   provinces, 27
   roads, 23
   thimbles, 26
Romano-British army, 28
   population, 26
Roses, Wars of, 173
Round church built, 110, 116
Round Moats at Fowlmere, 14
Royal roads, 23
Royal titles, 83
Royston Priory founded, 113
   Use of Bangor at, 182
   Priory Church bought for town, 189
   James I. resides there, 213
   Charles I. detained there, 225
   secedes from Cambridgeshire, 269
Royston Cave, origin of, 11
   used as hermitage, 113
   filled up at Reformation, 191

Salisbury, Assize of, 112
Samian ware, 26
Sanctuary, 114
Sawston, belonging to Hospitallers, 129
   Mary Tudor takes refuge there, 203
   incendiary fires, 259
   state of church (1685), 260
Saxons, special ferocity of, 33
   origin of name, 35
Scales, Lord, 144
Sceatta, 39

"Scholars of Ely," 147
School-dames, 261, 266
Schools, University, 124, 230
School Boards, 267
Seals introduced by Normans, 92
   in fourteenth century, 130
Seaton, 23
Seax, 34
Selwyn College, 126
Sempringham, 143
Senate House built, 247
Seneca, 21
Senlac, 93
Serfs, 151
Sergius, St., 143
Sexburga, Queen of Kent, 48
   Abbess of Ely, 51
Sexwulf, Abbot of Peterborough, 49
Shelford, belonging to Ely, 85
   hermitage, 144
   church desecrated (1643), 217
Sheppey, Danes in, 79
Shepreth, disturbance (1309), 139
Sherstone, battle of, 78
Shingay, Preceptory of, 128
   looted by rebels, 1381, 155
Ship-money, 222
Shuckburgh Castle, 14
Shudy Camps, 82
Sidney College, 210
Sidonius Apollinaris, 33
Sigbert, 45
Signatures, 50
Simeon, Abbot of Ely, 110
Siward Barn, 97
"Skegman," 285
Slavery, 105
"Smoke farthings," 167
"Snell," 76
Soham, Abbey of St. Felix, 46
   destroyed by Danes, 58
   belonging to Ely, 71
   dowry of Queen Margaret (1299), 138
Solere Hall, 166
Sophisters, 123
Sophistry, 228
Southampton sacked by Danes, 65
Special studies of Colleges, 164
Spindle-whorls, 39
Spinney, 143
Spinning-house, 245

Stage-waggons, 236
Stamford, battle of, 35
   Bridge, battle of, 93
   University, 122
Stapleford, state in 1685, 260
   belonging to Ely, 85
Star Chamber, 116
Steeple-Morden gallows, 139
Stephen, 113
Stigand, Archbishop, 82
Stilicho, 30
Stock of See, 167
Stocks, 268
Storm of 1704, 264
Stourbridge Fair, 240
Stretham parson ejected (1643), 222
Studium, 121
Suetonius, 22
Sunday-schools, 266
Surplice, 221, 284
Sutton, state in 1685, 261
Swaffham nunnery, 143
   church desecrated (1643), 217
Swavesey gallows and pillory, 140
   alien Priory, 143
Sweyn Forkbeard, 75
   King of Denmark, 95

Tabula Eliensis, 42, 101
"Tawdry," 50
Taxers, 125
Taxes at Conquest, 91
Teignmouth sacked by French, 263
Templars, 116, 128, 138, 139
"Tenants," 90, 129, 153
"Terra Ecclesiæ," 90, 191
"Terræ Filius," 228, 245
Teversham given to Ely, 71
   church desecrated (1643), 217
Thanes, 89
Theodore of Tarsus, 53
Thimbles, Roman, 26
Thirlby, Bishop, 168
Thirling, alien Priory at, 143
Thomas à Becket, 113
Thorney founded, 49
   destroyed by Danes, 58
   state in 1135, 141
   hospital, 144
Thorney, Bishop Pecocke confined there, 175

Thorney, present condition, 252
Thralls, 38
Tithes, 150, 151, 190
Tithings, 61
Toft, belonging to Ely, 85
   reredos destroyed, 191
   state in 1685, 260
Tokens, 234
Tonbert, King of Girvii, 47
Tory, 233
Townland, 256
T. R. E., 91
Tournaments, 136
Trinity College, foundation of, 194
   Hall, foundation of, 162
Trinobantes, 17
Triplow, 71
   belonging to Ely, 71, 85
   army encamped there, 224
Tripos, origin of name, 227
   assumes present form, 246
Trivium, 124
Trumpington, belonging to Ely, 71
   Charles I. passes through, 224
   Gate, 147, 288
Tydd, boundary of isle, 73
   in fourteenth century, 150, 151
Tyndall, 193

Uffa, King of East Anglia, 44
Ugrians, 9
Ulfkytel, Alderman of East Anglia, 75
   his death, 81
Undergraduates, 123, 124
University. See Cambridge
University Hall, 166
Upware, boundary of Isle, 73
Upwell Abbey, 143
Uses, 182

Vacarius, 121
Valence, Marie de, 165
Valentinian III., 27
Vandlebury, origin of name, 29
Vanity Fair, 240
Vaudois relieved by Brief, 263
Verulam, 22
Vespasian in Britain, 17
   coin of, 27
Via Devana, 23, 114
   Regalis, 23

20

Vicar of Britain, 28
Victorian prosperity of County, 256
Vigils, 146
Villages, Anglo-Saxon, 37
Villains in Doomsday, 90
   position, 106
   status in 1381, 154
Visitation of 1685, 260

Wages in 1338, 129
   in 1448, 171
   in 1500, 178
   in 1875, 259
   in 1897, 269
Walsingham, Alan, builds Ely Lantern, 154, 286
Waltheof, 90
Wareham, 59
Waterbeach, Rights of Templars in, 139
   parson ejected (1643), 165
Waterfowl, 253
Water-supply, 268
Watson, Bishop of Lincoln, 212
Wat Tyler, 154
Waynfleet, Bishop, 171
Wearmouth, 51
Weather in thirteenth century, 134
Wedmore, peace of, 59, 72
Welsh in fens, 67
Wendover, Roger of, 120, 133
Wendy, belonging to Hospitallers, 129
Werburga, 74
Westminster Abbey, 149
West, Bishop of Ely, 185
Whaddon, birthplace of Bishop Cox, 195
Whig, 233
Whitby Abbey, 48, 50
White Canons, 143
White Friars, 120
White Hill, 144
Whittlesea, 49, 147, 287
Whittlesford Hospital, 144
   cemetery reconciled, 151
Wicken Hospital, 144
   last remaining fen, 252

Wilbraham, Preceptory of Templars, 138
   made over to Hospitallers, 143
   parson ejected (1643), 222
" Wilkok," 284
Wilfrid, 50
Will of Henry VI., 170
William I., his theoretical position, 94
William Rufus, 112
Willingham, unlicensed teacher (1685), 261
Wimpole, parson ejected (1643), 222
Winchester, 17, 168
Winford, 54
Wisbeach, Clarkson monument, 105
   John's army destroyed, 131
   tidal wave (1237), 134
   whale cast ashore, 139
   hospital, 144
   in fourteenth century, 146
   episcopal residence, 167
   North German trade, 192
   heretics burnt, 204
   Catholic prisoners, 211
   parson ejected (1643), 222
   Quakers, 263
   fruit-culture, 269
Witan, East Anglian, 65
Witcham communicants (1685), 261
Witchford, at Conquest, 100
   fanatic schoolmaster (1685), 262
Woodlark founds St. Catharine's College, 176
Wool-trade in fourteenth century, 138
Wordsworth, sonnet to King's College Chapel, 174
Worsted Street, 14
Wranglers, 246
Wren, Bishop, 217
Wulfhere, King of Mercia, 48, 49
Wykeham, William of, 169

York, army of, 62

ERRATA.

Page 32, last line, *for* "in the thickest of" *read* "on the eve of."
,, 33, first line, *for* "423" *read* "446."
,, 36, note 1, *for* "xv" *read* "Book I., chap. xv."
,, 44, § 16, line 5, *for* "599" *read* "597."
,, 46, § 19, line 16, *for* "4" *read* "5."
,, 47, note, *for* "iii." *read* "vi."
,, 57, note 1, *for* "825" *read* "823."
,, 63, § 11, line 9, *for* "1537" *read* "1534."
,, 74, § 26, line 4, *for* "sister, Witburgha" *read* "ruler, Werburga."
,, 80, note 2, *for* "1925" *read* "25."
,, 80, note 2, *for* "1772" *read* "772."
,, 100, note 2, *for* "1072" *read* "1071."
,, 104, § 26, line 11, *for* "last English Abbot, Thurstan" *read* "first Norman nominee, Theodwin."
,, 119, § 2, line 5, *for* "1214" *read* "1224."
,, 122, note, *for* "84" *read* "79."
,, 130, line 3, *for* "1179" *read* "1187."
,, 130, line 6, *for* "1180" *read* "1190."
,, 131, note 3, *for* "§ 360" *read* "A.D. 1266."
,, 132, note, *for* "§ 367" *read* "A.D. 1267."
,, 140, last line, *for* "Magdalen" *read* "Magdalene."
,, 142, § 38, line 3, *for* "Pandionia" *read* "Pandiona."
,, 143, line 18, *for* "1439" *read* "1349."
,, 143, line 28, *for* "twenty-eight" *read* "twenty-nine."
,, 173, § 24, line 7, *for* "two" *read* "a few."
,, 176, § 29, line 9, *for* "north-west" *read* "north-east."
,, 186, line 9, *for* "1516" *read* "1511."
,, 209, § 43, line 5, *for* "1559" *read* "1558."

ADDENDA.

Page 112, at end of § 37, *add* "See page 284."
,, 141, after line 16, *add* "See page 286."
,, 143, after line 27, *add* "At Mirmond, near Upwell, was a Gilbertine nunnery."
,, 146, at end of § 43, *add* "See page 286."
,, 158, ,, ,, § 60, ,, ,, ,, 286.
,, 167, ,, ,, § 12, ,, ,, ,, 287.
,, 194, ,, ,, § 17, ,, ,, ,, 288.
,, 209, ,, ,, § 42, ,, ,, ,, 288.
,, 219, ,, ,, § 13, ,, ,, ,, 289.
,, 225, ,, ,, § 25, ,, ,, ,, 291.
,, 236, ,, ,, § 7, ,, ,, ,, 291.
,, 244, ,, ,, note 2 ,, ,, ,, 291.

In demy 8vo., cloth, 7s. 6d.; Roxburgh, 10s. 6d.; large-paper copies, 21s. net each volume.

THE NEW SERIES OF
COUNTY HISTORIES.

ALL those special features which go to make local history valuable and attractive will be found in this series, such as the state of the county in the Roman, Saxon, Danish and Norman times; its antiquities, customs, social peculiarities, folk-lore, dialects, the prominent part it has played in the history of England at various periods, the personal record of the noble and illustrious sons and daughters of the district, its notable churches, secular buildings, historical seats and mansions, and its natural features.

A HISTORY OF HAMPSHIRE.
By THOS. W. SHORE, F.G.S.

A HISTORY OF CUMBERLAND.
By RICHARD S. FERGUSON, M.A., LL.M., F.S.A.

A HISTORY OF WARWICKSHIRE.
By SAM. TIMMINS, F.S.A.

A HISTORY OF BERKSHIRE.
By LIEUT.-COL. COOPER KING.

THE HISTORY OF DERBYSHIRE.
By JOHN PENDLETON,
Author of "Old and New Chesterfield."

THE HISTORY OF DEVONSHIRE.
By R. N. WORTH, F.G.S.,
Author of the "West Country Garland," etc.

A HISTORY OF NORFOLK.
By WALTER RYE,
Author of "The Norfolk Antiquarian Miscellany," etc.

THE HISTORY OF NORTHUMBERLAND.
By CADWALLADER J. BATES,
Author of "Border-Holds of Northumberland."

THE HISTORY OF SUFFOLK.
By JNO. JAMES RAVEN, D.D., F.S.A.

A HISTORY OF LANCASHIRE.
By LIEUT.-COL. FISHWICK, F.S.A.,
Author of "The Lancashire Library."

A HISTORY OF WESTMORLAND.
By RICHARD S. FERGUSON, M.A., LL.M., F.S.A.

LONDON: ELLIOT STOCK, 62, PATERNOSTER ROW, E.C.

ELLIOT STOCK'S
New and Recent Publications.

NEW ILLUSTRATED WORK ON THE CIVIL WAR.

In demy 8vo., cloth gilt, price 10s. 6d. (Shortly.)

EAST ANGLIA AND THE GREAT CIVIL WAR.

The Rising of Cromwell's Ironsides in the Associated Counties of Cambridge, Huntingdon, Lincoln, Norfolk, Suffolk, Essex, and Hertford. With Appendices and Illustrations. By ALFRED KINGSTON, F.R.Hist.S., Author of "Hertfordshire during the Great Civil War," "Fragments of Two Centuries," etc.

In demy 8vo., cloth, price 8s. 6d.

THE HOUSE OF CROMWELL. A Genealogical

History of the Family and Descendants of the Protector. By JAMES WAYLEN, Sometime Secretary of Thomas Carlyle. A New Edition. Revised by JOHN GABRIEL CROMWELL, M.A. Oxon., Hon. Canon of Durham.

"To those who are interested in such quaint lore Mr. Waylen's book will yield a world of satisfaction."—*Morning Leader.*

In demy 8vo., cloth, price 9s.

THE STORY OF THE HOUSE OF LANCASTER.
By HENRY HARTWRIGHT.

"The events which took place in the fourteenth and fifteenth centuries are made particularly attractive by Mr. Henry Hartwright's method of relating them."—*Public Opinion.*

In demy 8vo., bound in cloth and Illustrated, price 5s.

SOME NOTES OF THE HISTORY OF THE PARISH
OF WHITCHURCH, OXON. By the Rev. JOHN SLATTER (Rector of the Parish).

"The contents are both curious and valuable."—*Times Weekly.*
"The volume is one of great and permanent value."—*Liberal.*
"It contains a great deal worthy of record, and well put together."—*Antiquary.*
"Of interest to the antiquary and local historian. Canon Slatter has done well to preserve these records."—*Scotsman.*

In demy 8vo., cloth, Illustrated, price 4s. 6d.

THE ANCIENT CROSSES AT GOSFORTH, CUM-
BERLAND. By CHARLES ARUNDEL PARKER, F.S.A. Scot.

"This well-written monograph is exceptionally interesting. Mr. Parker has brought together, and presented succinctly, pretty well everything that is required to make clear the symbolism of the sculpture to be interpreted."—*Literary World.*

In demy 8vo., cloth, price 7s. 6d.

A HISTORY OF THE MANOR OF BENSINGTON,
IN OXFORDSHIRE. By the Rev. M. T. PEARMAN.

"Very few men are competent to detail the descent of a manor. Mr. Pearman shows the student how such a task can be accomplished."—*Pall Mall Gazette.*

LONDON: ELLIOT STOCK, 62, PATERNOSTER ROW, E.C.

www.ingramcontent.com/pod-product-compliance
Lightning Source LLC
Chambersburg PA
CBHW021201230426
43667CB00006B/497